Visibl

Visible fictions
Cinema : television : video

John Ellis

London and New York

First published 1982
by Routledge & Kegan Paul
Reprinted 1989 by Routledge

Revised edition first published 1992 by Routledge
11 New Fetter Lane, London EC4P 4EE

Simultaneously published in the USA and Canada
by Routledge
a division of Routledge, Chapman and Hall, Inc.
29 West 35th Street, New York, NY 10001

© John Ellis 1982, 1992

Typeset in 11 on 12 point Journal by
Columns, Reading
Printed in Great Britain by
Hartnolls Limited, Bodmin, Cornwall

British Library Cataloguing in Publication Data

A CIP catalogue record for this book is available from the British Library

Library of Congress Cataloging in Publication Data

Ellis, John

Visible Fictions.
Bibliography: p.
Includes index.
1. Moving-pictures. 2. Television broadcasting.
1. Title
pn1995.E57 1982   791.43   82–11290

ISBN 0–415–07513–0

Contents

Illustrations

Acknowledgments

Everyone I know, friends, family and colleagues, have contributed in some way to this book: film and television are the stuff of everyday conversation, and every conversation I've had over this book's long gestation has had effects in it. But there are some more sustained and systematic contributions that have to be acknowledged. The first is that of all those involved with *Screen* magazine since the early 1970s; their work has formed much of my critical outlook. Similarly, the members of the Independent Film-makers' Association have taught me harder lessons about cinematic practice, as well as elaborating many of the ideas presented here about the continuing social importance of cinema. Next, teaching with Ben Brewster at the University of Kent has taught me a great deal. Many of this book's historical speculations derive from Ben's work. Teaching undergraduates and supervising graduate students had made me develop ways of explaining my ideas more clearly. Finally, there is the contribution of Rosalind Coward, one of criticising ideas and drafts in a straightforward and cogent way, and of support in the daily routines of life, perhaps the single contribution that made this book possible.

The stills which appear in the text are production stills from films produced by the following companies, to whom thanks are due: Anglo-EMI, Ealing Studios, Paramount, Rank Organisation, United Artists, Warner Bros, Alpha Productions, British Film Institute, Rampart Productions, Rome-Paris Film.

1 Preliminaries

Cinema and broadcast TV are often taken to be interchangeable media, in direct competition with each other. This book argues their differences from each other: differences in their social roles, their forms of institutional organisation, their general aesthetic procedures. Cinema and broadcast TV are seen as divergent and complementary, having developed distinctive aesthetic and commodity forms (the series and serial in TV; the single 'feature' film in cinema), and divergent forms of narration and representation of events and people. These divergent products are marketed differently and ask their spectators to treat them differently. The two media are not in direct competition with each other: broadcast TV cannot wipe out cinema any more than cinema was able to wipe out theatre. But there are vast areas of interdependence. Cinema needs TV's money invested in film production; TV needs cinema film as a reference point for its own production work, and also as fodder for broadcasting. This mutual dependence has given cinema possibilities that it scarcely possessed before the era of broadcast TV: it can deal with more adventurous topics, and deal with them more adventurously; it can appeal to (and even work with) a wide diversity of allegedly marginal tastes. But cinema has remained within a conception of what constitutes a film (a self-sufficient, universally intelligible unit of about two hours length). It inherited this conception from its past. This conception suits the needs of broadcast TV, but does not exploit the specific characteristics of cinema as a public event to any real extent. An independent cinema in

1

Britain has begun to explore this aspect of cinema, constructing a form of cinema that is appropriate for the age
beyond that of broadcast TV: the age of domestic video.
Finally, and hesitantly, then, this book peers into the video
future, testing some of its arguments against the almost
messianic predictions that are sometimes made.

There are some immediate remarks that must be made
about this argument, which relate to the position it is made
from. Broadcast TV is a notoriously difficult phenomenon to
write about except in the impressionistic way that Clive James
has made into a form of criticism. Broadcast TV is extensive
and ever-present: it gives the impression of carrying on
regardless of what anyone in its audience is doing. A critic's
attempt to catch all of broadcast TV is doomed to failure
like all paranoid attempts to pin everything down, to know
everything.

The same is true of commercial cinema, where the rate of
releases and screenings far exceeds any one critic's physical
possibilities of viewing them, even in a cinematically deprived
city like London. Yet the inheritance of many years of
serious research and historical work on the cinema have made
this far less of a problem than it seems to be with broadcast
TV. When writing about cinema in this book, I have been
very aware of the wealth of dependable reference material
that stands behind the arguments made, and the possibility of
easy access to a wide range of material from the history of
cinema. When writing about TV, I was far more aware of
searching through my own childhood memories in some
cases, or being dependent on sources that seemed in some
way suspect or implausible. The strategy I adopted in trying
to think through general aesthetic questions in relation to
broadcast TV was to trade on this unevenness of knowledge
and theory (which may be my own; though I suspect it is
not). The strategy was one of comparison: taking what is
now a relatively tried and tested conception of cinema,
developed from an initial semiotic approach to cinema in the
early 1970s, and seeing how it fitted my perceptions of
broadcast TV. The results are presented here, as explorations
rather than definitive statements, turning a fresh attention
on to broadcast TV.

The way in which some of the statements and arguments are made might seem to belie a sense of the incompleteness of this writing, and the current impossibility of going much further. The form I have adopted is able to summarise and is short (an advantage), but is one of generalisation: in this case, rather a disadvantage. The writing abounds with statements that begin 'Television is . . .'.

A strategy of producing generalisations seemed to be necessary, since there are very few attempts at coherent overall descriptions of either cinema or broadcast TV as aesthetic and economic institutions. Readers are able to test generalisations against their own experiences and preconceptions; on the other hand, anecdotes and specific accounts (the most usual mode of writing about both media) are able to claim a certain authority for themselves, the authority of the eye-witness. Generalisations parade themselves, asking to be knocked down because of their own arrogance; they try to embrace everything: past, present and future. But there seemed no point in being coy about the strategy once it had been embarked upon, by qualifying each statement and surrounding it with doubts and question marks, reducing whatever clarity of perception it might have contained. Instead, it seemed better to let loose a flock of generalisations in the hope that some might return, and to take refuge instead behind some kind of statement of the position from which the arguments have been made.

This work is based on critical work carried out on the cinema because that is my own cultural background, and source of livelihood. I have been involved with a series of cinematic organisations, ranging from the Independent Film-makers' Association to the committee of Cinema 3 in Canterbury, as well as the editorial board of *Screen* magazine. I approach broadcast TV from a more common position, as one of its anonymous and fragmented audience. My experiences with production for broadcast TV are limited to involvement in the production of 'access' programmes, and to general observation of TV's practices informed by my experiences of cinema. Such is the nature of broadcast TV, attempting to cover everything, that each individual member of its audience sometimes confronts it as an expert. At some point, TV's genial generalisations will cover something of which each viewer has personal experience and knowledge. At such points, broadcast TV suddenly seems rather threadbare and inadequate. In some sense, then, my limited experience of the practice of broadcast TV production, together with a far more informed conception of cinema can produce a series of ideas and criticisms of TV in exactly the same way as any TV viewer can produce ideas about TV. I am confronting TV as a member of the cinema audience; nevertheless, also as someone who can appreciate the distinctiveness of a series like *Hill Street Blues*.

My engagement with this subject (rather than any other) comes from my enduring fascination with images, a fascination that has been enhanced rather than destroyed by analytic and critical work. My parents acquired their first TV set and their first son (me) at about the same time, so I am one of the first generation that has grown up with TV, amidst the dire predictions of the effects that the box would have on us. But my viewing experiences were interrupted rather than continued, as from the age of thirteen to eighteen I attended a boarding school whose notion of education included a savage deprivation of all electronic media. The consumption of moving images was virtually prohibited for two-thirds of the year: what had been freely available suddenly became taboo. At this point, I discovered cinema, an illicit pleasure involving avoidance of compulsory sport. University brought a new twist to this intertwining with moving images: a wide range of films, old and new; a developing sense of distaste (which still remains to some degree) with the more self-consciously artistic intentions of some TV and cinema; and contact with the growing political culture that developed amongst intellectuals in the late 1960s. One of the aims of this culture was a thorough analysis of ideology, including the audio-visual media. So my own involvement with watching moving images is closely linked with pleasure and its prohibition, and with the demands of the super-ego that such pleasures should be analysed in a socially useful way.

The position from which I write might seem to disqualify me from writing about broadcast TV. Having been much more involved with cinema than TV, I have for long periods used broadcast TV as a rather haphazardly organised film archive rather than a medium in its own right. More seriously, I have had very little experience of watching any broadcast TV other than Britain's. In particular, I have never been to the United States, so many of the statements I have made here might need revision from the rather different perspective that US TV might provide. This really demonstrates an insuperable problem with all writing about broadcast TV: unlike cinema, which in its commercial sectors has a highly integrated international aspect, broadcast TV is an essentially national activity for the vast majority of its audience. Broadcast TV is the private life of a nation-state, defining the intimate and inconsequential sense of everyday life, forgotten quickly and incomprehensible for anyone who is outside its scope. This sense of privacy accruing to each nation state's broadcast TV is another problem for anyone writing about TV in general. It means that any research is difficult if it is a research that aims to go beyond viewing and analysing individual programmes and series. To look at the whole phenomenon of broadcast TV in a particular country, both how its output works and how it intersects with the economic and social life of that country, it would be necessary to live there for an extended period of time. It also means that any programmes used as examples may mean nothing to some readers, especially in writing likely to be read on both sides of the Atlantic.

Sudden exposure to the often bizarre practices of broadcast TV in another country can stimulate fresh thinking about the whole phenomenon of TV. This is the case with Raymond Williams's concept of 'flow' (criticised in Chapter 7) which resulted from his culture shock on seeing US TV. Seeing another country's broadcast TV has the effect of 'making strange' something we normally take for granted: TV, normally habitual and bound into the private life of the nation, suddenly becomes an alien and inexplicable series of events. Even without this 'culture shock', something of this distance can also be gained simply from being confronted with a repugnant or ridiculous view of the world which TV's presentation assumes to be a taken-for-granted attitude.

Parts of this book are inspired by such an experience.
Several of the presuppositions of this book need to be
explained. There are three general conceptions that haunt
many arguments about the mass media, which are not
directly confronted in the rest of the text; rather, a particular
position is assumed about them. These are: first, the assumption that both cinema and TV should conform to usually
unexpressed conceptions of realism; second, the assumption
that technology determines the uses that society puts it to;
and third, the conception that cinema and TV have certain
measurable effects in modern society. It is not the aim of this
book to develop arguments around these major conceptions,
but the ideas that the book does develop depend to a great
degree on the particular kinds of attitude that I adopt to each
of them.

Realism

Notions of realism are some of the most enduring means of
judgment of film and TV creations; they also form a powerful block to the development of new forms of use for the
two media, as well as to perception of how they work. The
word 'realism' is scarcely used in this book, except to denote
the presence of a set of conventions of portrayal that in a
certain time and place, are able to pass themselves off as
realistic. Whilst there is a certain truth in this position, it may
appear to some readers to do less than justice to the complexities of the notion of realism. This is indeed the case, but
only because the word 'realism' is used to cover a whole
series of ideas and expectations, some of which can conflict
with each other. The question of realism is indeed a complex
one, but it is complex because the word itself is being used to
describe a whole series of principles of artistic construction
and of audience expectation alike.

'Realism' denotes the expectation that a particular representation should present a 'realistic portrayal' of character
and event. Beneath this tautology can lie a series of expectations. The particular representation (film or TV programme), should have a surface accuracy; it should conform

to notions of what we expect to happen; it should explain itself adequately to us as audience; it should conform to particular notions of psychology and character motivation. Each of these expectations is different: there is nothing to stop more than one being demanded from a particular representation. Indeed, part of the complexity (or confusion) of the use of the term comes from the fact that when realism is demanded from a representation, it is always more than one type of realism that is demanded. So, to expand these summaries slightly further it becomes clear that the first, which is that the representation should have a surface accuracy, is not enough on its own. The kind of surface accuracy in question is an accuracy of costume, setting and props. This is often the subject of a particular 'know-all's' correspondence in the *Radio Times* about TV historical dramas: 'How could you get the buttons on the uniform wrong?' Other notions of realism are needed to supplement this type, though they can do so in different ways. The second, that a representation should conform to what we expect to happen, is perhaps the most conservative. It represents the spectator's desire that a representation should conform to common sense and taken-for-granted notions of events: it demands that politics is presented as a matter for powerful (male) politicians, not for popular struggle; it demands that the Second World War is shown as a conflict with the virtuous Allies pitted against satanic Germans and sub-human Japanese.

The third conception of realism is different again. It can quite cheerfully admit large-scale divergences from accepted notions, but it sets the terms on which such representations can be comprehensible to audiences as realistic representations. This criterion of realism can be regarded as quite anti-realist by those who believe that 'realism' equals the attempt to portray things as they are or were. The demand that a representation should explain itself adequately to its audience cuts right across the desire that it should show things 'as they were'. In practice (the practice of film- or programme-making) a compromise is always drawn between the two tendencies, a compromise that always favours the audience and explanation to that audience. The demand for explanation is a demand for adequate motivation of events in the sense that events should always be seen as·having explicable causes and being related to each other within the representation, rather than coming out of the blue. On a mundane level, if a character is walking down a street, with an open umbrella, then it should be raining; on a more complex level, the fatal fall of Scarlett and Rhett's daughter from her pony in *Gone With the Wind* (1939) is motivated at two levels. First, it should be prepared by Rhett coaching the child to be a good horsewoman; second, it should link to the way that Scarlett's father met his death, also by falling from a horse. This motivation explains and prepares for the event, which nevertheless comes as a surprise to the viewer until the child announces her intention to jump the fence. . . The fourth version of realism is a variant on this form. Instead of demanding that all events should be soldered together into a form that explains itself to the audience through clear motivation of each action, the motivation for events is placed centrally upon the psychology of individual characters, who are taken as the unifying point in a representation in which weird and 'unrealistic' events take place. This is what holds many films of the macabre within a realistic form; it is also what provides the unity for much comedy, whose events taken on their own would seem to be rather implausible.

Hence there is no realism, but there are realisms: a series of arguments, justifications, and procedures for the production of representations alike. The appeal to the idea of 'realism' to justify a particular representation will probably rest upon more than one of these arguments. But the situation is not as simple as this, since each of these conceptions is highly dependent upon changing conceptions of what is appropriate. The example from *Gone With the Wind* nowadays seems *too* obvious to most spectators, and thus is judged 'unrealistic'. Each notion depends on particular, historically dependent judgments. They are not absolutes: they depend upon convention. As conventions of portrayal, they tend to diversify still further. Each conception of realism will have its older and its newer conventions, each constituting a different 'taste', each providing the possibility of disagreements between individual spectators, even if the particular form of justification of realism can be mutually agreed. And further, it can be argued that a work is 'realistic' to the extent that it breaks these conventions of portrayal in order to get to a new sense of reality. So a film that shows events as arbitrary, not explaining them in the conventional way, like Rossellini's work, can be judged 'realistic' for these reasons. In not conforming to conventions of portrayal, it has found reality from behind the dead weight of representations. This is certainly the argument that André Bazin uses to explain Rossellini's work.

Enough has been said to indicate that the notion of realism is not a simple given, not a result simply of the camera's ability to record light and the tape's to register vibrations in the microphone. Instead, it can be seen as a complex network of conventions of portrayal and conventions of audience expectation alike. Yet, conventions or not, the idea of realism is still a powerful regime of reading sounds and moving images. It constitutes perhaps the basic demand that our society makes of its film and TV representations, apart from a very few licensed exceptions. The recourse to notions of realism by film-makers, by TV institutions, and by spectators alike is almost a reflex action. It ensures that film and video images continue to be treated in a particular way, as the unified image of a particular reality. The notion of realism tends to unify the diverse elements that go to make up a picture or sound track: it unifies them as the attempt to portray, according to whatever conventions of realism, a particular fragment of reality. Reality is taken as being the subject and object of the representation. This hinders various attempts to produce different uses for sound and image combinations, and different spectator attitudes. The conventions of realism (and the convention that there should be realism) prevent the realisation of Eisenstein's wild dream of a film of *Das Kapital*: the realisation, that is, of the desire to use images and sounds analytically, rather than as the presentation of a self-sufficient reality.

In essence, realism is a regime of unified portrayal: every criterion of realism aims at the same objective, to combine all the elements of the representation at any one point into a harmonious whole. This prevents the reading of the image, scanning it to see its different elements and their possible conflicts or combinations, which is a central feature of modernist tendencies in the other visual arts. Film and video both have a tremendous potential to produce such combinations of elements which are meaningful as combinations of meanings rather than unified into any particular reality. With the increasing availability and flexibility of video in the home, the attempt to create such forms becomes a more urgent one. With home video equipment it is possible for people to view material more than once, view selected fragments, to skip or repeat pieces. This allows a much more analytic attitude to video representations, rather than the serial attitude that has been the only one available, in cinema or broadcast TV, to the vast majority of the population. One possible development that can now begin to take place is the development of more sophisticated reading skills, and the habit of understanding images as combinations of meanings rather than as the imprint of an external reality. The beliefs traditionally associated with realism would seem to hinder rather than to promote such an attitude.

Technology

Sophisticated new technology always seems to provoke a flurry of wild and naive speculation about its effects. It is so currently with video technology of all kinds; it was so with the introduction and spread of cinema technology. All kinds of dire prognostications can be had, according to your taste. There is the media apocalypse prediction: that home video and cable diffusion of video between them will finish off both cinema and broadcast TV. There is the surveillance paranoia nightmare, with video technology in the home to keep an eye on every action, and computer centralisation of all possible kinds of information to abolish any remaining personal freedoms that Westerners might have. There is the domestic idyll promoted by some equipment manufacturers, where it will be possible to do everything by interactive cable video (shopping, voting, socialising) so that no one need go out on to the unsafe streets or the run-down public transport any more.

All of these operate by extrapolating the technical potential of an invention into the future, without regard to any factors that might intervene. In particular, the complexities and varieties of modern culture are neglected, together with the great capacity for people to resist or ignore many of the more unsavoury aspects of technology. These predictions ignore the fact that technology is used, adapted and implemented in particular ways by the society that has called it into being. Cinema and broadcast TV provide convenient examples of this process and its complexities. First, it was once fashionable to predict the imminent demise of cinema, any form of cinema, under the impact of broadcast TV. Nowadays, it is obvious that this apocalypse has not taken place: cinema may have changed because of the impact of broadcast TV, but this is a different matter. Second, there is nothing in the technologies themselves that dictated how they were used by the societies that invented them, though there is a great deal in the form that those societies took: turn-of-the-century America and Europe for cinema; post-war Western society for broadcast TV.

Domestic cinema is quite conceivable: easy-to-operate 16mm or 8mm projectors sold or rented to domestic units, wih film prints hired from local shops, is nowadays a perfectly conceivable form for cinema to take. At the time when the apparatus was introduced, however, the massive investment in domestic life that now characterises Western society had hardly begun to take place; the multiple production and household or individual ownership of technology similarly had not developed as an industrial strategy. Similarly, public TV is conceivable; and indeed does exist in Third World countries whose organisation makes ridiculous the notion of domestic ownership of TV receivers. Public TV has also had an airing in Britain in the 1950s, with major sporting events like boxing and racing relayed live to cinema audiences in major cities, and projected on to a cinema screen. The technology alone does not create the use to which it is put: technology is implemented (or, as with most inventions, *never* implemented) according to the prevailing patterns of use into which it can be fitted, and according to the emerging forms of social organisation with which it can align itself. So TV lines up with (and inflects) the increasing domestic use of technology, the emphasis on home and family as site of consumption; cinema lined up with (and superseded) public forms of entertainment like vaudeville and music hall, the sites of public enjoyment and of the development of non-religious mass ideologies. Currently, we are witnessing the development of new technologies associated with TV that may move the domestic consumption of TV away from the mode of broadcast TV. More than one technology is in an advanced stage of development and capitalisation, and experts have conflicting predictions for the future, most of which make fundamental mistakes simply because they base themselves on technologies alone, rather than on the institutional nature of the commodities involved.

There is equally a pervasive public belief in technological progress. It is generally thought that technology is continuously improving, under some kind of impulsion of its own. In cinema, this links with beliefs about realism, and the hazy perception of changes in the conventions of realism. Hence, the idea is generated that films are generally becoming 'more realistic' because old films are not very convincing any more. Technology and aesthetics combine together here in a lethal pair. In fact, it can be demonstrated that the complexities of the organisation of cinema, and the pressures of costs have combined to decrease the quality of the cinematic image rather than to improve it. The proliferation of wide-screen processes in the 1950s produced screens in cinemas that are less high than previously. In order to produce images to fit these screens, cinematographers began to leave wider 'space bars' between each frame of the filmstrip: effectively using less of the negative. In addition, the move in the early 1950s from the full Technicolor colour process (labour-intensive/ mechanical/dye-based) to the 'more advanced' Eastman-color process (based on Agfa's researches into dyes that change colour in contact with the light) have reduced the possibilities for colour cinematography. Eastmancolor is less intense (less saturated) and is prone to degeneration over time, eventually turning pink. This has overcome most East-mancolor films of the 1950s (negatives included), and occasionally much more recently made films, sometimes only a couple of years old. Considerations such as these emphasise the fact that the material differences between the images of cinema and TV are not ordained by the basic technological principles used, but by their specific implementations and developments. Cinema has reduced both screen size and the area of the negative used. This has been determined both by the confusion over standards of screen size following the experiments with wide screen (to combat TV), and by the awareness of the area of the image that would be visible when broadcast on TV (nowadays a large economic calculation in film production).

Cinema has adopted the Eastmancolor process with its lack of saturation and its tendency to degenerate simply because it is less expensive than the Technicolor process. The Techni-color process itself belongs to a more primitive level of tech-nology than the Eastmancolor one, yet it provided a more stable process and a process that could be manipulated to achieve complicated effects. Hence recent technological changes in cinema have tended to reduce the quality of the projected image rather than to improve it. The final death-blow to the cinematic image has been dealt by some exhibi-tion chains, which have constructed multiple cinema complexes containing screens so small that the image is little bigger than a TV screen.

Hence the question of technology is a more complex one than it might first appear. In particular, it is necessary to remember that comparisons made in this book between cinema and TV are not comparisons between their respective technologies but between the typical uses to which these technologies have been put by Western society.

Effects

Effects studies are the commonplace of TV research. Once it was possible to prove that children were conditioned into various attitudes or activities; now it is fashionable to be given large grants to carry out empirical research to prove that empirical research cannot prove very much either way. Effects studies ally with audience research to prove to potential advertisers that their advertisements might have a predictable effect at the supermarket shelf. In every case, the links that are sought are far too direct. Cinema and broadcast TV do indeed have effects of various kinds, but they are much more diffuse than effects research is usually willing to admit. They have more to do with the creation and sustaining of meanings in modern society (the realm of 'ideology') than they do with any direct action upon individuals.

Cinema and broadcast TV work over the meanings that modern society gives itself, the web of definitions and suppositions that give sense to the world. For each medium, it appears that these meanings come from elsewhere. They seem to exist already in the very air that we breathe, rather than being a creation of any one medium, or of any one person's speech. Very often, such meanings do not appear to be meanings at all. Rather, they appear as common sense, as the taken-for-granted, a kind of natural horizon to life, beyond which anything is unthinkable. This network of conceptions, beliefs and habitual definitions appears to have no particular source: it is always already there. Yet at the same time, it is subtly shifting to take account of new phenomena, to interpret new events. The strength of this common sense lies exactly in its suppleness and the invisibility of its suppleness: it changes but does not appear to change.

Cinema and TV contribute to this silent process of change that is ceaselessly taking place within the realm of ideology. These media — like all other media — do not reproduce ideology as has sometimes rashly been supposed. Instead, they are involved in a process of renewal or refreshment of society's layers of common sense, its basic understandings of the universe. The ideological meanings that a society creates for itself cannot be taken as being a perfect seamless whole, some kind of 'bourgeois ideology' that is a unitary series of definitions of everything that falls within its scope. Rather, there is a constant friction between different kinds of meanings and different beliefs, between new discoveries and old habits, between what goes on in one sector of knowledge and another. The effects of the media, if effects are sought, lie in the way in which they participate in this process, by presenting in their particular ways perpetually new variations on and recombinations of specific ideological meanings.

This book concentrates on the aspect of the above formulation represented by the phrase 'in their particular ways'. For the effect of broadcast TV in the area of production of social meanings is not the same as that of cinema in that broadcast TV is prone to create rather different regimes of knowledge from those favoured by cinema: in particular, it is able to sustain a category of 'news' as a definition of a significant proportion of its output. Cinema has never really been able to produce news. Its privileged form has been the self-contained fiction. Subsequent chapters detail the differences between broadcast TV and cinema as forms of representation. At this point, it is still necessary to make a few general comments about the ways in which both media inflect the process of creation and recreation of ideological meanings in which they participate.

The specific effects that cinema and broadcast TV have in ideological production are these: first, the direct effects of obsessional repetition of certain definitions and areas of concern, and the neglect of others; second, the creation of specific areas or modalities of meanings, the generic patterns of thought which both media have; third, the way in which they place the spectator in particular attitudes to events, creating a particular stance towards or view upon events.

Broadcast TV obsessively repeats, in its news coverage, a certain conception of 'important events' which gives pride of place to two categories: the activities of governments, and any action that could be considered to be exceptional. This definition is sometimes considered to be too narrow by the professionals who are concerned with the production of news. They consider that it produces an unduly dark picture of the world, lurching from crisis to crisis. Hence the broadcasters' solution of 'happy news', meaning the good actions of government and any action that could be considered to be exceptional and uplifting. The concentration on news as events outside the normal flow of life is thus maintained even by those who seek to change the news from within. The conception of the newsworthy that is shared by TV and most newspapers (the two forms feed off each other) produces an excessive concentration on one form of event (or one perception of what an event might be) and so neglects the events which occur 'in between', and provide the framework and basis for understanding how the isolated and exceptional events might have come about. Repetitions occur equally in the conception of the family that is assumed in TV advertisements, TV drama and cinema films alike. Each assumes a range of versions of the nuclear family (the couple and their children) that precludes any consideration of other forms of living as anything other than comic exceptions or personal tragedy.

The range of genres that cinema and TV dispose are a powerful means of classifying the world into types of action and types of response. Current affairs and situation comedy; melodrama and documentary; crime picture and pornography: all these incompatible generic indicators share a common medium. They each represent a particular form of attention and a particular range of emphases and blindnesses. These generic distinctions have very real effects in the way in which the media perceive and define events for us. Take, for instance, broadcast TV's treatment of twentieth-century history.

Historic fictions are presented as the personal dramas of a sequence of generations with momentous historical events as a background. *Roots* is an explicit example of this strategy; *Days of Hope* one that attempts to give more prominence to the historical events. In such series, the sequence of generations has a twenty-year periodicity: similar dramas tend to recur in each generation at about twenty-year intervals. In the construction of the TV historical narrative, these cycles tend to be set up so that they coincide with the 'common-sense' periodisation of history. So, in the case of a drama set in Germany, we would see the romance of a young couple at the end of the First World War (i.e. reconstruction); the Nazi education of their children and consequent estrangement in the late 1930s (i.e. chaos begins to reassert itself); the children fighting, marrying, being killed or imprisoned (i.e. repeating the parents' woes); their children subsequently being born as the symbol of new hope amongst the ruins (i.e. today's generation, free from guilt). Thus the ending of each of two world wars marks the ending of a historical epoch for the fiction. It is a return to zero, a new beginning. The fictional structure, pulling together the repetitive drama of the generations and the public drama of history, intimately supports a conception of history as repetitions or new beginnings. The effect of this particular regime of representation of history is a difficult one. We do not so much live *in* history according to it, as *with* history. As a result of its prevalence on broadcast TV (and it is a specialism of British TV), we all have a knowledge of what happened this century, hazy though it probably is. We are all acquainted with its key images: they have become part of our personal historical memories as well as public ones. Yet these memories are only solid up to the 1950s. As we come closer to the present, they begin to fade. We can conjure up images of miners striking in 1926; miners as the long-term unemployed of the 1930s; even miners coming to terms with state ownership of the pits after the Second World War. But the notions of miners as the mass pickets of 1972, miners who challenged the Conservative government in 1974, do not coalesce into memory images, even though the events are more recent and more current. The first three sets of images are composites in the memory created by innumerable fictional and historical representations. The images of the 1970s are virtually absent, especially from broadcast TV. Current affairs and news do not construct history, and hardly ever situate the present in terms of the past: indeed, it can be said that those TV programmes that attempt this task have not yet succeeded in developing a form adequate to it. The problem is that much of the descriptive rhetoric used (the handy division between 'moderates' and 'extremists' for example) would tend to fall apart when the origins of current situations were examined. TV is persistent in working over history for us, yet at the same time it cuts us off from our history. It has two very separate forms of historical time: the history-fiction-epic with its broad scope and its twenty-

year periodisation; the current affairs programme which deals
with the events of the immediate present and loses its grip at
the distance of one year, where it becomes amnesiac. In this
coverage, with fiction ending in the 1950s and current affairs
beginning this year, a twenty-year period falls into neglect:
the previous twenty years more or less: the almost-present,
not-quite-past. Broadcast TV's generic distinctions, therefore, create a particular kind of historic blindness that has
effects in the perception of a radical gap between the
immediate present and the distant past.

The two media of cinema and broadcast TV have one
further effect. They create particular ways of viewing events,
each in slightly different ways. Broadcast TV and cinema do
not constitute events, even when they stage particular occur-
rences for the camera and tape recorder. The events and
meanings that they record have sources elsewhere. The two
media do, however, constitute those events and meanings
for a particular point of view: they organise them so that
they are comprehensible for a spectator taking a particular
attitude. The fundamental effect of cinema and broadcast
TV lies in this effect of organising events for a viewer who
adopts a position of knowledge-in-security. Events are explained to the viewer in that the way in which they are outlined provides the viewer with all the elements necessary
to understand them. Cinema and TV thus operate regimes
of intelligibility: certain knowledges are assumed in the
viewer, others always have to be established. A TV news
bulletin will always state 'The Prime Minister, Mrs
Thatcher. . .', rather than just her name; but it is assumed
that the viewer will know what the office of Prime Minister
is. This comprehensibility aims to place the viewer in a
position that enables him or her to understand the totality
of events that are presented. The viewer is provided with a
panoramic view of the events that are being laid out in a
series for that viewer. The actual course of the accumulation
of those events one after another can involve uncertainty or
even confusion: the thriller and mystery genres thrive on
exactly this state and the pleasure that it provides. But the
pleasure is provided by the certainty that eventually a
position of complete knowledge will be provided: everything

will fall into place. The viewer is provided with a view: one that is comprehensive. The viewer is equally kept separate from the events involved: editing will provide a mobility of physical viewpoint that is always more than the sum of the physical points of view of any one character in a fiction; the narration will provide more information than that possessed by any one character. Equally, factual programmes will provide terms which place every individual contribution, either by the techniques of voice-over in a documentary, or by the privilege that the presenter of a studio discussion has to speak directly to the viewer. The viewer is placed in separation from events, called upon to judge rather than to be a participant, to assess rather than to be partisan. If anything is to be considered the effect of cinema and broadcast TV, then it is this: the constitution of events for a particular form of comprehension, and the production of a particular form of point of view for the spectator. From the constitution of such a position come all the possibilities for bias towards particular interests and against others; and the massive investment in particular forms of subject matter both in fiction and non-fiction.

The weight of repetition of particular definitions, the construction of a network of generic organisation and the constitution of particular positions for the spectator can be taken to be the effects of cinema and broadcast TV. The examination of these three aspects has taken place rather more thoroughly in the study of cinema than it has in the study of TV, not least because of the relative ease of access to old cinema films and various kinds of information regarding cinema. Hence this book summarises the central conceptions of this work on cinema, and subsequently measures them against the particular way in which broadcast TV is currently constituted.

The attention of this book is not directed to the effects or technologies of broadcast TV and of cinema so much as to their *forms*. Often, use of this word indicates an attention to films or programmes alone, a particular deviation of critical work (convenient for academic analysis) that looks at films or, less often, programmes from the point of view of their

internal structure only. This attention to form is a characteristic of a wide range of critical thought: it is common to
both Leavisite criticism of literature, as it is normally practised nowadays, and to a certain version of structuralism
and semiology. However, the forms that are explored here are
at once economic and textual. They are concerned with the
institutions that produce films and programmes, with the
institutions that create conditions for their consumption,
as well as with the so-called internal questions such as narrative processes. In this sense, this is an attempt to sketch out
cinema and broadcast TV as social forms, particular forms of
organisation of meanings for particular forms of spectator
attention.

The final contention of this book is that the social forms
of each medium determine the ways in which each can
contribute to the production of representations in our
society: the way in which they can operate as institutions
mainly concerned with the production of ideology. It is the
characteristic form of each medium that is in question, not
so much those valiant exceptions and brave experiments
that so often have a limited and tragic life because of the
hostile institutional terrain in which they work. The conditions of reception of cinema and broadcast TV play a large
part in creating and maintaining these characteristic forms.
It is an element of popular wisdom that the development of
new domestic video technologies will change both cinema
and broadcast TV, though no one is very sure how. Instead
of joining in this area of speculation, a concrete example of
the unexplored formal and social possibilities of cinema is
examined in Chapter 16: the example of British independent
cinema's work over the past decade and more.

Part I

Cinema

2 Cinema as cultural event

Cinema and broadcast TV are distinct forms of representation, with distinct forms of production. The aim of this section is to produce a generalised characterisation of cinema as a distinct mode of representation. Most of this characterisation is gained from existing work in the area of cinema semiotics and aesthetics. The aim of the second section is to apply this model to broadcast TV, and to measure the distances from it, so that a characterisation of broadcast TV as a distinct means of representation can begin to develop. The third section examines the differences between the two forms of production that the two media have developed, based upon these distinct forms of representation.

The demands of making a distinction between two media that are often seen as interchangeable have meant that, particularly in dealing with cinema, the whole medium has been portrayed monolithically. General statements are made about 'cinema' as though 'cinema' were a mass of virtually undifferentiated material. The central focus of these generalisations is upon the cinema that has been economically and aesthetically dominant in world cinema since the period of the First World War. This is the American entertainment cinema, a cinema that coincides with virtually everyone's common-sense notion of 'a film'. The economic form of this notion of cinema is examined in Chapter 13. Its form as the predominant experience of cinema is explored here; many of the statements refer simply to 'entertainment' cinema, a notion that refers to films in the Hollywood mould that are made outside America, by national cinemas that see themselves as developing a style distinct from that of American cinema. However, these cinemas too retain many of the fundamental features of the Hollywood film when they produce entertainment films. Not until the final chapters of this book are forms of cinema considered which break with the fundamental conceptions of the Hollywood film: and these forms of cinema are still in their early stages of development.

The form of the entertainment film is one reason for the confusion between cinema and broadcast TV. The entertainment film can be broadcast on TV, hence it seems as though there is little real difference between the two media. Two immediate objections can be made to this assumption. First, a film on TV yields a very different experience to its viewer, unless that viewer is able to suspend the sense of watching TV and imagine instead the sense of being in a cinema. Second, it is not possible to show broadcast TV material in a cinema in the way that it is possible to show films on TV. Broadcast TV has developed its own forms, those of the serial and the series, which resist showing in the 'single work' form that cinema imposes.

There are four main areas into which the distinct aesthetics of cinema and broadcast TV can be divided. First, there is that of the ways in which the experiences take place, with cinema offering a public event which offers, through advertising, a narrative image to provoke the spectator to see a particular film. Its mode is that of the individual text, the single event of film performance. Broadcast TV characteristically offers the serial or series; it is watched in domestic conditions on a casual basis. The second series of distinctions concerns the forms of image and sound combinations that each medium offers. Cinema offers a large-scale, highly detailed and photographic image to a spectator who is engaged in an activity of intense and relatively sustained attention to it. Broadcast TV offers a small image of low definition, to which sound is crucial in holding the spectator's attention. The spectator glances rather than gazes at the screen; attention is sporadic rather than sustained. These forms of attention enable different modes of narration to develop in each medium. Entertainment cinema characteristically adopts a tightly organised narration, organised around a particular problem or disruption that is resolved at the ending of the film. Events and characters are integrated into the continuous narration of this progression in its logical sequence. Broadcast TV normally does not adopt this self-enclosed narrational form. It is more concerned with open-ended forms like the series and serial, which run through a number of variations on the same basic narrative problem. Each episode is highly divided into segments, which are relatively self-contained events which have slight connections with ensuing events in their separate segments. Finally, each medium proposes a rather different attitude to its spectators. Cinema proposes a curious and expectant spectator, anxious to find out, the resolution of whose anxiety becomes the point of intelligibility of the film, where everything falls into place. The viewer for broadcast TV is rather more a figure who has delegated their look to the TV institution. TV is a diversion: the viewer is able to glance at a TV look on the world outside, a world separate from the domestic place of the TV viewer and their complicity with TV's look at it.

There are a number of levels upon which cinema and broadcast TV differ. These are not textual levels alone: they are a matter of the whole context in which each text (film or programme) is produced and seen. Hence, the examination of cinema begins not with the structure of the single film, but with the conditions in which 'a film' exists as a separate entity in our current culture, for this itself is one distinction between cinema and broadcast TV. Broadcast TV can transmit and even produce single films, but only by reference to a notion of 'cinema'. The notion of cinema that entertainment cinema has developed is able, by a series of means, to differentiate sufficiently between single films so that an audience can be generated for each one. This is largely a matter of marketing. Cinema marketing sells two rather distinct things: the single film in its uniqueness and its similarity to other films; and the experience of cinema itself. Cinema and film are both sold at the same point, at the point of sale of an admission ticket. It is not the film that is sold at this point, it is the possibility of viewing a film or films; it is not cinema as an object that is sold, but cinema as an anticipated experience. The moment at which the capital involved in cinema is turned over is therefore a special moment, quite dissimilar to the sale of a particular item to a consumer, be it a cabbage or a videotape. Cinematic capital is turned over, tickets are sold, on the expectation of pleasure. A particular individual is buying something that he or she has not seen: in fact, entertainment cinema hinges on the fact that its audience has not seen the particular film before. Films are generally constructed to be seen once and once only. To see a film again is usually accounted either as a sign of great devotion to the person accompanied, or as a rather suspect devotion to cinema itself. So the possibility of pleasure in cinema, and in a particular film, is what characteristically motivates the purchase of a ticket for the cinema. Anticipation prompts the exchange of money. If the anticipated pleasure is not experienced money is not usually returned except in the case of a mechanical fault in the projection: even then, a refund is difficult to come by. What is bought in the cinema is the possibility of a pleasurable performance: the performance of a particular film and the performance of cinema itself, both together.

It is necessary to distinguish the two performances whose expectation is sold at the box office. Cinema is enjoyed whether the film is or not (hence no refund on a dissatisfying film), and often people 'go to the cinema' regardless of what film is showing, and sometimes even with little intention of watching the film at all. Cinema, in this sense, is the relative privacy and anonymity of a darkened public space in which various kinds of activities can take place. At some historical moments, and for some particular cinemas, this definition of cinema has been of considerable economic importance. Yet this is only a minimal definition of cinema as an institution. More central perhaps is the experience of watching a fiction (it usually is a fiction in entertainment cinema) with an anonymous group of people, who need have nothing more in common than the fact that they have been attracted to that particular place and that particular fiction. Cinema in this way becomes a very precise urban experience, that of the crowd with its sense of belonging and of loneliness. Alterna-

1 Inside a picture palace, 1928: the orchestra pit, stage and screen of
the Camden Hippodrome, London

tively, cinema in smaller communities tends to perform a
different function when most of the audience are acquainted with each other. Here the entertainment is related to
particular characteristics of individuals or of the place itself.
The film comes from outside, the cinema belongs to the
particular place. However, such group experiences of cinema
are becoming more and more rare, and cinema is now characteristically an urban phenomenon, especially in Britain.

Cinema also functions as a special event, as a particular
conception of an evening's entertainment. The massive investment in cinema-building, in America from the mid-1910s
and in Europe with the boom after the First World War, was
predicated on this conception of cinema. The buildings that
were constructed were the 'picture palaces', now the subject
of nostalgic photo-books: simple brick shells decorated in
bizarre and rich styles, and usually of a massive size to
emphasise the grandeur of the cinematic experience. Most

2 The view from the screen: Camden Hippodrome, 1928

of them also included a restaurant so that 'going to the cinema' became an integrated social occasion whose conception of its typical audience was that of a (heterosexual) couple. The conception of cinema offered was not limited to that of an impressive place where films were shown: film appeared as the culmination of a series of entertainment events, especially in the period before the introduction of sound in the late 1920s and of the 'double bill' in the early 1930s. Here, the presence of a small band or orchestra in the picture palace produced forms of musical entertainment, stage acts, community singing, and even competitions with prizes (bingo has a long association with cinema). The couple visiting the cinema during this period experienced cinema as an integrated succession of entertainments that went far beyond the simple experience of viewing a film together in a more or less anonymous crowd.

This conception of the cinema event is historically very varied. It has fluctuated according to very specific social

3 The cinema as catering institution: the café in the Whitechapel Rivoli, London, 1928

conditions in various countries. In Britain, the cinema-restaurant mixture became very difficult to sustain during and after the Second World War because of the costs involved. Cinema exhibition still depends upon catering as an economic fact: the profits on the sales of sweets, hot dogs, ice-cream and drinks are habitually the cinema's major source of profit (hence the prices). But cinema for the commercial entertainment sector has increasingly been narrowed to a conception of film-viewing in a public hall. The specificity of the collective experience has been minimised. It has been left in Britain to the emergent independent sector of cinema (minimal though it currently is) to begin to rescue cinema as an integrated series of experiences, but in a very new form.

The sale of cinema tickets depends upon the public knowledge of the cinema experience. The expectation of a particular kind of entertainment, with a particular social role, is one crucial factor in the kind of commodity that cinema offers. It runs as a kind of groundbase, ensuring that cinema is a known constant in the anticipation that surrounds ticket sales. Within this reassuring context of cinema, the film (or film programme) is less certain. The entertainment film depends on being unknown if it is to provide pleasure; yet it also depends upon being known to some extent if it is to be understood. Cinema provides a certain degree of knowledge: the film is likely to be a complete work, it may be accompanied by subsidiary material (adverts, shorts, an episode of a serial), and will conform to certain basic and known stylistic features (the conventions of classical narration). This knowledge is not enough; a crucial further element is needed in the process. An idea of the film is widely circulated and promoted, an idea which can be called the 'narrative image' of the film, the cinema industry's anticipatory reply to the question 'What is this film like?' If anything is bought at the box office that is already known by the audience, it is this narrative image. Payment for a ticket is not an endorsement of a film, nor is it an endorsement of a particular performance of a film in a particular place. It is an endorsement of the narrative image of the film, together with the general sense of the cinematic experience. Payment at the box-office of a cinema is an act of approving the promise that the film offers through the mechanism of the narrative image. The narrative image created for (and from) a film is the deciding factor in its commercial success, and a considerable factor in the success of the actual performance of the film.

The narrative image is decidedly less than the whole film: it is the promise, and the film is the performance and realisation of that promise. However, it is a remarkable phenomenon, and crucial to the operation of entertainment cinema. It enables cinema to offer single texts, films which have a high degree of difference each one from the next. Unlike broadcast TV, which thrives on the repetition of formats and of narrative situations, repetition of 'formulae' in cinema is a more perilous business. Cinema demands single films, complete in themselves and distinct from other films. The mechanism of the narrative image is crucial to this process, as it offers a publicly circulating definition of a particular film, attempting to specify it out from other films in the market-place.

The narrative image of a film is a complex phenomenon that occurs in a number of media: it is the film's circulation outside its performance in cinemas. It consists of the direct publicity created by the film's distributors and producers; the general public knowledge of ingredients involved in the film (stars, brand identifications, generic qualities); and the more diffuse but equally vital ways in which the film enters into ordinary conversation and becomes the subject of news and of chat. The narrative image that appears through this network is a mass of references to other films and cultural phenomena (a mass of repetitions, therefore), and a series of enigmas, of questions whose answer can (usually) be found in the film itself.

The film's enigma is most obviously posed by the title itself: witness the number of film titles that are questions: *Whatever Happened to Baby Jane?*, *Guess Who's Coming to Dinner?* Other title forms include the paradox (*The Passionate Friends*), the partially indecipherable (*The Big Red One*), the portentous (*A Matter of Life and Death*), and the invitation (*Meet Me in St Louis*). Sometimes a title can be sufficient to indicate the whole problematic, the subject matter, of the film: *A Time to Love and a Time to Die*, *I Am a Fugitive from a Chain Gang*. More often, the title is one fragment in a series which combine to produce an enigma. Hence the film's publicity (posters, newspaper advertisements, front-of-house material) will provide images and slogans which provide further information. So the film *Alien* (1979) is specified on its poster by the slogan, 'In Space No-one Can Hear You Scream', and a graphic of an egg-like object which draws upon one of the film's scenes and themes, reproductive sexuality as a natural process inevitably corroded by any technological procedure. Screaming, interestingly, does not feature much in the movie (surprisingly, since it relies on the horror-film plot device of a confined space where terrified individuals still contrive to separate from each other). Screaming is an attribute not of the film's characters but of the film's promise to its audience. Yet this is not clear from the slogan, since its other function is to stress the science-fiction nature of the story ('In Space. . .').

4 The narrative image as enigma: the poster for *Alien*

The narrative image formed from this material does not produce an accurate summary or thumb-nail sketch: indeed, the slogan could be said to mislead, with a promise of (female) hysteria rather than the heroine's sang-froid. But such is not the function of the narrative image of the film. It does not summarise the film, it indicates it. Hence, the title *Alien*, the slogan and the graphic deliberately refuse to coalesce into a single description. They gesture towards various elements or directions (horror/space/birth/nature/helplessness, etc.); they do not allow them to fall together into a single enunciation, a synopsis of the film. Hence the enigma offered by the narrative image is that of how the various elements do indeed coalesce. The narrative image proposes a certain area of investigation which the film will carry out; it states the thematic of the film, but refuses to do more than that. The narrative image is an enigma, an offer; the film is offered as the resolution of the narrative image.

The second area of the narrative image is the way in which the film is specified as a particular kind of product: its brand identification. This includes the very potent and resonant naming of stars, the subject of another chapter; the identification of the director, especially in those areas of cinema which identify the director as author of a film; and the identification of past successes. Hence *Raiders of the Lost Ark* (1981) comes 'from the creators of *Jaws* and *Star Wars*'. Other brand identifications that come with the publicity for some films include the studio's self-image (as with Ealing Studio's use of a particular culturally respectable graphic style), and the identification of the film's generic classification. Sometimes again the title is enough to indicate a generic classification, like *All Quiet on the Western Front* or *Stagecoach*. At other times, the title and graphic

5 The narrative image as generic indicator: the poster for *All That Heaven Allows*

provide a joint indicator: *All That Heaven Allows* with Jane Wyman being embraced but looking longingly over Rock Hudson's shoulder to the infinite beyond of desire. This generic indication nowadays extends to indications of the kind of cinema that is involved: the name *Emmanuelle* invoking a whole system of soft-core pornographic cinema; the use of quotation from newspaper critics usually indicating that the film has certain cultural pretensions.

Generic indications point to the similarity between the particular film being advertised and other films. It locates the film. However, the demands of marketing also dictate that the film should be able to function as a distinct entity. It cannot be simply the repetition of other films. In some sense, the uniqueness of the particular film has to be emphasised across its similarity to other films. Hence the degree of emphasis on disparaging comparisons like 'Bigger Than *Ben Hur*'. It is perhaps the conflicting demands for uniqueness and for marking of generic similarities that contribute to a large extent to the enigmatic nature of many narrative images, which show the strain of trying to do both things at once.

In recent marketing, the brand image of the film has become more than the marking of generic similarities. The film itself has become a kind of brand name. The integrated publicity campaign for expensive major 'blockbuster' films centres on the creation of a particular logo or trade-mark for the film. This logo is then used on a series of other products: record sleeves, toys, books, magazines, confectionery. This is the logical extension of the marketing of a particular film on the basis of a narrative image, as Walt Disney was one of the first to realise with Mickey Mouse. The particular film-product is not the only product that can be sold through the circulation of a narrative image: indeed, the marketing of a film is enhanced by the presence of other disparate objects in the market-place that claim to have a connection with the film. This form of marketing, the quintessence of the process of creation of a narrative image, is only possible with a relatively small number of films over any one period: the so-called blockbusters. It is a process that leads to a greater expenditure on the promotion of the film (the creation of the narrative image) than on the production of the film itself. A vague frisson of scandal attaches to this statement, as though this inverted a long-standing balance in cinema. However, the use of cinema's institutional arrangements to provide a focus for selling a series of diverse commodities has a long (if not exactly honourable) history. Hollywood studios of the 1930s had tie-ins with electrical goods manufacturers: the appliances seen in films were simultaneously seen in local stores, with a cardboard cut-out of the film's star endorsing them.

Cinema's developed marketing strategies, with all the critical and public attention to them, mark cinema out from every other medium. All of cinema's products in the entertainment sector go through the processes of marketing in the same kinds of ways. The difference between a blockbuster and a routine film being one of the different intensities of marketing rather than of kind. Indeed, cinema's marketing through the narrative image contributes to the attraction of its films as material for broadcast TV. The audience for a TV transmission of a major film marketed even some years before can be assumed to have some kind of memory of the narrative image that can be revived. The cinematic means of marketing may well mean that entertainment cinema will be preserved as a loss-making arena for promotion of individual films which will then make their real profits in other areas: in the sale or hire of videotapes or discs; in satellite or cable transmissions.

The elements in the creation of the narrative image all have one feature in common, they are willed by the distributors (who are normally entrusted with marketing a film), and paid for by them. However, equally important in the creation and circulation of the narrative image of a film are those activities that are not directly paid for by the marketing agencies. The most intimately connected are those of journalism, which includes the activities of film reviewers. Film reviewers provide descriptions and classifications of films as much as judgments: indeed, the newspaper reviewer's very judgments tend to become a form of generic classification when keen cinema-goers identify a particular critic's view as close to their own. Broadcast TV's coverage of contemporary cinema perhaps best indicates this close relationship between marketing, the creation of a narrative image, and the activities of film journalism and reviewing. TV does little more than screen clips of commercial releases and make jokes about them, providing in the process a particular inflection of the narrative image. A reviewer who goes further and makes critical comments is in danger of being refused clips from new films for the programme. A similar threat has been wielded against newspaper and radio reviewers: most spectacularly in the case of E. Arnot Robertson in Britain in 1946. M.G.M. refused her entrance to its press shows after a particularly unfavourable review; the subsequent court case reached the House of Lords, where she lost the day.

Newspaper reviewers have a limited degree of autonomy from the direct forms of marketing, and are regarded by industry and public alike as useful means of spreading information about films: as another aspect of the creation of a narrative image. Other forms, less organised, also have a role. These are the forms of casual reference to particular films that takes place right across the media, and in ordinary conversation. It is these references that constitute a particular film as a cultural event, as a particular fragment of the ceaseless ideological work of a society. Hence a radio disc jockey makes a casual reference to a film he saw the previous evening (sometimes at a specially arranged show); a newspaper speaks of the star of a particular film; a magazine runs a feature on a particular aspect of the film, or on the particular question that the film raises (e.g. *Kramer vs Kramer* (1979)) and the problem of fathers not gaining custody of their children after divorce). This more diffuse, less organised, process occasionally reaches the point where a particular film becomes the slogan or title for a particular kind of event: *A Clockwork Orange* (1971) for urban street violence, *The China Syndrome* (1978) for the problem of nuclear energy. This process eventually forms a part of everyday conversation: the film becomes a rhetorical point, its title becomes a verbal shorthand.

Most narrative images do not achieve this degree of informal circulation. They rest at the level of the formal mechanisms of cinema marketing and reviewing. Nevertheless, the creation of a narrative image for each film has a crucial role in cinema, and is central in defining its particular commodity form. Cinema deals in individual texts, in single films which have a distinct problematic and area of concern, even if some particular areas are more fashionable at one time than another. This concentration on the single text is an early and consistent feature of entertainment cinema: the massive institutions of stars and genres are both dependent upon it. The means of marketing through the circulation of a narrative image in turn creates a particular pattern in the distribution of a film. The cinema institution puts a particular emphasis on the newness of a film, and films are released so that they are seen first in particularly luxurious locations, and for a substantially higher price: in the West End cinemas of London; then the city centre screens around the country; and finally the local cinemas (if any). Occasionally, especially for an 'exploitation' or pot-boiling film, this pattern is abandoned in favour of a blanket release in as many cinemas as possible. But in the main, Mae D. Huettig's definition of the cinema-commodity still holds true: 'In its entirety the product (of cinema) consists of the right to look at a film in a given type of theatre, at a given time with reference to the original release date of the film.'

The newness of a film that Mae D. Huettig identifies is a result of the creation and launching of the narrative image, and the consequent critical and public attention to it. Novelty and familiarity, knowledge and expectation are the elements that cinema trades upon. The sale of a ticket is an endorsement of the narrative image of the film, together with an indication of a desire to see a film in the particular *ambiance* of a cinema. The experience offered is one in which an individual film will complete the enigma of the narrative image. The experience of cinema that is offered is one of the public viewing of images with their supporting sounds. These images and sounds, viewed in the particular circumstances of the cinema, produce a particular kind of spectating that is intense and sustained.

3 Cinema as image and sound

Cinema, broadcast TV and non-broadcast video are often gathered under one heading: the audio-visual. This definition elides much that is different about the three forms. They have a common concern with images and sounds, but each has different visual and audible materialities. The cinema image is instantly perceived as different from a video image: the cinema image is photographic; the video image electronic. These distinctions bring with them a series of different attentions to the images and sounds, and therefore a rather different set of possibilities for representations.

Cinema as a photographic medium instantly poses its images and sounds as recorded phenomena, whose construction occurred in another time and another place. Yet though the figures, objects and places represented are absent from the space in which the viewing takes place, they are also (and astoundingly) present. The regime of cinematography presents an image which can claim a far higher fidelity and level of complication than any current video system, broadcast or not. The cinematic image is therefore in some sense the perfection of photography: superior in its ranges of nuance of colour or black-and-white to video; firmly within the paradoxical regime of presence-yet-absence that can be called the 'photo effect'. This effect is by no means so established with broadcast TV, which assiduously maintains a general sense of the live and instantaneous nature of its representations. Perhaps it should be said immediately that these comparisons are not to the detriment of broadcast TV and video as technical forms: they would only be to their detriment if they tried to achieve exactly the same effects and to use exactly the same aesthetic forms as cinema. The purpose is rather to examine the characteristic differences between the forms and practices of the two media of cinema and broadcast TV.

The photo effect of the cinematic image is one characteristic that is intensified by the form in which cinema images are consumed in our society. The characteristic mode of cinema has been described in the last chapter. Essentially, this mode, closely associated with a commercial entertainment cinema, is one in which the form of the narrative image provides an incentive or incitement to attend a particular cinema. Cinemas are arranged so that a public exhibition of a film or films takes place, without any particular contact between the individuals who comprise the audience. Classic entertainment cinema did tend to offer forms of exhibition event that went beyond the simple anonymity of a crowd that tends to dominate nowadays. Live entertainment, community singing, bingo games, and so on, tended to move the entertainment into a more active sense of communality. This sense can sometimes be found within the films themselves, often those films that explicitly call upon conventions from live entertainment. Hence Basil Dean's *Sing As We Go* (1934), starring Gracie Fields, uses extensive references to music hall conventions and to individual acts (dialogue references to Stanley Holloway's 'Sam, Pick Up Tha' Musket', etc.). The extent of the film's assumption of its audience as an active group is indicated by the form of sound mix for the title song that occurs at both the beginning and the end of the film. Gracie Fields' voice can hardly be heard: the singing of the group she is leading, and the sound of the accompanying band predominate. The film assumes that the audience will be singing as they go, not listening to Gracie. This mix is different from that of other numbers in the film, which all demonstrate Gracie's virtuosity as singer. However, such examples are largely limited to particular genres like musical or comedy, or to the activities that take place 'at the edges' of the performance of the film itself. The performance of a film characteristically assumes an audience giving rapt attention to the images and sound that are projected for them. This is the fundamental mode of entertainment cinema: it is economically convenient in that it means that the audience will leave the cinema immediately after the performance, and feel satisfied. This leaves room for another audience, another performance. It is convenient, too, because it enables film-makers to make broad calculations about the effects of their films: commercial cinema, in increasing its scale and scope as far as possible, tries to standardise its audiences to the same kinds of attention to the screen. This use of cinema, not the only possible use for public exhibition of images, has become predominant in society: it is both what cinema expects of its audience and what the audience expects of cinema.

Commercial cinema, our standard model for cinema, proposes an image that is the perfection of the photographic. It provides an image that is large, usually substantially larger than the individuals watching it. It also provides a particular set of circumstances for watching this image: the audience is seated in rows, separated from each other to some degree, and the image is projected in near-darkness. This induces a particular kind of mental state in the commercial cinema viewer: a concentration of psychic activity into a state of hyper-receptivity. Christian Metz has demonstrated that the peculiar circumstances to which we submit ourselves in entertainment cinema (sitting still — or reasonably still — in the dark) produce a particular attitude to the representation on the screen. Sitting still in the dark has overtones of sleep and dreaming: indeed, it is easier to fall asleep in a film than is often admitted. But it is dreaming from the outside: the images are coming from a source other than that of dream images, which are produced from the unconscious. The spectator's activities are confined to those of watching and listening, and these activities are correspondingly intensified. Images and sounds are received in a state where the normal judging functions of the ego are suspended to some degree (near to sleep), so that what is seen is not subject to the usual expectations of plausibility that we apply to everyday life. In cinema, it is perfectly possible to believe that a man can fly. What is more, the depiction of this activity captures almost all of the attention of the spectator, whose

only other activities tend to be oral stimulation of one kind
or another (e.g. eating confectionery to keep the cinema
in profit). The image is larger than the spectator, the sounds
are loud and usually well-balanced. The spectator looks up
towards the image: image dominates the proceedings. It is the
reason for cinema, and the reason for the spectator's presence
at the event of the film's projection. This concentration on
the image and the lack of distractions for the average
spectator have a series of consequences that define the entertainment cinema event.

The first is that the spectator produces a series of identifications with the images and figures within them. This
process is more complex than the conventional meanings of
the word 'identification' might indicate, as the process is often
taken to be simply a sense of being with (accompanying/
taking the side of/liking) one or perhaps a few of the central
characters. It is a process that has two distinct phases. The
first is an identification with the cinematic apparatus itself;
the second is the narcissistic identification that can take
place in relation to *any* human figure on the screen, or even
with anthropomorphised figures like robots or animals.
Identification with the cinematic apparatus is a precondition
for any cinematic event: it represents the spectator's desire
to concentrate him- or herself into the activities of visual
and aural perception. Predominant anyway in our culture,
cinema further intensifies the experience of these senses.
The beam of light from the projector to the screen is crucial
in this respect. It provides a parallel with the way that we
spontaneously think of our own activity of vision. The
ideology of vision that we inhabit is one that thinks of the
eyes as projecting a beam of light, like a torch-beam, that
illuminates what we look at, making it visible and perceptible. The arrangement of projection in the entertainment
cinema that developed in the West exactly parallels this
ideology of vision: it too presents a beam of light, coming
from a source behind the spectator's head, which widens out
to illuminate a scene for perception. The beam of light from
the projector parallels the beam of light from the eyes. On
this basis, it can be said that the first identification that
takes place in cinema is with the apparatus of projection.

A profound homology is experienced between the cinematic spectacle and the activity of perception of it. They are identified, rather than perceived as complementary activities, or opposed forms of activity. Identification with figures on the screen is the result of cinema's similarities with a series of psychic processes, described by psychoanalysis. First, there is the experience of perception of self as an image: an image separate from the individual's sense of their own body, an image outside of self, in the other. Freud uses the parallel of the myth of Narcissus, falling in love with his own reflection, to describe this process. This account has two emphases: first, the image of self is perceived as though it were the image of another, outside of self; second, it is an image that is desired. Lacan has taken this to be one of the fundamental moments in the construction of a sense of self for the small child, who until this point had no particular conception of its own body as having distinct boundaries and interrelations between its various parts. In this account, the ideal nature of the perceived image is stressed: it is perceived as being more coordinated, more perfect, than the child's existing sense of self. Both these accounts, Lacan's and Freud's, use the literal perception of an image as a convenient mode of explanation rather than a literal account of the processes involved. However, it is clear that part of the point of the account is the description of the processes involved in setting up the possibilities of coherent and comprehensible vision for the infant. The infant is set up as an individual capable of vision of the outside at the same time as having a vision of self in the outside.

Cinema is not simply a narcissistic process. Narcissism is overlaid in the construction of the individual with other processes, some of which find echoes in the way that cinema is constituted. The conditions of cinema viewing mimic to some extent the activities of dreaming, and are certainly close to the partial suspension of the judging function of the ego necessary for the activities of day-dreaming and the construction of phantasies. In both these activities, dreaming and phantasy, the particular individual whose psychic activity is involved does not see him- or herself as a unified individual.

Central to these activities is the perception of possible positions, elements of personality, conflicting tendencies within the individual. Hence both dreaming and phantasy deal with fragmented and contradictory representations of figures. They involve the dreamer or phantasiser in conceptions of self as bisexual, as occupying *both* positions within a representation of heterosexual activity, not just that of active or passive participant. Even less does it involve the dreamer or phantasiser in seeing him- or herself as exclusively 'male' or 'female' in the terms provided by our culture.

Cinematic identification involves two different tendencies. First, there is that of dreaming and phantasy that involve the multiple and contradictory tendencies within the construction of the individual. Second, there is the experience of narcissistic identification with the image of a human figure perceived as other. Both these processes are invoked in the conditions of entertainment cinema. The spectator does not therefore 'identify' with the hero or heroine: an identification that would, if put in its conventional sense, involve socially constructed males identifying with male heroes, and socially constructed females identifying with women heroines. The situation is more complex than this, as identification involves both the recognition of self in the image on the screen, a narcissistic identification, and the identification of self with the various positions that are involved in the fictional narration: those of hero and heroine, villain, bit-part player, active and passive character. It involves the identification of the public, external phantasies of the fiction with personal phantasies. Identification is therefore multiple and fractured, a sense of seeing the constituent parts of the spectator's own psyche paraded before her or him; a sense also of experiencing desire for the perfected images of individuals that are presented over and above their particular phantasy roles.

These forms of identification, through narcissism and through the playing-out of phantasies, are not identical in every individual by any means. They are overlaid by many other processes: I may see a particular phantasy-position of myself in Leslie Howard, but this does not prevent me from finding unsympathetic a whole representation like that of *The Petrified Forest* (1936) for reasons that have far more to do with its construction as a fiction and the particular modality of Howard's performance in it. More important, the forms of narcissism and phantasy are themselves subject to a series of sexual divisions, between men and women. Psychic and social construction both tend to make an equivalence between 'male' and 'active', 'female' and 'passive'. They tend also to play down elements of narcissism in men, through forms of construction of looking which tend to place men as subjects, operators, of the look, and women as objects of the look. Other problems in the construction of the individual intervene in the process: the problem for men of castration, which provokes a tendency towards phantasies of dismemberment, physical harm to men within representations like those of war movies. Often, such films provide no women characters whatsoever: they provide representations of men as active and destructive, condemning or excusing manifestations of 'passivity'. Crucial to the war film is the notion of survival through a series of threats of physical mutilation, to which many characters succumb. It is a phantasy that is characteristic of males; and a phantasy (like many more phantasies than we realise) that is based upon the fear of that which it represents.

The particular conditions of cinema therefore provoke a series of identifications on the part of the spectator: identification with the cinematic apparatus itself; narcissistic identifications with all of the figures (to some degree) who are presented on the screen; identifications across filmic narratives with the various phantasy positions that these narratives invoke. Such identifications tend to be specified according to the sexual construction of the individual spectator, but are by no means exclusively male and female in the conventional sense because they are multiple and shifting, involving different registers in the psychic construction of the individual.

Identification with the cinematic apparatus involves the spectator's concentration of her or his activities into looking and listening. It involves the phantasy of self as a pure perceiving being. The forms of visual perception involved in cinema are yet another psychic level in the construction of the cinema event. The spectator is involved in looking at something that does not (except in very exceptional circumstances) look back at the spectator: this is implied in the identification with the beam of light from the projector. This activity of looking can be described as voyeurism. This is the activity of looking at something without being seen looking. It also implies an irreducible distance between the looker and the thing seen. In cinema, the screen is light and the source of action and sound; the space of the audience is dark, the locus of inaction and relative lack of sound. This defines the separation from the image which is constitutive of voyeurism. The individual spectator is secure in the knowledge that his or her position as voyeur is unthreatened: everyone else present is committing the same offence, if, indeed, it can be called an offence in these circumstances. This sense is completed by the way in which the characters within the fiction, known at some level to be actors, do not look directly at the audience. They acknowledge their role in the process, which is to agree to be seen without showing that they know they are seen.

Voyeurism implies the power of the spectator over what is seen. Not the power to change it, but the knowledge that the actions being undertaken are played out for the spectator. This is so too with cinema, where the cinema spectacle itself clearly has only one aim, that of performing itself for an audience. The spectacle is separate from the spectator, with an unbridgable gulf between the seer and what is seen. This sense of separation permits the spectator to maintain a particular relation of power over what he or she sees, and constructs the need for a continuous change and development in what is seen. The characteristic voyeuristic attitude in cinema is that of wanting to see what happens, to see things unrolling. It demands that these things take place for the spectator, are offered or dedicated to the spectator, and in that sense implies a consent by the representation (and the figures in it) to the act of being watched. The voyeuristic activity is active and inquiring when defined in this way. The activities of peeping toms are a particular, intensified and socially unacceptable variant of voyeurism. Cinema provides a socially sanctioned version, and fosters

6 Photographic voyeurism: the hidden, exotic look (*The Big Sleep*)

it. The concept of voyeurism, derived from psychoanalytic theory, is useful to describe the kind of looking that cinema specialises in, that is the specific pleasure and fascination of cinema. Psychoanalysis is also useful because it indicates the way in which voyeurism, as just described, is never a pure form. It tends to shade into a particular variant, or blockage, of its activity: the fetishistic activity of looking. Where voyeurism maintains (depends upon) a separation between the seer and the object seen, fetishism tries to abolish that gulf. The fetishistic process, taken to its conclusion, is thus the abolition of looking itself: bridging the gulf that separates viewer and object. This process implies a different position and attitude of the spectator to the image: it represents the opposite tendency to that of voyeurism. Any act of looking in the cinema is constituted in the tension between voyeurism and fetishism. Fetishistic looking implies the direct acknowledgment and participation of the object viewed. This contrasts with the voyeuristic emphasis on the film pretending that it is not seen whilst all the time constructing itself for the viewer. With the fetishistic attitude, the look of the character towards the viewer (i.e. down the camera) is a central feature. Each participant, the absent actor and the present viewer, gaze at each other. It is the gaze of longing, asking for the impossible abolition of the distance that separates spectator and fiction. This implies a lack of the secure knowledge that the voyeuristic attitude gives the spectator over the fiction. It implies an equality, a directness, and a level of delicious frustration. It also implies a lack of change and of action. The voyeuristic look is curious, inquiring, demanding to know. The fetishistic gaze is captivated by what it sees, does not wish to inquire further, to see more, to find out. Hence those films which incline towards a fetishistic attitude, like those of Josef von Sternberg, tend to have cyclic plot structures, which repeat variants on the same scenes of desire and rejection. The fetishistic look has much to do with display and the spectacular. It is present in our enjoyment of displays of landscape, of technology. But it is centrally concerned with the display of the female body, a body to be looked at, to be desired, but dangerous in its mystery. The fetishistic attitude will not seek to discover the (impossible) mystery of female sexuality, but will always stop short and become fascinated with this or that detail or display. The voyeuristic look seeks to discover the mystery: 'what is it that women want?' being the question behind the ostensible narrative of many entertainment films.

Such an attitude, the centring of the question of female desire, assumes that male desire is unproblematic. It attempts a definition, a discovery, of female desire from the position of a certainty. In a society where roles are defined in terms of the masculine, the female becomes a problem. The masculine is assumed to be a set of positive definitions: action towards a goal, activity in the world, aggressiveness, heterosexual desire. This implies an opposite: the feminine. However, the definition of this opposite remains a problem, and this problem is obsessively worked over in narrative fiction films. The ubiquitous 'love interest' (never generalisable, always specific) points to this concern. The definition of looking in the cinema is thus a definition which, in entertainment cinema, depends upon the assumption of a masculine norm and the relentless demand to know what the female counterpart to that norm is. Is it an exception, an aberration? This is implied in the numerous films − of great sensitivity, naturally − in which individual women end up mad precisely because they cannot find a place in the world of the fiction, a genre in which Robert Altman specialises. Or is it pure negativity, the opposite to male activity: passivity, waiting behind the scenes, wanting to be wanted but unable to desire actively? Such a thematic appears particularly in films of the Second World War, where men's activity took place in another world, and women waited, supported, contributed what they could, and (tried to) remain faithful. Or is the female counterpart to the constructive male norm the destructive, the dangerous, as the post-war genre of *film noir* tended to imply?

These are impossible questions that are doomed to remain unanswered. They are based on particular assumptions of a sexual difference that then validates one term in that difference to the detriment of the other: the male is assumed as

natural and relatively unproblematic. The problems of male-
ness (insecurity or weakness, for example) are problems that
narratives can solve in phantasy for their spectators. The
assumption of the male as norm underpins something as
fundamental to entertainment cinema as its regime of looking.
The processes of voyeurism and fetishism that it mobilises
are oriented from the male position. This is not to conclude
that only men enjoy films, that women can find no place in
entertainment cinema, for processes of identification (narcissism) involve bisexual positions that are not the exclusive
prerogative of either socially defined sex. Rather, it is to
argue that some of the fundamental terms of entertainment
cinema, like many other representations in our culture, are
oriented towards men rather than women. The terms in
which the representations tend to take place assume the
masculine as a relatively unproblematic given, and the female
as somehow an object to be investigated. The voyeuristic,
investigatory look investigates the female body. There are
therefore numberless sequences that show details of the
female body in an explicitly erotic way; yet the sequence
near the beginning of *Saturday Night Fever* (1977) of John
Travolta dressing is still a rarity in entertainment cinema.
The fetishistic look tends to fasten on to the figure of a
female performer: Marlene Dietrich, Greta Garbo, Marilyn
Monroe; performers whose invitation is precisely that they
should be desired, without knowing beyond that what their
own desire might be. Men and women alike participate in
these structures of looking. Men and women alike have to
assume the terms and definitions of male and female that
they are based upon. Men can see themselves and the objects
of their (socially sanctioned heterosexual) desire; women are
presented with more of a problem. The question 'What do
women really want?' that haunts entertainment cinema (and
many other representations as well) is not one that recognises them in its terms.

Hence voyeurism and fetishism, as the two contrary impulsions in the cinematic organisation of looking, have gained
a common central focus. They are both modalities of the
gaze, of the intense activity of looking, that the circumstances of cinema (sitting still in the dark) are suited to

encourage. They are both profoundly inflected (or perhaps even formed) by the regime of representation which tends to centre the female body as the object of its voyeuristic curiosity and its fetishistic fascination. These two tendencies in looking are both forms of the gaze rather than the glance (momentary and casual).

Gazing at someone is a slightly uncomfortable experience for the person looked at, and a sign of intensity of attention on the part of the person seen. Gazing is the constitutive activity of cinema. Broadcast TV demands a rather different kind of looking: that of the glance. Gazing at the TV is a sign of intensity of attention that is usually considered slightly inappropriate to the medium. Its most active proponents are children, watching despite their domestic circumstances, learning the ways of the world and its narratives.

There are several characteristic ways in which cinema's concentration on the gaze has produced aesthetic effects and consequent technological developments. Entertainment cinema claims a photographic realism for its images, but this claim always conceals more than it reveals. Because of the particular circumstances of spectator concentration and separation from the image (a voyeuristic relation to the image), no naive theory of realism (it's just like real life') can really be applied to cinema. Instead, cinema presents something that contemporary audiences will recognise as 'the real' under a spectacular guise. As the conventions for the depiction of reality change, so audiences tend to deride what once was taken as 'the real' as being spectacular or a fake. Most, then, seeing another film that conforms to the current canons of realism, assume that cinema is making a long march towards ever-increasing realism. This is hardly true: the conventions of depiction of reality are changing all the time, and will continue to change so long as we put the demand upon fictions that they should mimic what we choose to call 'reality'. What is really happening behind this supposed development of realism is a development of the spectacular effects of cinematic vision. When the attempt is made to present reality, we are in awe at the fidelity of the representation. We say it is *so* real (not just it is real), revealing the fetishistic tinge to the desire to investigate reality.

We are fascinated by the fact of the portrayal itself: the image captivates us and holds us. The very fact of desiring to see reality from the position that entertainment cinema provides (secure separation), brings with it a sense of the spectacular, the marvellous nature of what is being seen, a fetishistic undertow.

In many senses, entertainment cinema has been concerned more with the spectacle than with reality. Or rather, it has been concerned to play between the two, to make the real spectacular and the spectacle plausible. Hence entertainment cinema (to the disgust of some) has massively devoted itself to fiction, which plays between reality and the extraordinary, always using one to support the other. The state of the cinematic spectator, with the judging function of the ego temporarily suspended, is ideal for this circumstance. Cinema fictions present extraordinary events, ones that we know to be impossible, or at least highly unlikely. It then performs a fantastic trick upon these unlikely things: it succeeds in making them credible. Cinema's predisposition to the forms of narcissistic and phantasy identification predisposes spectators to accept its representations as plausible. The so-called realism of the cinema (itself a changing convention) is based on the sense of cinema as phantasy, a multiple and fragmented imagining of the self. It is based on the position of the viewer as gazing at the cinema screen, and it is based upon a further characteristic of cinema: its photo effect, discussed later in this chapter.

Sound remains, in relation to the cinematic image, relatively under-researched, both at the level of technological and filmic sophistication, and at the level of theoretical exploration.

Sound lacks directionality in the vast majority of films: it comes from a single point in relation to the spectator. The source of the sound is then detected in relation to the image: if a figure on screen is moving their lips when speech is heard, we assume that the sound is being uttered from that point. Even when, for some reason, the loudspeaker is at the back of the hall rather than behind or very near the screen, the discordant effect produced is very short-term. The habits of expecting sound to issue from a point on the screen soon

make hearers discount the disparity of sound and image
positions. They are discounted in favour of the image: the
sound' is imagined to be coming from the screen. Sound,
then, is placed in relation to the image, it is oriented by
vision. Experiments both with high-fidelity sound and with
directional sound (stereo/quadrophonic) are still at the
stage of wondering how far they can free sound from the
image and invade the space of the audience who are nevertheless faced by a screen separate from them and in a particular place, showing a two-dimensional image. Such effects
break the separation of the audience from the spectacle to a
certain extent, yet no useful effect seems to have been
achieved by them. The image still remains, with its characteristic patterns of attention, at the centre of the cinematic
experience.

The forms of attention that are involved in looking and
listening in the cinema are fundamentally similar. Hearing
involves a distance and separation from the source of the
sound heard; it is prone to similar structures to those of
voyeurism and fetishism. Indeed, many accounts of these
two activities of looking stress the importance of hearing
as constituent parts. Voyeurism is intensified by the activity
of overhearing, of listening to sounds that are not intended
to be heard. The makers of pornographic films have not been
slow to capitalise upon this, providing a little genre of sexual
sounds that are as mythical as the exploits presented for
the gaze of the viewer. Similarly, certain forms of music and
sound become cyclic and repetitive in a fetishistic manner.
The use of repeated words, voices or musical themes in melodrama is a common way of representing absence and the
impossibility of fulfilment of desire. Hence the lost lover's
most poignantly significant line will be repeated after their
death, supposedly 'in the mind' of the bereaved; actually
for the audience. Claudia Allemann's *Blind Spot* (*Reise nach
Lyon*) (1980) develops the logic of this fetishistic attitude to
sound. A woman seeks the truth about Flora Tristan by
recording the sounds of the city where she spent her last
days. The obsessive act of recording promises, but never
manages, to abolish the real historic distance between the
woman and the object of her curiosity and desire.

Hence sound can be seen to participate in the same kinds of structure as those of vision in the cinema. This particular regime of intensified gazing and listening enables cinema to develop in certain directions: towards the elaboration of detail of image and sound, and elaborate forms of attention to them towards spectacular long takes and forms of ellipsis.

The cinema image is routinely more elaborate and detailed than the TV image. In commercial cinema, the budgets for fiction films have increased steadily since the 1930s, especially with American-based or financed films. This budgetary increase has largely gone towards detail in the image: towards larger, more sumptuous sets and set dressings, to special effects, to costumes, to intricate camera-work. The main reason why Hollywood films of the 1930s look inferior to those of the 1940s and 1950s lies in this level of expenditure upon the illusion within the image. This elaboration is largely one of detail: more objects appear in a scene, street scenes are no longer staged with a few passers-by but a whole street with traffic, ancillary activities, crowds. Later comes an elaboration of the sound track, with the increasing possibilities for multiple tracks brought about with magnetic tape recording. Background noises become more complex, sound registration and reproduction becomes more sensitive. Often carried out in the name of 'increased realism', this tendency towards elaboration of the image and soundtracks has two major effects. The first is one of increasing the spectacular nature of the image, which sometimes is overwhelmed with detail; the second is one of tending to introduce a level of ambiguity within the image.

Ambiguity in the image (and, more recently, in sound) occurs when the viewer is presented with more than one area of activity and interest simultaneously. André Bazin makes great claims for this effect in the name of realism. He presents scenes of Welles or Wyler as an advance on the realism of their contemporaries because they give the viewer a choice of areas of interest. The viewer is not presented with one meaning only in any one shot; the image is to be scanned for its areas of importance. In most cases, this is really an overdetermined process. The viewer is not free to select any of the events in the image as attention is still directed towards one particular event, even if only by the fact that it is performed by the characters who are the centre of the narrative interest. Other events, though sometimes fascinating, function more as an attempt to reduce the amount of attention given to the narratively central events in the hope of providing some kind of context for them. Hence in the films of Altman, a superfluity of events is provided in many scenes, especially on the soundtrack: the ridiculous movie announcements over the *M*A*S*H* (1969) camp public address, or the simultaneous wisecracking from three teams of surgeons in the operating theatre. This last is matched by the composition of shots in depth to frame all three teams; the surgical masks making it impossible to tell minor characters from the film's central duo.

Ambiguity in the image relies on a particular form of audience attention. It requires that the viewer scans the image to take in more than one focus of attention, even if the relative importance of those areas of attention is almost always made clear. This process of scanning the image is an important component of the complexity of the cinema image, and relies both on image size and on the intensity of the audience's attention. Scanning the image is taken by Bazin as similar to the attitude of an individual (voyeur?) in relation to real events; however, in relation to the cinema image it is more an activity of relating various aspects of the image together than one of picking out a particular area of interest and discarding others.

Everything in the cinema image (at least the fiction film image) can be assumed to be calculated. Hence everything tends to be pulled into the process of meaning. Everything is assumed to be related to everything else, at least in terms of a common thematic.

Pure irrelevancy is extremely difficult to achieve because the particular detail used as 'irrelevant' will tend to attribute itself with some kind of reason for its existence. It will attract some kind of motivation. Hence the pure irrelevancies that appear in Rossellini's historical reconstruction TV films become illustrations of the period and its strangeness in relation to our own. The elaborate sequence of bone-setting (using munched-up spinach) in *Blaise Pascal* (1971) has no narrative function (the bone-setters left Jansenist tracts that converted Pascal: a fact briefly noted later in the film). But the process of bone-setting tends to become a metaphor for the state of science in seventeenth century France, even though it appears to be (and, narratively, is) suspended as a digression. Hence, ambiguity in the image (and in sound) is not so much a matter of providing an image which is to be scanned and selected from, as providing an image to be scanned, analysed in some way, and then constructed into a meaningful whole.

Independent cinema in Britain pushes this aspect of the cinematic image much further. The final guarantee for an ambiguous image that occurs in entertainment cinema is that it represents a reality. Reality provides the coherence of the image ('It must be true because it's real'). For independent films, the image is to be scanned and seen as fragments of meaning related to each other. But the relation between the elements is often one of contrast or of ironic juxtaposition. It refuses to coalesce into a single coherence of meaning. Further, the image provided is often deliberately 'unreal'. It refuses to be a representation of reality; instead it is a mosaic to be deciphered. In Roger Buck's *Industrial Britain* (1979), a man and a woman (a couple?) sit in an ordinary contemporary living room and quote long sections of the writings of Marx at his most Hegelian. Clearly, this is being offered as a position from which to analyse industrial Britain; yet it is also being undercut by the incongruity of the event. There is a disparity between action and setting that cannot be attributed to any notion of 'realism'. Nevertheless, it is meaningful as a filmic event, and its meaning is somewhat open: it can indicate the irrelevance of Marx's particular analysis to the situation which can provide ordinary people with their current level of material expectancies (three piece suite, stone-effect chimney piece); it can indicate the difficulties (yet the necessity) of applying Marx's analysis, or of using it as an agitational weapon. The film, seeing itself as posing a problem and detailing it, refuses to provide other sequences that make this ambiguity clear. Instead, it provides materials for constructing an understanding of Britain's industrial decline rather than a specific all-embracing analysis. This represents a different attitude from entertainment cinema's; none the less, it depends to some degree upon the cinematic use of image and sound.

The elaboration of the image and consequent uses of ambiguity within it is the result of the particular kind of image size and audience attention that cinema can provide. Similarly, the close attention given to cinema enables sophisticated forms of editing to be carried out, which paradoxically remain virtually unnoticed. In cinema it is routine to cut out parts of scenes that have no particular narrative function: the time it takes a character to enter a door and cross a room, for instance. In cinema, it is enough to show the beginning and end of the action, disguising the missing elements with a change of shot and camera angle, and perhaps providing continuity at another level: dialogue continuing over the cut, or continuous music. This process is known as ellipsis, and is extremely common, especially in the classic period of American fiction films, 1915-55. Close study of most scenes in films of this period will reveal some element of ellipsis of this kind, partly because editing is used to a much greater degree than today. This consistent use of ellipsis tends to give a greater density and concentration to cinematic events compared to events on a theatre stage. It also enables precise forms of pacing to be provided in editing. It also means that once long takes are used instead of highly edited scenes, a great effect of reality is achieved: there is very little ellipsis possible in a long take. The result of the tendency towards long takes, a feature of the entertainment film since the Second World War, has not been a change in the level of audience attention and of density of action, however. The tendency towards long takes has brought with it a new attitude to staging of events for the camera, and of staging the camera in relation to events. It has enabled the concentration of events to take place within one single take (hence intensifying an effect of reality, as Bazin indicates) and has led to a multiplication of events within one take and scene. Instead of ellipses, there are now things in the frame which effectively cover the movements which were once elided in editing. Sometimes this is an increase in the surface detail of sets (especially in period dramas), sometimes a development of ensemble playing. In addition, the staging of the camera in relation to the events has become a major feature. In a long take, the camera and its movements, its pans or zooms, becomes an important feature. The camera reveals a scene, moves around in it, hiding and showing things in the frame. This very quickly becomes a spectacular effect, providing a fluid mobility of the gaze for the viewer which tends to replace the fragmented vision of the highly edited scene. This mobility of the gaze is intensely voyeuristic because it seems to provide a stability for the position of the viewer by providing a continuity of camera vision. The development of the zoom in the 1950s intensified this sense, as the zoom gives a mobility of gaze from a fixed position: hence the repeated habit of latter-day Westerns of constructing pursuit sequences by placing the camera on a high point, framing pursuers, close shot, in a cloud of dust at the very limit of the zoom; then zooming out to frame the pursued much closer to the camera. The zoom thus gives a mobility of gaze to the fixed position of camera at a particular vantage point. Cinema here becomes the perfection of vision: much better than a spectator at that point could possibly see.

Cinema's image, its material quality, its size when projected and the concentration it requires and enables the viewer to have thus all contribute to a specifically cinematic form of seeing. It emphasises the voyeuristic position of the spectator, with its inevitable counterpart of fetishistic tendencies. This has enabled the vast majority of entertainment films to centre their attention upon the investigation of female sexuality, posed as an enigma from a masculine position. It also enables a particular development of representation in image and sound: one that is taken as 'realist', but is so only by convention. The cinematic regime of visual and aural representation is spectacular in its effects, because its effects are sure to be noticed. It is also concentrated, by means of ellipsis in editing or of elaborate staging for spectacular long takes. It produces ambiguity in the image, more than one area of attention, which in entertainment cinema is a controlled effect, and in independent cinema becomes a structuring principle for the viewer's attention.

All of this takes place within a particular regime of representation: the photographic. This is particularly marked in relation to TV, where the image has a very different quality, even if it has been recorded on film. TV appears to be live; the film appears to be recorded. It is important to stress 'appears to be', for much TV is recorded as well, a fact that is often hidden under its apparent immediacy. Yet film is known to be photographed, elsewhere and at an earlier time to the projected performance of the film. The institution of cinema assumes this in all of its workings: the practice of marketing by narrative image, the fact that films are still 'new' for several months after their initial release, the reluctance to place precise dates on filmic events that are vaguely contemporary. Cinema is profoundly marked by what Roland Barthes has called the 'photo effect', the specific and poignant way in which photographs create their sense of reality. In some sense, what has already been said about voyeurism, fetishism and identification in relation to the gaze has specified some features of the photo effect, especially the elements of irreducible distance between viewer and object. But this is only one aspect of the photo effect, which in its full definition again calls into question any simple notion of cinema as an essentially realist medium.

The photograph is always already a record. Even a polaroid photo appears after the moment of which it is a token. For cinematography, this process is even more marked, as image has to be married with sound, scene constructed from fragments, film text from scenes. From the point of view of the spectator (the point of view for which cinema exists) the cinematic illusion is a very particular one: it is the illusion of something that has passed, which probably no longer exists. The cinema image is marked by a particular half-magic feat in that it makes present something that is absent. The moment shown on the screen is passed and gone when it is called back into being as illusion. The figures and places shown are not present in the same space as the viewer. The cinema makes present the absent: this is the irreducible separation that cinema maintains (and attempts to abolish), the fact that objects and people are conjured up yet known

7 The photograph effect: Rote Fahne perform to an audience whose
fate we suspect was tragic (*Kuhle Wampe*)

not to be present. Cinema is present absence: it says 'This
is was.'

This photo effect of present absence can produce an
almost intolerable nostalgia: seeing the faces of young
Germans enjoying a Communist Party Sports rally in *Kuhle
Wampe* (1931) brings with it an appalling sense of loss and
separation, wondering what became of these individuals,
temporarily united in a crowd. Such an effect also contributes to the idolisation of certain stars like Marilyn Monroe,
each of whose gestures can be reinterpreted according to her
tragic persona. More than these passing effects, however, the
present absence of the cinematic image and sound enables
cinema to adopt a particular mode of narration which can be
called 'historic'.

The historic mode of narration involves the use of forms
that do not explicitly acknowledge the presence of the
viewer.

Such forms as direct address (where a character speaks

directly 'out' of the screen as 'I' to a 'you', the audience)
are extremely rare in cinema, however common they may be
in TV. Direct address makes explicit the relationship between
viewer and the subject of the look; the historic mode does
the opposite. Events take place as though they came from
nowhere. Events told in the historic mode of narration are
told by no one, they have no origin, no motivating intelli-
gence. 'Who is telling this story?' is not a question that is
addressed to a classic entertainment film in the way that it
can be addressed to a TV documentary. Instead, the story
unfolds: it seems as though reality itself is telling itself,
almost unaware that it is being watched. This characterises
the historic mode of narration: reality unfolds itself, addressed
implicitly to a voyeur whose presence is acknowledged by the
film's pretence that it is not overlooked. The effect of
historic narration depends upon the photo effect. It depends
on the sense that the photo effect brings of the completeness of the actions before the projection of the film begins.
The film is always already complete, a record of something
that predates the projection. The historic mode depends
upon the fact that it has a story to tell, a story which is
completed at the outset, yet unrolls as though it were in the
present. Present absence thus creates a sense of the presence
yet self-containedness of the cinematic fiction, taking place
in its spaces and times, in a separation from the viewer who
nevertheless can experience the spurious presence of those
events and people.

The historic mode, characterised by its sense of reality
narrating itself, can thus be seen to rely upon the photo
effect. The historic mode is one of the lynchpins of the
notion of cinema-as-reality, because it enables discussion of
cinematic events to take place without any acknowledgment of their status as cinematic fictions. Standard (newspaper) criticism will divide into a substantial set of remarks
about the film's themes, its events, its morality and so on,
concluding with a few asides about style. Cinema, in the
historic mode of narration, can be discussed as though it
were events and characters alone. This is the product of one
theory of realism, the theory of the transparency of cinema
as a window on the world. However, the historic mode is

not this simple. It is not an absence of narration, but the appearance of the absence of narration. It crucially depends upon the photo effect, that is, on the absence of the events represented as much as on the illusion of their presence. The historic mode needs the irreducible separation of viewer from event, and the ability of the event to unroll as though the viewer were not present. The historic mode, therefore, needs the voyeuristic attention of the cinema viewer, concentrating gaze upon illusion.

4 Cinema narration

It is a dangerous undertaking to generalise about narrative procedures; but it is necessary, especially in the area of cinema and TV. A generalised model of narration in each medium is a necessary initial gesture because it then enables specific examples to be compared with the model, to produce a sense of their place in relation to the general run of film or programme productions. However, this process does not work smoothly. The generalised model tends to become normative. Either it is seen as describing the ideal kind of film or programme, or it becomes a series of rules which admit no exceptions. This is not the case with the generalisations put forward here. They should be taken as generalisations, and therefore as (necessary) risks: they are to be compared to 'exceptions' to their rules, as these exceptions often indicate points of change or development. They are not even to be seen as necessities for success in economic or even aesthetic terms. There are several notable films which take very little notice of the model of narration proposed here for cinema: Blake Edwards's productions for instance.

The real value of a generalised model of narrative forms is that it demonstrates that cinema and TV are precisely composed as forms. They are not neutral mechanisms that convey a truth from the world beyond. On the contrary, they work very hard and very subtly to convey an impression of truth. They do so through mechanisms of narration of events which tend to operate in 'documentary' modes as much as 'fictional' ones. The work that these forms of narration do to convey their impressions of truth is not perceived as such, to the extent that the form of narration is able to return to the audience the audience's own assumptions about what life is like. This process has many degrees: there are those films and programmes that return these notions with something added, returning them, as it were, refreshed, rejuvenated, with a slight spice of surprise, a frisson of scandal that indicates that the programme or film is going beyond the purely taken-for-granted conceptions of its audience. Such a TV programme is *A Bouquet of Barbed Wire*. At another point occurs the soap opera whose effect is only to confirm existing conceptions, making some series seem gestural, going through the motions for the sake of it. Part of this effect can be attributed to the fact that the soap opera really does not need to explain its characters' actions and reactions most of the time. The TV series that plays at the edges of or transgresses, common-sense notions of human behaviour tends to spend much of its time explaining these transgressions, with characters endlessly discussing their own and each other's possible motives and feelings.

Behind, or beneath, such nuances can be found a generalised narrative form, a model of narration working through the medium at any particular time, with quite specific effects in terms of what can and cannot be thought and shown by the medium at that moment. A model has been developed over the last few years for the classic Hollywood film, the kind of entertainment film that dominated world markets from about 1915 to 1955. This model of narration in the 'classic' Hollywood film has had the valuable effect of demonstrating the unity that underlies the diversity of generic differences in entertainment films. It has demonstrated the ways in which certain forms of common-sense conceptions of society and individuals have dominated entertainment cinema, and beyond that how it has certain characteristic worries and blind-spots. In effect, what has been shown is that the famous 'realism' of Hollywood films (and their equally famous status as 'mere entertainment') are both the product of a generalisable narrative procedure.

Beyond this, the development of this model has had appreciable effects in the way that classic Hollywood films can be viewed. From being perceived as a form of realism, they become a form of beauty. They can still be enjoyed, but not naively. No longer celebrated simply for their depiction and its truth-to-life, the films can now be seen as mechanisms of a surprising delicacy. The enjoyment lies not in the fact that a certain sense of reality is conveyed, but rather in the way that that result was achieved. Historic distance certainly helps here, as anyone seeing the films now is not caught up in their meanings and their problems in the way that their contemporary audience tended to be. It is more difficult — and hence more urgent — to try to develop a model for contemporary cinema and TV that is capable of a similar release from the immediate hold of cinema and TV productions. Such a release would tend not to aestheticise these films and programmes (as is the case with many older works), but rather to reveal their often corrosive preconceptions.

It has been vaguely assumed (though not really practised) that the model of classic film narration could be applied to TV programmes. This is encouraged by the general assumption of a kind of genealogy of novelistic narration that Colin MacCabe's version of classic realism at least is explicitly based upon. MacCabe demonstrates a continuity of narrational devices from the nineteenth century novel into cinema, a notion confirmed by the general perception that cinema largely came to occupy the place of the novel in the social consumption of fictions in the advanced Western countries. This perception is extended by implication to TV, which is seen as taking cinema's place in its turn. However, vital qualifications need to be added to this schema, attractive as it may seem. First, the material and organisational differences between the three media have had a central effect in determining the modes of narration that can conveniently be accommodated in each. Cinema does not take over the nineteenth-century novel's form, only certain aspects of it. It has to develop its own procedures and emphases. Similarly, TV does not inherit from its predecessors, it develops its own distinctive modes of narration. There is a passing resemblance between TV serials and series and the massive, often serialised, novels that are the high point of the nineteenth century. Each is prone to the development of incident and detail rather than the concise narrative development

8 The narrative image lying in wait: Mile End Empire, London 1928

exemplified by cinema films. Yet their overall architecture is very different, with the novel's majestic synthesis of its characters and incidents (a characteristic of Dickens) contrasting with the fragmentary and often open-ended structure of the TV series.

The following model of classic cinema narrational forms depends for its efficacy on the institutional and material nature of cinema. It relies upon the fact of a single text that is viewed in a sustained and intense way, and its characteristic procedures are initiated by the circulation of a narrative image of that text beyond the text itself. Cinema narration performs and completes a narrative image. Classic cinema narration also relies upon a certain size of image in relation to the spectator; a gaze from the spectator that is able to inspect the image and move around in it. Finally, it is a form of narration that depends upon the sense of present-past that invades the cinematic image. Cinema narrates events that have already completed themselves before the film begins. This is by no means so with TV narration.

Filmic narration is marked by a coherence at the level of textual organisation and of the problematic of the film: its ostensible and hidden subject matters. The filmic narrative is composed of intricate patterns of repetition and innovation of material at all levels, from locations to gestures and camera angles. It appears as though events narrate themselves: there is no voice or agency that specifically addresses the viewer like the 'I' of a narrator that so frequently appears in a novel, or the immediacy of the direct address to TV viewer from programme presenter. Instead, the cinema image is presented as embodying truth, or, perhaps more nowadays, as allowing a closer access to truth than any other medium. This often becomes explicit in modern American films, where cinema is able to reveal truth where the TV images shown within the film's fictional world are trivial or even on occasions dishonest (e.g. the use of TV in *All The President's Men* (1976), showing the surface events beneath which the film's characters are investigating).

The cinema film is explicitly about a particular set of concerns: the narrative image that is inevitably encountered on entrance to a cinema (and usually before) tells us this much. So films are about crimes, espionage, what would happen if . . . , the male menopause, city life, rock music, government corruption, divorce, what really happened in famous historical events. Behind these subject matters comes another series, equally present in the narrative image: the relations between men and women, or more precisely, the problem of understanding the feminine, female sexuality, from a male perspective. Obsessively in classical narrative films, it is women who cannot be fitted in, who represent a problem or a threat to the male self-definitions and masculine positions. So women are eliminated from the story entirely (an early 1970s tendency); threatened and brutally assaulted (the beginning of the 1980s tendency); punished for embodying a sexuality that is as puzzling and threatening to the males as it is desired (*The Postman Always Rings Twice* in its various manifestations); or are tamed into a secondary role, a safe role by the 'happy end'. Habitually, for classical narratives, it is the figure of a woman or more than one woman around whom disruption and imbalance is concentrated. And it is disruption and imbalance that the filmic narrative is constructed to work over and resolve.

Vincente Minnelli's *The Cobweb* (1955) begins with writing snaking across the screen: 'And the Trouble Began'. Or to be precise, it does so after the film has run for a couple of minutes, with credits played over shots of a boy (John Kerr) escaping from a formidable institution and running through the fields, accompanied by a 'crazy' duodecaphonic music. The inscription arrives when he has met a car and hitched a lift. It arrives at the moment that he meets a woman, Gloria Grahame. In a particularly transparent way this opening has demonstrated how classical narrative films propose themselves. They begin with trouble, with a disruption which often orients itself around a female figure; the film then works through this disruption until the trouble is resolved, everything returns to a safe place. *The Cobweb* ends with the inscription 'The Trouble was Over', writing itself across a scene of relationships resolved: Gloria Grahame reunited with her husband, playing surrogate parents to John Kerr. Classic narrative films begin by stating a disruption of a stable state; sometimes they begin by showing that stable state (a small town street on a hot and peaceful afternoon, *Charley Varrick*, 1973), sometimes it is merely implied by the disruption that is presented initially (Bogart's character in *Casablanca* (1942) 'already' disillusioned). This disruption constitutes the problematic of the film, the series of problems that it will proceed to work through, both explicit and implicit. The disruption also constitutes the way that the film will work through these problems: in its beginning is its end. Characteristically, the initiation of a film will specify the kinds of relationships that will be permissible for the characters. Normally these are heterosexual relations. Each man and each woman relate sexually and other sexual permutations will be unthinkable in the terms that the film sets itself. The proviso that this is normally the case has to be emphasised, because the pervasive sexualisation of filmic narratives combined with the obsessive worry about female sexuality make it difficult for encounters within each sex not to be sexualised in some way. Hence the very close (and occasionally explicitly homosexualised) relationships between men in the films of Hawks or Wilder. The film's initial statement of its terms will make clear both the terms of its problematic, and the way it will work through them. The initial disruption, with its stated or implied balance which is disrupted, states the film's problematic, that is, both its concerns and the terms in which they will be worked through.

From the initial disruption, the film works to achieve a rebalancing of elements, a new resolution, a new steady state. A film is a risk, setting our expectations of the world in doubt, stirring up emotions and hazarding things we would not dream of doing or would not like to be done in real life. It is a contained risk because these disruptions are paraded for a short while and then brought back into line, sorted out in a way that fulfils the wish that we could perform similar miracles of reconciliation and reordering in our own lives. This process is not always as cut and dried as these statements might suggest. The strength of the system of filmic narration lies exactly in the way in which it can produce its own variants and exceptions. There are the spectacularly unhappy ends where central characters die a violent death as the only plausible solution for the narrative. *Bonnie and Clyde* (1967) die in a hail of bullets which literally force the film to grind to a halt. Their brief spree of lawlessness, spurious stardom and thwarted tenderness for which we are the privileged spectators ends with a resolution that reinforces the law (and affirms historical fact) just at the moment when we know them and sympathise with them, despite their violence. The film's resolution of its initial disruption is a difficult one: the pair are eradicated precisely because they have placed their audience in an impossible position of understanding the reasons for their actions without being able to condone them. *Bonnie and Clyde* proposes an impossible problematic which taunts its audience with the impossibility of finding a satisfactory resolution for it. Either our human sympathy will be hurt, or our sense of social responsibility. Human sympathy, with its propensity for the tragic, eventually loses out.

Other films propose impossible solutions in rather different ways. It is a characteristic of melodrama that it is capable of producing situations that cannot receive a satisfactory resolution: both desire and social constraint cry out to be appeased in this genre. Hence those films which have a transparently 'stuck on' happy ending in which husband and wife, who have hated each other throughout, are reunited as a conventional caring couple at the film's closure. Sometimes the case is not even as clear as this, with a film declining into incoherence under the pressure of its own contradictions. Any narrative resolution is bound to be inadequate. Often, these cases are extremely interesting for what they reveal of how their society thinks of itself. In some sense they have touched deep ideological problems, indicated by the fact that they can find no mode in which to resolve them.

The movement from initial disruption to final resolution, effective or not, takes place through a progression from event to event. In this sense, the narrative traces a series of consequences, a chain of events that leads from initial disruption to final resolution. Each event follows on from the last and gives rise to the next. The intensity of the experience of watching a film text makes possible a refinement of this process, which is common to all narrational forms. As the film text is watched at a sitting, usually without interruption, the chain of narrative events can be compressed and complicated at the same time. Events can be displayed in a closely connected sequence over a comparatively long attention span. The 'caper' film is an example, where complex thefts of valuables by evading sophisticated security devices occur in a long series of events charted in meticulous detail (e.g. the twenty-minute jewel theft in *Rififi*, *Du Rififi chez les hommes*, 1954). A compelling sequential logic unrolls, accumulating tension as it goes. The filmic narrative tends to be characterised by the movement 'and then . . . and so . . . and then', a consequential logic that runs towards its own resolution. It is set in motion by the repercussions of the initial disruption. One result is that life beyond the narrative (life before disruption and after resolution) tends to appear as inaction or stasis compared to the action and movement of the narrative itself. It becomes difficult, if not downright disruptive, to produce a sense of everyday life in a narrative film as a result. The experience of watching Akerman's *Jeanne Dielmann, 23 Quai du Commerce, 1080 Bruxelles* (1975) reveals this problem, as some people find it intolerable in the way it cuts across their sense of the cinematic. A narrative movement does occur, but at a slow pace; for three hours the film is mainly concerned with documenting the minutiae of a woman's domestic work. The film evades the compression of events that is so characteristic of the narrative film, relaxing the consequential onward movement so as to show the collapse of the careful (if not obsessive) domestic routine that produces the woman's final dramatic act. *Jeanne Dielmann* reveals the characteristic compression and sequencing of events in the filmic narrative by refusing to perform them, and refusing their structuring of attention.

Jeanne Dielmann does depend upon another crucial aspect of cinematic narration, and in this sense it is not a refusal of cinema (as some have claimed), merely of some of the effects of the normal regime of cinematic narration. The film of Jeanne Dielmann shows three days in her life. It repeats

9 Repetition: Jeanne Dielmann's everyday life, an intolerable spectacle
for those more used to seeing food eaten in films

events over those three days: cooking, cleaning, meals with
her son, a series of visits from men who are her sexual clients.
A pattern of repetition is set up, and such patterns of repetition are characteristic of the working of filmic narration.
However, the repetition is not uniform and unvaried: daily
events are repeated but differently. They begin to go wrong,
she forgets things, misplaces objects, loses her sense of order
after she has suddenly and unexpectedly experienced sexual
pleasure with one of her clients. In this sense, *Jeanne Dielmann* is a repetition of events with variation, with novelty,
introducing a central element of the unexpected into the
progression of events. This, too, is a central feature of cinematic narration. With *Jeanne Dielmann* this process is crucially altered, so that the elements of repetition weigh more
heavily than usual, and variation and novel material is a
matter of nuance. However, it could be said that *Jeanne
Dielmann* foregrounds this aspect of filmic narration through

its refusal of the conventional compressed chain of events.

Meaning is attributed to the onward movement of narrative events by patterns of repetition and novelty. The repetition of a particular face and body provides us with a sense of a character who occurs in the various settings that the film offers us; the variation of this character's expressions provides us with indications of his or her moods and thoughts. Such an example is deliberately banal (except that we tend to take it for granted), but such patterns can be found across the whole of the film, and reach out to contain everything in it. Lines of dialogue tend to be repeated for effect, having a slightly different (or sometimes contradictory) meaning each time. Gestures similarly carry such meanings, like Cary Grant's perpetual lack of a match in *Only Angels Have Wings* (1939), a repetition that gains its narrative purpose from the different people who reflexively offer him a light. This charts the true emotions of the hardboiled characters towards their 'leader'.

Repetition and innovation are fundamental to the way that filmic narration works. Narration works to lay out meanings in front of the viewer, meanings which are in some way jumbled or incomplete (i.e. the problematic). The narration then reintegrates these elements (or as many as possible) into a new harmony that is the ending of the film. The way in which this process takes place has to be clear at all points to the viewer in the system of classic narration. So neither too much nor too little new information should be presented at any one time. A balance is reached between repetition of known and familiar information and the new and unfamiliar. At the beginning of the film, where everything (apart from the enigmatic information in the narrative image) remains to be seen, a classic film will typically take the form of long, well separated sequences. These introduce both characters and their basic relations and the spaces in which the action is to take place. These locations are clearly indicated: in *The Big Sleep* (1946), a hand rings a doorbell, above which is a plate reading 'Sternwood'; the butler opens the door, and ushers Marlowe in to see General Sternwood. When the action returns to the Sternwood Mansion, no such heavy indicators are needed. The space being known, the action moves straight into it. This repetition at the level of location allows an innovation at another level: Marlowe is able, through repartee, to test out the butler (another known element) to explore and dismiss his possible involvement in the plot. This, an innovation, is also an exhaustion of an element in the film. The butler, not having an active plot function, is now 'exhausted', and so disappears from the film. This process of repetition of locations need not be literal. Once the action has been established as taking place in a certain type of location (seedy offices or bars), then any seedy office or bar is instantly recognised as such. It becomes an element of repetition, with an edge of innovation. These patterns play across the whole of a classic film: gestures, lines of dialogue, actions, significant clues and glances are all drawn into the accumulation of repetitions. These patterns establish continuities of meaning across the film, and allow changes or innovations in meaning to take place at other levels.

This system of novelty and repetition, delicately balanced, is an economic system. It enables the film to move faster between locations as the film progresses; being familiar, they no longer need to be introduced, the viewer knows where the action is taking place. Being familiar, too, they carry memories of the events that have already been staged there, and so intensify the accumulation of meaning within the film. An increasing fluidity is possible as the film progresses. This suits the increasing tempo of action which is characteristic of the narrative film as it moves towards a conclusion. Patterns of repetition across the text produce an effect of rhyming, whereby any element, however small, that recurs in the film gains a specific meaning from being repeated. This specific meaning is a product of the film itself: the repetition of a particular camera angle in *Letter from an Unknown Woman* (1948) — once framing the child Lisa's view of her fantasy-lover bringing a woman home, then framing Lisa herself in that position later when they have met as adults — owes everything to the particular circumstance of the film, and very little to any generalised notion of 'high angle shots'. In another sense, then, the pattern of balancing repetition and innovation is an economic one: it allows as much as

possible that appears in a film to be used, and to contribute
to the meaning of the film by being used again.

A balance between repetition and novelty can be said to
characterise a narrative film's relationship to the general
cultural knowledges that it assumes of its viewers. A film
takes a lot for granted in what it refers to as well as in the
way it is constructed internally. It assumes we think it
normal that everyone owns cars, smokes cigarettes, avoids
talking about politics, and much else besides. It assumes that
the audience will make certain recognitions, whether it be
that the Eiffel Tower equals Paris, or that in a film of the
1940s a man lying on a couch smoking a cigarette whilst a
woman adjusts her make-up indicates that 'intimacy has
occurred'. General ideological notions and ones drawn
from the specific domain of film are assumed by narrative
films. These assumptions are established through repetition,
a characteristic of ideological production which leads us to
assume things unless they are specifically contradicted. Yet
mere repetition alone is not the characteristic of the film
text. It may take for granted certain meanings, certain
assumptions, but it exists to take risks, to work through
ideological problems. Hence the innovatory character of
the filmic in relation to ideological meanings. They are not
reproduced so much as refreshed, not so much repeated as
reworked.

Filmic narration is an economic system: balancing familiar
elements of meaning against the unfamiliar, it moves forward
by a succession of events linked in a causal chain. The basic
terms of this movement which recur throughout are those
produced in an initial disruption of a stable state. The narration works through these terms, changing and rearranging
them across the movement of events until a new stable state
is reached. Overall, this process gives a very specific impression: an impression of reality. It appears that events narrate
themselves. There is no voice which tells the story, there
does not appear to be a controlling consciousness that is
writing the narrative for the audience, however much we may
know about the director or whoever. This effect of impersonal narration is specifically filmic, and, further, belongs
to the form of the classic narrative film. It is a product

of the way that the films pretend that they are being overlooked (showing intimate events at which strangers should
not be present), yet at the same time constructing this overlooking very carefully so that it is comprehensible to the
mythical average spectator. Comprehensibility is provided by
the balancing of repetition and novelty, which construct a
level of attention and an accumulation of meaning on the
part of the spectator: neither too much that is new, nor too
little. This careful construction presents itself as agentless:
events telling themselves, falling into their natural progression and inevitable consequences. This impersonal narration,
carefully constructed, is responsible for the particular effect
of reality that the classic narrative film has.

Nowadays, large sections of entertainment cinema have
radically revised some of the basic workings of the classic
narrative cinema, in the pursuit of several aims: increased
realism, artistry, increased spectacular effects. In particular,
the impersonal mode of narration has been eroded in favour
of a cinema which marks its narrative of events at certain
points as an effect of a system. In many cases, this is little
more than showing off what Hollywood once took for
granted; in others, it marks a genuine unease with the effects
of impersonal narration. Hence the tendency of 'New
American Cinema' to make itself slightly incomprehensible:
the mumbled dialogue of a Marlon Brando giving way to the
straightforward inaudibility of much of the dialogue in a film
like *Mean Streets* (1973). Again, there is a tendency to multiply incidental details so that they tend to overwhelm the
narrative drive. Narratively important events appear in the
same mode as, in the interstices of, the everyday (usually the
everyday of fairly exotic characters). Hence a film like
Killing of a Chinese Bookie (1976), where it is never certain
which events are providing the onward movement of the film,
though the centrality of the male strip-club owner is never
in question. Nicholas Roeg's films tend to follow another
strategy. They multiply the possible connections across the
text and fragment what is usually a simple narrative line into
a series of scenes and shots which make explicit certain connections, and generate others. Not only are subjective
memories included, but also a series of connections between

images which defy rational explanation: the series around the colour red in *Don't Look Now* (1973), the obsession with Teresa Russell's throat in *Bad Timing* (1980). To some extent the stylisation, or exaggeration, of one or another trait of the classical narrative procedure, such films (which often have difficult commercial careers) demonstrate both the tenacity of the classicial regime as our basic model for what a film should be, and a certain impatience with it.

The model of classical narrative cinema has certain characteristics that mark it out as a distinctive mode of constituting fictional events. It is heavily centred towards a particular problematic, and thus tends to be centred upon particular individuals rather than a wide group. This concentration on one problematic also leads to a strong impulsion towards a final coherence (which is not always delivered): towards a sense in which everything falls back into place, repeated, worked through and resolved. The classical filmic narrative constructs events as consequential, producing a chain of cause and effect between successive sequences. It presents itself as a record of events, events which narrate themselves rather than relying on any perceptible agency of narration. With its economic construction, in which anything present on image or sound tracks tends to be incorporated into patterns of repetition, it tends to emphasise *mise en scène*, the use of every element within the world of the fiction to contribute to an overall system of meaning. Such is the regime of narration of the classical fiction film, a regime that owes much to the specific conditions of cinema that were constructed by and produced for the American studio system between 1915 and 1955. It still tends to underlie our basic preconceptions of cinema.

5 The cinema spectator

The predominant myth of cinema, fostered by cinema itself, is that its images and sounds present reality. The equivalent myth of TV is that its broadcasts are immediate and live. Each myth reveals something of how the medium concerned wants to be watched. It reveals the kind of spectator that the medium proposes that we should be, what state of mind we should have, what kinds of pleasure and satisfaction we should achieve. Each medium proposes an ideal spectator and a position for that spectator; and it is habitual in our society to occupy that position more or less when using the particular medium. Cinema proposes its image of reality to a spectator who wishes to resolve an enigma, who is concerned to gain the answer to particular questions, the resolution to specific problems. TV proposes its sense of immediacy to a spectator who is concerned to remain in touch with events, to keep abreast of current concerns and fashions, to extend his or her horizons of knowledge and acquaintance. When each medium represents itself, when TV shows us a TV studio, when a film shows us film-makers, they are more or less explicit about these expected attitudes on the part of their spectators. The assumptions are even more pronounced when one medium describes the other: when cinema shows the TV image and its uses, when TV calls upon the category 'film' to justify certain aspects of its programming.

To describe the assumed spectator of each medium is to run the same risks as those found in characterising their respective regimes of narration. Any generalisation tends to wipe out nuances, to eradicate differences so that both historical variations and present points of change are obscured. As a result, TV and cinema seem to have monolithic attitudes which are incapable of changing. Hence a profound pessimism is the only responsible political attitude to them from a variety of points of view. However, generalisations of this order do have an initial power of revelation, which, properly used, can help to generate a coherent sense of the general characteristics of a particular medium. Features that hitherto had seemed piecemeal and unrelated begin to fall into some kind of relation to each other. General statements can accomplish this much. From then on, it is a matter of discovering the nuances and points of real change which will eventually lead to a radical revision (if not replacement) of the initial generalisations. The generalisations gathered here are (and always were) intended to be of such an order: to reveal rather than to proscribe, to incite further perceptions rather than to induce pessimism. This is particularly so with the characterisation of the spectator presupposed by cinema, a characterisation that has been in circulation for some time. It is not intended as a dismissal of particular kinds of cinema, nor as an exhaustive definition of all the potential of cinema, but rather as a broad characterisation of the dominant forms of entertainment cinema that have developed both in the USA and, now, internationally.

Cinema habitually proposes a particular enigma to its spectators through the operation of the narrative image which offers scrambled meanings to be sorted out by the film itself. These meanings are always particular and specific. The spectator is therefore already specified in her or his turn: a spectator who is curious or expectant about the particular problem with which the film promises to concern itself. Such a specification can be highly defined (as with an anthropological documentary for example), or it can be of the vaguest kind. With entertainment cinema, it is usually vague because of the institutional demands of a cinema that conceives of itself as a mass medium. To get twelve million or more people to see a film dictates that the narrative image should produce the most general possible specification of the audience. However, this general spectator specification still has to be specific, it still has to provide something that will produce curiosity or expectancy. This is perhaps the most difficult ideological calculation in the whole of the film industry: not what to make a film about, but how to offer that film to as wide as possible a range of curiosities without losing the specificity of the film itself. The narrative image will therefore confine itself to known and safe ideological trends in society, producing, for example, a spectator who is curious about displays of masculinity, or is curious about the phenomenon of the 'liberated woman' from a position of scepticism.

Mass entertainment cinema of the classic period was able to offer narrative images which could specify audiences in two principal ways: through genre and through the star. Never imagining that the possible audience for any routine film could be more than a fraction of the mass audience, these two means were enough to create an expectancy. Nowadays, the diversification of cinema into a series of rather separate kinds of audience has made the publicity specification of the potential spectator a little more difficult. First, the type of cinema involved (art cinema, adventure, thoughtful entertainment, pornography) has to be marked. Then this initial definition has to be deprived of exclusivity so that other potential viewers can be attracted. Hence the campaign for Just Jaecken's *Emmanuelle* (1974) in Britain featured respectable, homely Katie Boyle's radio commercial offering it as 'The film that makes you feel good without feeling bad.' The spectator was specified by the formula Pornography minus Shame equals Eroticism.

The institution of the narrative entertainment film itself proposes a definite kind of spectator. It proposes a type of film (the 'Hollywood film'), so the spectator for that film is already specified on entering the cinema as someone who is curious or expectant about a particular enigma, and demands that this curiosity should be satisfied in a particular way. The institution therefore specifies someone as its spectator who demands satisfaction of a curiosity in a way that cannot be gained from a newspaper or a novel, from TV or radio.

Entertainment cinema satisfies the curiosity it provokes by its particular process of narration. Satisfaction is found through the charting of a causal series, the consequences of an initial disruption. The general enigma posed by the narrative image is immediately specified by the particular forms of disruption that the film proposes to work through. It works through them by a process of repetition and innovation of meanings, a process that constantly balances and rebalances itself. Narration constantly provides surprises, its twists and turns, but these surprises reveal themselves as another aspect of a whole, as both causal consequences of previous actions, and as thematically linked to the major patterns of meaning that emerge progressively. The narration's final action of balancing is the final reintegration of as many elements as possible into a new stable order. So there is a specific form to the satisfaction of curiosity excited by the narrative image and by the institution of cinema. It is a satisfaction of order, balance and exhaustion of narrative elements. It provides links and answers, and settles the question that initially provoked the narrative as far as it is possible to settle it within a particular set of circumstances.

Narrative exhaustion and satisfaction is the general aim of cinema's entertainment narratives, but this process is always subject to historical constraints. Very obviously, films produced in Britain during the Second World War, are not able to provide the answer to the major enigma that provoked them as films in the first place. They cannot predict the answer to the question 'Will we win the war?' let alone to the question that increasingly began to replace it, that of 'What will happen when the war is over?' Hence *Millions Like Us* (1943) opens the question of the unprecedented displacement of class differences taking place during the war, but can provide no prediction of what its consequences might be. A romance develops between the blunt North Country factory foreman and the woman worker with aristocratic manners. Its resolution is left suspended, with him telling her that they will have to wait to see what the war's consequences for British class structure will be. A similar effect is found in the Ministry of Information's short *The Tyneside Story* (1944). The euphoric voice-over telling of the revitalisation of Tyneside shipyards after the mass unemployment of the 1930s is interrupted by a Tynesider who asks, in direct address, whether the same thing will happen again after the war. Some films go to extraordinary lengths to ensure the satisfaction of the basic enigma that surrounds them. Cavalcanti's *Went the Day Well?* (1942) is surrounded by a flash-forward to postwar days, with the complacent churchwarden speaking, again in direct address, as though the spectator were a tourist who has come to visit the site of the famous Battle of Bramley End. He shows us the grave of the German invaders, informing us that this was the only piece of British soil that they managed to capture. Each film is in some way unable to provide a full resolution of its basic enigma, although each works as a satisfying narrative. They manage to balance and reintegrate the elements that they propose for themselves (their particularities), but are unable to include in this reintegration the satisfaction of the wider enigma that provoked them. They are still satisfying entertainment because of the internal reintegration that they manage to achieve.

The process of narration is able to provide such satisfaction even when it is unable to satisfy underlying questions. This is because of the particular kind of position it gives the spectator towards the events and meanings that it presents. This position is qualitatively different from those positions that are normally available in everyday life (particularly in the everyday life of wartime). The spectator is given a position of spectatorship, of voyeurism. The spectator is specified not only as someone whose curiosity is to be satisfied by the rebalancing of an initial disruption, but also, more centrally, as someone who is to occupy a particular position in relation to those events. Entertainment cinema offers the possibility of seeing events and comprehending them from a position of separation and of mastery. The film is offered to the spectator, but the spectator does not have anything to offer to the film apart from the desire to see and hear. Hence the spectator's position is one of power, specifically the power to understand events rather than to change them. This is the position of mastery that the voyeuristic process gives to the cinema spectator. It is a mastery that can shade into fascination, into the fetishistic desire to abolish the very distance and separation that makes the process of seeing possible. The mastery offered by the process of narrative

10 The cinematic image, separate and unattainable (*Les Carabiniers*)

cinema is one of being able to make sense of disparate
images and sounds, to knit them together into a coherent and
meaningful whole. Hence the mastery is one of separation
and of totalisation. The spectator's position is that of the
seer, who is able both to see and comprehend what is seen.
The film itself is constructed for and offered to this spectator,
who becomes the point of intelligibility for the film. Hence
a film (fiction or documentary) is not simply constructed out
of reality, nor to show reality, but rather to offer an intelligible reality to a curious spectator who remains separate
from the illusion.

So habitual are the processes of construction of films for
a spectator in this position that theories of 'realism' and
cinema habitually ignore them. These theories ignore the
complex and subtle forms of organisation of material in both
fiction and documentary which aim to organise them as
intelligible wholes for a spectator. They ignore, for instance,
the shifting conventions of dialogue which have only an
incidental relationship with the ways that people speak to

each other, but have a central function of being intelligible
to the spectator. The search for an increased effect of reality
often means providing dialogue that is less comprehensible
than the prevailing conventions would dictate, whether this
be by providing regional accents (Renoir's *Toni* (1934) or
Henzell's *The Harder They Come* (1972), subtitled for
British release), or by the famous effects of mumbling promoted by Marlon Brando. However, as Brando's early
mumbles nowadays demonstrate, the conventions of dialogue
depiction tend to change to absorb these exceptions into a
new set of dialogue conventions. Even in these cases, where
delivery of dialogue may be innovatory, the basic construction
of dialogue remains the same: it assumes a viewer whose
acquaintance with the situation portrayed began at the beginning of the film. Hence dialogue, along with other elements,
will tend to provide information that can be used to construct an adequate notion of what is happening and of the
general relationships between characters and situations.
The regime of classic narration developed in Hollywood
tended towards an extremely explicit regime of construction
of information for the cinematic spectator, where everything
was directed towards intelligibility with the effect of reality
sometimes severely sacrificed in the process. Nowadays, the
'New American Cinema' provides a certain amount of dialogue whose meanings are incidental to the drift of the
narrative. Altman provides scenes of overlapping dialogue
that consists mainly of inconsequential remarks, gags, incomplete utterances and so on. But he is careful to provide
certain conversations and remarks that have a greater audi-
bility, and it is these which provide necessary narrative
information. Hence those films that are praised for their
'realism' at particular points are also constructed for a viewer
as the point of their intelligibility: they do not only (as
sarcastic critics sometimes claim) mumble away to themselves.

The position offered to the spectator is that of the seer
who renders the film intelligible. It is a position of knowledge which constructs the spectator as able to produce
a vision of the truth through the film. Often, the truth that
the spectator apprehends is nothing other than vision, a

vision whose mastery is based on the fact that it can see more
than anyone or anything else. Habitually in a fiction film,
vision is equated with access to truth: those who can see
more know more of the truth (conversely, those who are
blind 'see' truth that the sighted overlook, and offer their
'vision' for the spectator as well). The position of ultimate
vision in any fiction film is not that of any of the characters,
but that of the spectator. The spectator can see everything
the characters see, together with both the characters' acts of
seeing, and those things that are kept hidden from the gaze
of the characters. Sometimes, the sight of a particular detail
is deliberately withheld from the spectator, so that its revelation constitutes the final resolution of the film, the point at
which vision, knowledge and truth coalesce in the spectator.
At the end of *Psycho* (1960) it is the sight of the shrivelled
corpse of Norman Bates's mother that proves he is insane,
and explains his behaviour for us. At this point, the film is
closed. The ensuing explanation by the psychiatrist is strictly
speaking redundant: it only verbalises what we have already
seen as the truth about Norman Bates's character.

Such instances point to an important facet of the process
of cinematic narration. The position of knowledge, intelligibility and truth is not held all through the film to the same
degree. The process of a narrative film is usually an extended
game with the spectator, offering the promise of such a position, but witholding fulfilment of that promise until the end
of the film. In effect, just as the process of narration is a
constant balancing of repetition and novelty, so too the
spectator's position is one of balancing and rebalancing, of
achievement and loss of a position of knowledge and vision.
Hence the spectator is constantly in a state of anxiety, of
wanting to know but being unable to find out instantly. This
anxiety is not total, because the loss of position of mastery
is never total, but always concerned with one particular
aspect of knowledge.

Thus, in *La Règle du Jeu* (1939) we are always sure of the
characteristics of each person, which very often reduce to a
cliché: the champion pilot who is as hopeless at human relations as he is a genius with machines; the aristocrat who
treats his wife as a rather inferior possession; the jealous

gamekeeper husband and his flirtatious wife. However, what these characteristics will produce in terms of human interactions is never quite so certain. The viewer is constantly surprised by the particularities of relationships in the plot, even though those relationships themselves tend to belong to quite familiar theatrical and filmic conventions. The state of knowledge that the spectator has concerns the general characteristics and disposition of characters, together with the general social background of the whole drama. This background is familiar enough from both French and foreign films of the 1930s: the upper-class house-party, the background for farce and crazy comedy. However, the spectator's anxiety, the lack of knowledge which is undergone through the film, concerns the motives of characters and the eventual outcome of Christine's affair with the pilot. Motives can be revealed both intentionally, by one character to another, and unintentionally, by moments and gestures that are visible only to the spectator. Hence the spectator gains a greater knowledge than any character, even Octave. But finally motives cannot be known in their totality, not even by the spectator, so the film manages its closure by both the accidental shooting of Jurieu, the pilot, which reduces the weekend from farce to minor tragedy, and by Octave's remark that 'The most puzzling thing is that everyone has their reasons.' The film closes by affirming the radical impossibility of knowing fully what human motives are, whilst having given the spectator a wide range of insights into the motives of a particular group of characters. Hence a position of knowledge relative to the characters is held by the spectator throughout the film; finally, this particular knowledge is subsumed into a generalised wisdom, a general knowledge about humanity.

The spectator's anxiety is an anxiety that is provoked in safety, because its resolution is guaranteed by the institution of cinema itself, which is not in the habit of presenting incomplete films. The spectator's anxiety is thus the result of contradictory desires: the desire that the film should continue, and the desire that the film should end satisfactorily. The mechanisms of narration foster and accomplish this second desire, the desire for an ending. The activities of phantasy and narcissistic identification are directed towards the open continuance of the film, with its multiple presentations and representations of different figures of people, different possible positions in various kinds of encounter. The film provides the spectator with various scenarios, one or more in each scene as well as more general ones governing the whole narrative, which correspond to a greater or lesser degree with the spectator's own phantasies and identifications. Some of the satisfaction that is gained from a particular film comes from its correspondence, or lack of correspondence, with a particular spectator's own phantasies. These are by no means only pleasurable phantasies. It is equally possible for pleasure to be gained from scenes of humiliation and defeat as it is from scenes of success and victory. In both cases, the pleasure comes from the fulfilment of a wish (for we wish what we fear as well as what we desire), and from seeing the fulfilment of that wish in the other. What happens on the screen does not happen directly to the spectator. It represents the fulfilment of phantasies without extinguishing the desires that support them. The cinematic fiction is not only a wish-fulfilment, it is a wish-fulfilment that takes place in the very particular conditions of voyeuristic separation and narcissistic identification, and in the circumstances of narration for a generalised public rather than for each spectator alone. For the spectator, the anxiety that is produced comes from the contradictory desires that the film should achieve a satisfactory narrative conclusion, and that it should continue its multivalent statements and restatements of situations and figures that have echoes in the spectator's own phantasies.

This whole process, taking place for a large and differentiated audience, is a delicate balancing act. Sometimes films fail to achieve it for particular spectators, whose anger at the film's failure to hold their interest or to be intelligible enough is out of all proportion to the amount of time and/or money they may have expended upon it. Dislike of a film is usually a very aggressive feeling, directed towards the film itself, the institution of cinema, and sometimes even those who shared the experience of the particular performance. A film which fails for a spectator usually fails because it does not provide the necessary play with phantasies, and final closing accomplishment of a position of mastery and knowledge. The anxiety produced in the expectation of its satisfaction is not dissipated; it returns as a kind of aggression.

The anxiety inherent in the experience of entertainment cinema could be called the work of the spectator. It is a work because it involves the expenditure of emotional energy and the taking of emotional risks in order to produce a sense of pleasurable satisfaction at the conclusion of the process. The process itself is a constant teasing: a position of partial mastery is held throughout the film by the viewer, who sees something of truth throughout. But the film refuses to reveal all of its truth until its conclusion, where everything falls into place for the spectator. The truth that is perceived at any one point can, of course, be erroneous. The famous twists of a good suspense plot prove this: the revelation of a supposed truth as partial or even false serves to reconfirm the spectator's position in relation to the fiction. It seems as though, in the words of many fictional police investigators, '*now* we're getting somewhere'.

The form of spectatorship offered by entertainment cinema is open to various kinds of social manifestation. In entertainment cinema, it tends to remain an individual experience: the more adept at understanding the demands that cinematic narration makes upon an individual, the more engrossed each separate member of the audience becomes. Two points emerge when members of the audience relate directly to each other during the projection of a film. First, when one or more members of an audience demand an explanation of a particular aspect of the plot, and someone volunteers this. Sometimes, even this process is left until the end of the film, when in conversation someone will hazard 'I didn't understand it when . . .'. The other moment of direct relation is when some part or all of the audience refuse the illusion that the film is offering. They make fun of it, laughing, mocking the film for being an ineffective piece of work. But if a film is intelligible to its viewers, and is able to provide a satisfying balance of knowledge and promise of further knowledge, then the audience will relate to the film as individuals, each placed separately by the film in a similar position of secure seeing. The physical arrangement of the cinema intensifies this individuation. All face forward in the dark, awareness of anyone else unknown is reduced to a general awareness of the presence of a crowd, everyone and no one. Yet the complicity of the crowd in the experience of a film is very necessary. It is not only the film itself that licenses the activity of the spectator, silently watching, but also the presence of others who are engaged in a similar activity without disturbing each other, without watching each other. The experience of watching a film in an empty cinema is curiously desolate, and the feeling of being watched watching a film is curiously disturbing. The presence of the crowd in the cinema is vital to the operation of the regime of cinematic representation. It enables a voyeuristic activity to take place that is necessary to produce the individual spectator as the point of intelligibility of the film. Perhaps it is to ensure the presence of co-voyeurs that people seek company to go to the cinema. The audience of an entertainment film is very seldom composed of isolated individuals, but rather of couples, groups of friends and sometimes even family groups. Many people feel a profound sense of shame at watching a film alone, not principally during the projection, but during those interminable minutes devoted to the sales of ice-cream or advertisements for sundry items not permitted TV advertising. At these moments the house lights are up: it is possible to be seen clearly by other members of the audience, and to see them clearly. It is no longer a crowd, but a gathering of individuals, mutually suspicious rather than mutually affirming.

The voyeuristic activity, inquiring and powerful, is central to the cinematic process. Voyeurism implies the consent of the object watched, as well as, in the case of cinema, the complicity of an anonymous crowd. In these circumstances, the spectator can participate in a process which awakens curiosity through the operation of the narrative image, and satisfies that curiosity in a particular way through the operation of the narrative film. Entertainment cinema puts the spectator in a particular relation to the enigmas it poses. The spectator is the point of intelligibility of the film, where it coalesces meaning, vision and truth. The film works by constructing and reconstructing a position of relative knowledge and relative vision for the spectator throughout. It perpetually promises to make this vision full, to totalise the various partial visions and scattered knowledge at the end of the film's projection. Hence narrative entertainment cinema produces a temporary and partial anxiety in the spectator that it promises to dissipate. It does so through the final reintegration of as much as possible of its narrative materials in the film's conclusion.

This, then, is the institution of entertainment cinema, the predominant form of cinema in our culture. It projects films as a public event, and offers single separate fictions. These are offered to spectators through the mechanism of the narrative image, an enigmatic statement of some of the particular film's concerns. The cinematic image is large and high definition, and it is watched in conditions of relatively intense and sustained attention. This produces a concentration upon the activities of looking: the activities of identification, of voyeurism and its variant, the fetishistic attitude. Cinematic narration uses this regime of looking to produce tightly organised narratives, centring on a particular problematic that is resolved and exhausted through a pattern of repetition and novelty. These hold the spectator in a process of pleasurable anxiety, wanting to know, being provided with information, but not all the information in the correct form until the end of the film. This spectator is maintained in a position of mastery in relation to the film: the film is directed towards the spectator, even whilst it pretends that it has no agency of narration. This direction towards the spectator sets the spectator as the point of intelligibility of the film, the point where its meanings will coalesce into an order and a knowledge. The spectator is separate from the film's fiction, able to judge and to assess; separate from the filmic image, which is absent even whilst it presents itself as present.
This is the regime of classic cinema, a whole institution that includes both films and the ways in which those films are made available and govern the way they are watched. It is a regime that has a wider social and aesthetic effect than

its own scope might indicate. In particular, it has formed a cultural institution that has spread far beyond the cinema, even though it still crucially depends upon cinema: the institution of the star system.

6 Stars as a cinematic phenomenon

Stars have a similar function in the film industry to the creation of a 'narrative image': they provide a foreknowledge of the fiction, an invitation to cinema. Stars are incomplete images outside the cinema: the performance of the film is the moment of completion of images in subsidiary circulation, in newspapers, fanzines, etc. Further, a paradox is present in these subsidiary forms. The star is at once ordinary and extraordinary, available for desire and unattainable. This paradox is repeated and intensified in cinema by the regime of presence-yet-absence that is the filmic image. Further, the star's particular performance in a film is always more than the culmination of the star images in subsidiary circulation: it is a balancing act between fiction and cultism. It may well be that a similar creation of stars is impossible for broadcast TV (which fosters 'personalities'), but does take place in the rock music industry.

The basic definition of a star is that of a performer in a particular medium whose figure enters into subsidiary forms of circulation, and then feeds back into future performances. Hence the tradition of the 'star' stretches back beyond cinema, into theatre, and especially into opera. The discovery of stars by cinema is a well-documented legend. The 'Trust', the MPPC set up by the manufacturers of equipment in 1908 to muscle in on the profits of the nickelodeon boom, had a primitive concept of marketing. They relied on selling the experience of cinema (and the newer experience of cinema fiction) alone: all films were treated as fundamentally similar. However, exhibitors realised that some performers had a greater value than others, and some producers began to offer them in roles with the same name: Little Mary, Bronco Bill, etc. The Trust could see perfectly well where this would lead, but other independent producers decided that they were willing to take the risk, so they offered some hitherto anonymous performers a billing with the film's title, subsidiary publicity, and substantially more pay. The Trust were indeed correct in their supposition that inflation in salaries to performers would result. Amongst a small group it was astronomic. Some (Chaplin, Pickford, Fairbanks) pricing themselves out of the market entirely (hence United Artists). However, the star became very quickly a standard item of marketing: so much so that films like DeMille's post-1918 'scandal + haute couture' specials were billed as 'all-star' productions (i.e. no-star productions).

The star arrived as a marketing strategy in American cinema at the point at which the initial expansion of cinema had taken place. The nickelodeon boom was over: basic patterns had been established (centralised production, distribution by rental, atomised exhibition) which were to last almost to the 1920s. Marketing of films began to develop. Films needed to be distinguished from each other so that they could be recognisable to exhibitors and audiences, so that they could attract their particular fragments of the mass audience. Increasingly, narrative forms settled into genres, recognisable from posters, reviews and gossip, if not named by a specific label. Increasingly, the supposed personality of the performer became a means of describing or specifying a particular film. The performer's supposed personality was not the ostensible subject of many films, however. It was discussed and promoted elsewhere, in other media, and very quickly it became one of the staple functions of the film industry to supply 'appropriate' material to those other media. The 'image' of the star began to become a major part of the creation of narrative images. The importance of the star image in the creation of narrative images is that the star is also an incomplete and paradoxical phenomenon.

There is always a temptation to think of a 'star image' as some kind of fixed repertory of fixed meanings (Joan Crawford = tough, independent, ruthless, threateningly sexy, etc.). However, this seems to simplify the process, and to misstate the role of the star in producing meanings in films and beyond films. Star images are paradoxical. They are composed of elements which do not cohere, of contradictory tendencies. They are composed of clues rather than complete meanings, of representations that are less complete, less stunning, than those offered by cinema. The star image is an *incoherent* image. It shows the star both as an ordinary person and as an extraordinary person. It is also an *incomplete* image. It offers only the face, only the voice, only the still photo, where cinema offers the synthesis of voice, body and motion. The star image is paradoxical and incomplete so that it functions as an invitation to cinema, like the narrative image. It proposes cinema as the completion of its lacks, the synthesis of its separate fragments.

The relationship is not, however, only that of star-image = incomplete: film performance = completion. It is also one where the process of the star image echoes, repeats and develops a fundamental aspect of cinema itself. The star image rests on the paradox that the star is ordinary and extraordinary at the same time. The cinematic image (and the film performance) rests on the photo effect, the paradox that the photograph presents an absence that is present. In this sense, the star image is not completed by the film performance, because they both rest on the same paradox. Instead, the star image promises cinema. It restates the terms of the photo effect, renews the desire to experience this very particular sense of present-absence. So the star image is incomplete and paradoxical. It has a double relationship to the film performance: it proposes that the film performance will be more complete than the star image; and it echoes and promotes the photo effect which is fundamental to cinema as a regime of representation.

The process of circulation of a star image has been broadly the same whether it has been undertaken by a centralised studio agency (the form of classic Hollywood) or by a specialised enterprise contracted by the star themselves (the current form). The star's activities are presented in a number of media, some associated quite directly with the film industry, others using the film industry as one raw material amongst many. In the classic period of Hollywood, stars would 'feature' both in newspapers and magazines of general interest, and in magazines associated with cinema, fan magazines (or as we can now call them, fanzines). They appeared in advertisements, endorsing products. They appeared on radio, both in news, chat-shows and fiction. At certain points, they appeared directly as products and merchandise effects. The first star to do so was (probably) Mickey Mouse. In all of these media, the star appears directly as face, body and voice; and as a figure constructed by writing. There are photographs of the star; there are written descriptions of the star's activities; there are the voices of stars speaking (or singing) on the radio, from the mid-1920s onward. Each of these forms of appearance is less than that offered by sound cinema, which will present the animated, talking figure of the star. So on the simplest level, through the presentation of the star in photos, writing and radio, the elements of the star's person are offered to the public, but in discrete bits and without movement. The promise of these various presentations is that the film performance will present the completeness of the star, the real mystery at which these only hint. Hence the presentation of Marlene Dietrich to the American audience. Already a star in Europe because of *The Blue Angel* (1930), a film not then released in America, she arrived to film *Morocco* (1930). Her image (photographic and written) appeared in the press; she had already 'proved' herself in another unavailable film; her mystery was well cultivated. So *Morocco* appeared, its narrative multiply punning on that of *The Blue Angel*, and its publicity announced: 'Now you can see . . .'. The film revealed what the star image in its subsidiary circulation could only hint at or describe in a veiled meta-language.

The particular nature of the copy, the photos and the broadcasts made by/from stars reveals the other side of the star image's relation to the cinema. The stars are presented both as stars and as ordinary people: as very special beings, and as beings just like the readers. This seems to be the case both for male and for female stars, but sexual difference inevitably colours what kinds of roles are shown. Thus we

11 The final unveiling of the enigma: *Morocco* opens at Grauman's Chinese, Hollywood, 1930

have Bette Davis's recipes but Tyrone Power's baseball achievements; Audrey Hepburn's affinity for Givenchy clothes but Errol Flynn's big game hunting. Photographs similarly will show stars in the most mundane of postures, feeding babies or just relaxing in old clothes; and then in the most exotic, performing stunts at a lavish party or meeting the King of England. These are the general rules that govern the specific coverage given to stars: there are two aspects, one the ordinariness of the star and the other the totally exceptional nature of the star, endowed with some special talent and position.

These general characteristics of the coverage are inflected in different ways by the different kinds of publications which make use of stars. It could be said that mass circulation daily and sunday newspapers tend to use stars as a kind of moral barometer, whereas fanzines push the paradoxical constitution of the star image to its limits. Mass newspapers use stars for their own ends: they can be the occasion of scandals, and they provide a repertory of figures who are in the public eye, yet have no political power. Stars provide newspapers with the vehicle for discussion of sexuality, of the domain of the personal and the familial. This is relatively absent from public political life, so the stars perform a valuable function in newspapers: they provide the dimension of the personal. This dimension is that which is inhabited by most of their readers, yet is not that of the events portrayed in the news. Stars have a soldering function: they hold the news and the personal together by being both public and intimate, by being news only in so far as they are persons.

Fanzines are a different kind of publication, very much more directly linked in to the industry itself. They emphasise stars-as-workers much more than other publications, with details of the punishing studio schedules, the indignities of make-up and costume for some parts, the hard training for dancing and stunts, even the lousy facilities offered by studios. Yet at the same time they can present the extraordinary aspects of the star as well, because they are generally high-quality printing jobs with glossy, high-definition full-page photos. These photos present both male and female stars with all the sophisticated techniques that are available. These are images of faces (sometimes bodies as well) in all their impossibility: smooth, free of blemishes, clear-eyed, every feature perfect. Often, the two aspects cross over each other in the same feature: pieces about the hard work of rehearsal dive into sentences which stress 'nevertheless' the exceptional talent of the performer.

Perhaps the living and dynamic paradox that is the star image was captured in Ophuls's *Caught* (1948): we are shown a page of a fanzine covered by a photo of a luxurious mansion with pool, accompanied by the headline: 'Would you be happy in these surroundings? *We would.*' The photo is then animated into a moving picture, the camera dollies in to reveal Barbara Bel Geddes a former shopgirl who, having married into this luxury, is indeed miserable, and for very good reasons. *Caught* constantly plays on the paradox in the star image that it can oscillate between two opposing poles. A desperately attractive James Mason is cast as the ordinary doctor in a poor district with whom Bel Geddes falls in love. Mason, the matinee idol, is meant to incarnate the ordinary and the honest against Robert Ryan's neurotic millionaire. The film multiplies the indications of ordinariness around him, spectacularly since this is an Ophuls film. Yet it only succeeds in intensifying the paradox of the star image, perhaps expressed by the melodrama's audience as 'if only *my* boss was like James Mason'.

The star image functions in two ways. First it is the invitation to cinema, posing cinema as synthesising all the disparate and scattered elements of the star image. Second, it repeats the cinematic experience by presenting an impossible paradox: people who are both ordinary and extraordinary. This is the same paradox as the photo effect. The oscillation between the ordinariness and the extraordinariness of the star implies a whole series of features which echo the photo effect. The star is ordinary, and hence leads a life like other people, is close to them, shares their hopes and fears: in short, the star is present in the same social universe as the potential film viewer. At the same time the star is extraordinary, removed from the life of mere mortals, has rarified and magnified emotions, is separate from the world of the potential film viewer. The circulation of the contradictory star image therefore operates a kind of summary or reminder of the photo effect of cinema. Yet it is more than that as well. The figure of the star crystallises the equivocal relationship to the viewer's desire that can be said to be produced by the photo effect.

By presenting a present-absence, by making statements in the impossible mode of 'this is was', the photo effect awakens a series of psychic mechanisms which involve various impossible images: the narcissistic experience of the mirror phase; the masculine fetishistic refusal (yet acknowledgment) of the fact of sexual difference; and at the same time, a particular variant of the voyeuristic contract. The photo effect can be said to be involved with a series of psychic mechanisms which participate in the construction of the polyvalent desires of both male and female viewers. The star is an impossible image, like the cinematic image. The star is tantalisingly close and similar, yet at the same time

remote and dissimilar. Further, the star is a legitimate object
for the desire of the viewer in so far as the star is like the
viewer, and an impossible object for the desire of the viewer
in so far as the star is extraordinary, unlike the viewer. There
is a complicated game of desires that plays around the figure
of the star: every feature in it is counteracted by another
feature. The male and female star can be desired by either
sex, yet that desire has access to its object only on condition
that its object is presented as absent. Desire is both permitted
and encouraged, yet knows it cannot achieve any tangible
form of satisfaction, except the satisfactions of looking. The
phenomenon of stardom relies on the photo effect for its
full expression; it is equally a summary of the photo effect,
making explicit the relationship between the photographic
and the realm of desire. Constituted by a central paradox, the
star system is both a promise of cinema ('this is the photo
effect'), and an invitation to cinema ('these are clues; cinema
synthesises them'). The film performance of a star both
animates the desire that plays around the star's published
image, yet holds that desire in place by the operations of the
fiction. The use of the fiction always exceeds the star's image
and the star's presence in a film, except at that single point
where the fiction is suspended in favour of the pure performance: the 'fetishistic' moment.

The star's performances in individual films have a particular
relationship with the images in subsidiary circulation. In the
period of classic Hollywood at least, each star's figure was
around all the time in subsidiary forms of circulation, but
was seen in the cinema only occasionally: in two or three
films a year. The film performance was therefore rare; the
subsidiary circulation was commonplace. The film performance was a special event. The film performance of a
star also involved a large degree of overt fiction, which the
star in circulation outside the cinema did not. The construction of a star's image in subsidiary circulation must
have routinely involved forms of fiction, but these were
offered as though they were true facts. The fictional element of a star's film performance is acknowledged by all
concerned, performers, film-makers and audiences alike.
These two features of the film performance, its comparative

rarity and its explicit use of fiction, mark it out as a rather separate phenomenon from the circulation of star images in other areas. The film performance of the star takes up and furthers the star image from other media. The relation between the figure of the star and the desire of the spectator is animated and intensified. The play between the possibility and impossibility of the star as an object of desire is intensified by the photo effect of presence-absence. The star finally appears as a physical figure observable over an extended period by the film audience: no longer a disembodied radio voice, a frozen photo image or a character in a piece of journalistic writing. Introduced here is a whole new dimension of the star: not just the star-in-movement, but also the incidental aspects of that movement. The star's performance in a film reveals to the viewer all those small gestures, particular aspects of movement and expression, unexpected similarities to acquaintances or even to self. Acres of writing have been produced to celebrate this or that phenomenon in such or such a star: Garbo's laugh, Cary Grant's eyes, the way Rock Hudson bites his lip in *All That Heaven Allows* (1955). . . . The journalistic apotheosis of these moments witnesses the feeling that the star is caught unawares in them. They are things, it seems, that could hardly have been planned or foreseen. They mark the absorption of the star into the fictional character. The star seems to be feeling the emotion of the role at that point as his or her own emotion. The star is not performing here, so much as 'being'. In other words, what the film performance permits is moments of pure voyeurism for the spectator, the sense of overlooking something which is not designed for the onlooker but passively allows itself to be seen. This is different from the star's image in other forms of circulation, where the elements of intentionality are very marked. The fanzine photo is obviously constructed for the look; the magazine interview or the radio broadcast participate in forms of direct address where the star is present as an intentional 'I'.

This sense of overlooking the incidental and the unmotivated aspects of the star's figure has two consequences which tend to outrun the film-as-fiction. First, it pushes the photo effect to its limits, especially with a star who is dead. This effect is an epidemic with stars like Garland or Monroe, whose presence on the screen brings with it the widespread myths of their tragic lives, the stories of their absence. It also radically compromises the stoic strength of Agnes Moorehead or the shrill complaints of Gloria Grahame. Less spectacular tragedies both of these: the tragedies of women who always inhabited the films of others, whose careers never provided them with a definitive role. In both cases, the combination of the extra-filmic circulation of a star's tragic story with their film performance promotes a voyeuristic relation to the performance. Rather than identifying the role in the fiction with the life of the star (a comparatively rare possibility), the incidental moments are promoted to the forefront of attention. These 'poignant' moments thus become the only remaining route to the truth or the essence of the star's personality. The incidental moments of the star caught unawares seem to provide a glimpse of the secret personality that disappeared (or destroyed itself) leaving behind the perpetual, unresolvable paradox of the star image. The film photograph constructs the possibility of a voyeuristic effect of catching the star unawares. The paradox of the star's image (especially Monroe's) exacerbates this effect, sending the desiring viewer off to the film itself as the only remaining physical manifestation of the star amid the welter of photo sessions, TV and film biographies, memoirs of associates both would-be and real. The viewer glimpses something, perhaps only a trick of the light. But it is only glimpsed during the film performance. Then the circuit begins again: more consumption of forms of subsidiary circulation, the desire to see more films, and even films-that-never-were: the out-takes, the screen-tests and so on.

There is one further effect that can result from the star's performance being taken as the indicator of some kind of psychic truth. This is a more fetishistic tendency. At its limits, this results in the expression of the desire to halt the movement of the film, to freeze one of the actions of the star. Hence some films come in damaged prints simply because some fetishist has cut out a favourite section. Sometimes this effect can be seen in the construction of the film itself: in the performances of songs by Marlene Dietrich which litter Von Sternberg's films. Further, the plots of some Von Sternberg films can be seen as cyclic rather than progressing from beginning to end. They repeat the same scenarios of desire, circling around a neuralgic point. That point is the figure of the star, and of the female star rather than the male star.

These examples indicate how a star's film performance can expand the realm of desire, the incidental relations between audience and photo effect, to proportions that can be deemed arcane or even anti-social. As a rule, it is the fact of fiction in the film which contains the star's performance. The star's performance is held in place by the fiction. Fiction provides a double perspective. The fiction is always more than the star or the stars (sometimes only just, though, e.g. *Hollywood Canteen* (1944)), and provides the star with a role that is to a greater or lesser extent different from the star's public image. The public image consists of a series of more or less paradoxical attributes; very little of a stable identity emerges from them apart from that of the star-paradox itself, ordinary and extraordinary. In the fiction, however, the star has to incarnate some kind of identity, be it Mildred Pierce, Sam Spade, La Bessière (or is it Le Bessier?), Stuart McIver. These names (rather more than those of the stars) designate stable points of identity, characters caught in webs of narrative circumstance through which they chart a path. To this extent, then, the fiction imposes a different regime of being upon the star. We have to know where the fictional character incarnated by the star actually stands. So there is a certain attenuation of the star image in the star's film performance. Certainly, there is still some element of the oscillation between the extraordinary and the ordinary, but this oscillation is fixed for the duration of the film to provide fairly stable reference points. Hence Joan Crawford in *The Bride Wore Red* (1937) has a stunningly ordinary emotional life to match her extraordinary situation: a prostitute masquerading as a titled society lady. As *Mildred Pierce* (1944) her aspirations towards an ordinary family where she would happily bake all day for her children are frustrated,

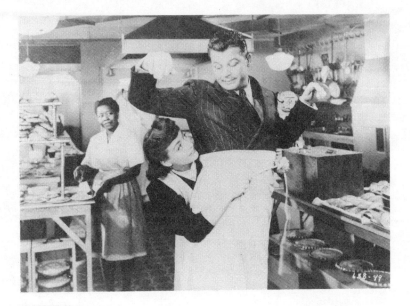

12 One of the crimes for which Mildred Pierce must be punished

forcing her into a series of extraordinary activities: running
a business, running around with a playboy.

The star performance in the fiction can have three kinds of
relation to the star image in subsidiary circulation. The
fiction can content itself with performing the image in those
rare cases where the star's image outside of cinema is fairly
stable. This is perhaps more possible for male stars, whose
characters can be defined by their activities. Such is the case
perhaps with Errol Flynn, whose roles seem to a large extent
the kind of exploit for which he became famous. The second,
more usual, relation is that in which the fiction exceeds the
circulated image. At its limits, the fictional figure can go
against the grain of the circulated image, creating a specific
tension in the film. Such is the case with Hitchcock's *Suspicion* (1941) where Cary Grant is cast as the likely murderer
and swindler. The whole film is constructed on this dislocation in order to render Joan Fontaine's suspicions in-
congruous at first, and then increasingly irrefutable even to

the most incredulous audience as the 'evidence' mounts. Despite the reconciliatory ending, this film represents something more than 'casting against type'. *Suspicion* needs the star image of Cary Grant in order to function at all. Its effect would have been totally different with Reginald Denny. More usually, the fictional figure is 'to one side' of the star's general image, where this can be established. Certain elements of the publicly circulated star image complex are used by the film, other elements are refused, further elements are added. Doris Day's films display her in a much wider range of characters than her image would suggest. Certain elements of her image are always present (sometimes her pervasive ordinariness or directness of approach to people), but they are not always the same elements. Further characteristics are accumulated to her fictional personas that have little or nothing to do with her star images. Yet the star image continues in circulation, feeding off the films where it can, trying to ignore aspects of her past as well as aspects of her fictional roles. The importance of Doris Day as a star phenomenon is the way in which her star images have obliterated the memory of her films. Doris Day's fictional roles are very much 'to one side' of her circulated images. It is possible that the circulated images are unperformable in a film: they provided so little scope for any dramatic action that there were few attempts to narrativise them. However, they provided acceptable and 'useful' themes in other, less narrative, less fictional, forms of circulation. Hence the endurance of 'Doris Day' as a touchstone of respectability, moral probity, young Americanicity, unrestrained enthusiasm and other characteristics that play around her figure without constituting a fixed identity.

The star's place in a film thus seems to be a difficult one. The film is constructed by the process of the star image as the point at which the paradox of the image will be explicated, and the disparate elements of the image will come together. The star performance thus animates the star image, and animates the desire which circulates in it. In doing so, the performance exceeds the circulated image in two usually mutually compensating ways. First, the performance is fictional, placing the star in a role whose characteristics

have to be fairly stable. This role can have a number of
different relationships to the circulated image: it can
resemble it to a large degree; it can contradict it; it can be to
one side of it In most cases, the fictional context of the
star's performance is enough to hold in check or to balance
a second way in which the star's performance exceeds the
star's circulated image. This second excess is the way in
which desire is animated towards the performing figure. The
performance produces the effect that, in its incidental rather
than intended moments, it reveals something of the essence
of the star's personality. Occasionally, effects either from
within the film (Von Sternberg) or from beyond the film
(Monroe) foster this effect and allow it to escape the effects
of the fiction. The result is a cultism, of an inquisitive
voyeuristic kind, or a fascinated fetishistic type.

For the star him- or herself, two options for performance
are offered by this regime. One is that of drastically under-
performing in comparison to the 'unknown' section of the
cast; and the other is to overperform in order to emphasise
the work of acting. Underperformance is not a question of
restraint or lack of histrionics. It is a question of producing
the effect of behaving rather than performing. This is always
a comparative effect, generated by a disparity within any
one film between the styles of acting of the star-group and
the supporting group. The supporting group have to produce
emphases in their gestures, delivery of lines and expression
simply in order to signify the required meanings. For the star,
it is different. The star has the attention of the audience and
is a recognised figure, with a recognised voice, face and
figure, even if no stable meanings accumulate to those
features in the star image. Having the audience's attention,
(and the camera's, and the fiction's), anything that the star
does becomes significant. Hence the star is permitted to
underact, compared to the supporting cast, and this underacting produces the effect that the star behaves rather than
acts. However, some stars have been dissatisfied with this
state of affairs and the whispered remarks that it produces
('so-and-so can't act', etc.). So a certain section of the star
firmament at any one time will be seeking to reverse this
tendency towards underacting in order to produce an effect

of 'performance'. Some stars produce a very explicit regime of expression which is again divergent from that of the supporting cast. In Hollywood, it has often been those actors who are most concerned with the artistic nature of their work (Bette Davis, for instance). More recently, a craft approach has been adopted to performance under the influence of the Method Acting theory. Examples are the antics of Marlon Brando or the disguises of Peter Sellers. Finally, a more traditional overacting is characteristic of certain stars, especially those from the British stage: Glenda Jackson for instance. All of these stars tend to offer a supplementary signification: they are there as star; they are there as fictional role; but they are also there as actor, saying, 'Look at me, I can perform.'

For the fiction film, the star and the places that the star can adopt produce a commendable narrative economy. Stars are recognisable; stars are the centre of the action. So the narration need waste very little time and space in pointing out who the central characters are. The regime of stardom that I have described here is found in its most straightforward form in the commercial cinema, and particularly in that of classic Hollywood. It is qualitatively different from any phenomenon found in television. Television has used the word 'star' to apply to anybody who appeared on its screen: even the weather forecasters. But television does not produce a play between the ordinariness and extraordinariness of its performers because it does not participate in the photo effect, and it cannot present the lives of its performers as anything particularly glamorous. The *TV Times* (29/1/1981) feature on Susannah York, appearing in the series *Second Chance* was revealing. Here is a woman who lives by Wandsworth Common and has gone through a divorce, just like the character she is playing. The profile was unable to generate any other sense of Susannah York: no sense of the extraordinary, no sense of glamour, even. There was a sense in which the dimension of desire was being written out of the piece. The institution of television (at least in Britain) seems at pains to reduce the star phenomenon by reducing the extraordinariness of its performers, and their status as figures of an equivocal attraction and identification by viewers both male and female.

Centrally lacking in television is the photo effect. Television presents itself as an immediate presence, except when it is borrowing the cinema with transmissions that are labelled 'films'. Television pretends to actuality, to immediacy; the television image in many transmissions (news, current affairs, chat shows, announcements) behaves as though it were live and uses the techniques of direct address. Its narrative regime is different. It hardly ever presents its performers in comparison to their presence in subsidiary forms of circulation in the way that is characteristic of cinema's use of its stars. Instead, the television performer appears regularly for a series which itself is constituted on the basis of repetition of a particular character and/or situation. The television performer appears in subsidiary forms of circulation (newspapers, magazines) mostly during the time that the series of performances is being broadcast. The result is a drastic reduction in the distance between the circulated image and the performance. The two become very much entangled, so that the performer's image is equated with that of the fictional role (rather than vice versa). The television performer exists very much more in the same space as the television audience, as a known and familiar person rather than as a paradoxical figure, both ordinary and extra-ordinary.

There is no way that the image in subsidiary circulation is a promise of television as the synthesis of its disparate parts. The image in subsidiary circulation is present in the culture rather less than the television performance, which has no real rarity value. The exchange is the other way about than in cinema: the television performance provides the basic materials and the basic enigma ('Is there a person different from the role in the fiction?') and the magazine profile provides the solution of it. Television's regime is rather more straightforward than cinema's, and its stress is rather more on the ordinariness of its performers, using them with greater abandon than cinema could ever conceive, presenting them as much more of an immediate presence.

What television does present is the 'personality'. The

personality is someone who is famous for being famous, and is famous only in so far as he or she makes frequent television appearances. Such is the case of Zsa Zsa Gabor, often mistaken as a cinema star. The personality on British television has been taken to new heights by Michael Parkinson and Russell Harty, whose secret is that they have no known identity of any kind. In some ways, they are the opposite of stars, agreeable voids rather than sites of conflicting meanings. More usually, the television personality is equated with a particular genre of character in fiction, or a particular area of knowledge or interest in factual programmes. Hence the scientist-personalities of Magnus Pyke or Patrick Moore; the political personality of Robin Day. These are personalities or celebrities rather than stars in the cinematic sense. Their notoriety results from their fairly constant presence on the medium rather than their rarity; they are familiar rather than remote; they are present in the actuality of the television image rather than the photo effect of the cinema image; they activate no conflict of meanings and no real enigmas; they bear a fairly minimal relationship to the desire of the spectator, the subsidiary circulation of material about them is more concerned with discovering if there is a personality separate from that of the television role than it is with the paradox of ordinary-but-extraordinary.

Television may yield personalities rather than stars, but the structure of the star system seems still to be present in the rock music industry. Here, the live performance takes the place of the film performance. It, too, is rare compared to other forms of circulation; it, too, is more complete in relation to other forms, including that of the disc (some groups excepted) and the tantalising television appearance. The journalism that surrounds the rock star works in a similar paradoxical register to that of film star journalism. Mick Jagger is one of its outstanding creations: the uncouth lad integrated with the jet-set. More often, journalism provides its sense of the ordinariness of the star through pronouncements like 'I mostly eat baked beans when it comes down to it, really' balanced against details of musicianship and statistical information ('Number one for six weeks', 'two gold discs', 'three-quarters of a million pounds').

Stars in classic Hollywood cinema exist as marketing devices, specifying a film in order to encourage attendance at its performances. As a marketing device, the star image in subsidiary forms of circulation is not a complete and settled identity. If it was, it would be a satisfactory phenomenon and would not produce the curiosity necessary to encourage cinema attendances. This curiosity seems to be produced in two ways: first by the enigma of star paradox (ordinary-extraordinary) and second by the resultant promise of cinema (of presence-absence). In its turn, this star phenomenon outside the film has certain effects within the film. It produces the star's film performance as the completion and potential explanation of the star phenomenon. It produces a relationship of desire between spectator and star performer that is intensified by the photo effect of cinema itself. These effects are almost always held in place by the operation of the fiction which suspends the oscillations of the star paradox in favour of a relatively stable fictional identity for the star performer. On rare occasions, whose reasons are both textual and extra-textual, the effects of desire outrun the effects of the fiction, producing cultism or fetishism. Finally, the star's film performance does not exhaust the paradoxes of the star's circulated image.

Part II

Broadcast TV

7 Broadcast TV as cultural form

The very obviousness of the differences between cinema and broadcast TV means that they are often overlooked. Cinema revolves around the purchase of the right to attend a performance of a single film text. The performance is public; the audience is prepared for it by the widespread circulation of the narrative image. Broadcast TV emits a series of signals that are available to anyone who possesses or rents a TV set. Broadcast TV is received overwhelmingly in domestic surroundings. The images involved are different: cinema's is large and projected; broadcast TV's is characteristically small and luminous. This much is obvious. However, the consequences of these differences for each medium are less obvious.

This section argues that broadcast TV has developed distinctive aesthetic forms to suit the circumstances within which it is used. These forms are distinct to broadcast TV as a phenomenon, rather than to video as a phenomenon. They have as much to do with the fact that broadcasting presents a continuous set of signals that are either received or missed by their potential audience. There is hardly any chance of catching a particular TV programme 'tomorrow' or 'next week sometime' as there is with a cinema film. There is no reason to infer that the forms outlined here will dominate the growing market for videotapes and discs. In the early stages, this might be the case through sheer imitation, but new forms should develop very quickly. Currently, broadcast TV is the predominant use of the video image in our culture. There is evidence (like all evidence in this area, not particularly reliable) that home video is overwhelmingly used as a 'time shift' phenomenon, moving a particular broadcast programme to a point when it is convenient to watch it.

Broadcast TV has developed a distinctive aesthetic form. Instead of the single, coherent text that is characteristic of entertainment cinema, broadcast TV offers relatively discrete segments: small sequential unities of images and sounds whose maximum duration seems to be about five minutes. These segments are organised into groups, which are either simply cumulative, like news broadcast items and advertisements, or have some kind of repetitive or sequential connection, like the groups of segments that make up the serial or series. Broadcast TV narration takes place across these segments, characteristically in series or serials which repeat a basic problematic or dilemma rather than resolving it finally. The broadcast images depend upon sound to a rather greater degree than cinema's images. The image is characteristically pared down, and appears as though it is immediate or live. This generates a kind of complicity with the TV viewer, a complicity that tends to produce the events represented as an 'outside world', beyond the broadcast TV institution and the viewer's home alike. The predominant forms in which this 'outside world' is presented tend to be those of the hostile or the bizarre. The viewer tends to delegate his or her look to the TV itself: it is as though the TV institution looks, the viewer passes his or her gaze across the sights in the TV eye. Such is the regime of representation that broadcast TV seems to have: a general description that is no doubt profoundly inflected by my experience of British TV.

This model of the functioning of TV seems to apply indiscriminately to fiction and non-fiction alike. It is one of Jean-Luc Godard's characteristic throw-away lines to inquire why it is that we divide cinema and TV so rigidly into 'fiction' and 'non-fiction', when we do not regard this distinction as fundamental to other means of representation. Indeed, for the purposes of this model of broadcast TV's characteristic procedures, examples are drawn indiscriminately from factual and fictional work. Both narrate events to a viewer who is in a particular relation to them. In this sense, there is no difference. The distinction rests on another level altogether, a level at which we simply have to trust the integrity of the programme-makers. The distinction between fact and fiction depends on the source of the material that is manufactured into narrating images and sounds. If fact, it is supposed to come from the world that exists beyond the TV institution and the home of the viewer. If fiction, it is the imagined and created vision of a particular person or persons. Hence arguments about documentaries and their supposed truthfulness very quickly become arguments about the integrity of the programme-makers involved, for it is with their guarantee of the source of the material that the distinction between fact and fiction rests.

Broadcast TV is a profoundly domestic phenomenon. The TV set has to be acquired by a person or persons before TV signals can be received, and the manufacture of TV sets has long assumed that its market is the domestic unit. In some countries, a licence to view (which contributes to the costs of producing some broadcasts) has to be purchased as well. This is the case in Britain. Unlike entertainment cinema, which characteristically addresses the couple seeking an evening's entertainment outside the home, broadcast TV is already in the home. The TV set is another domestic object, often the place where family photos are put: the direction of the glance towards the personalities on the TV screen being supplemented by the presence of 'loved ones' immediately above. Broadcast TV is also intimate and everyday, a part of home life rather than any kind of special event.

Broadcast TV institutions respond by conceiving of this domestic and everyday audience in a specific way. Broadcast TV, its institutions and many of its practitioners alike assume that its domestic audience takes the form of families. 'The home' and 'the family' are terms which have become tangled together in the commercial culture of the twentieth century. They both point to a powerful cultural construct, a set of deeply held assumptions about the nature of 'normal' human existence. The family is held to consist of a particular unit of parents and children: broadcast TV assumes that this is the basis and heart of its audience. Broadcast TV's conventional notion of the family is of two parents, the father

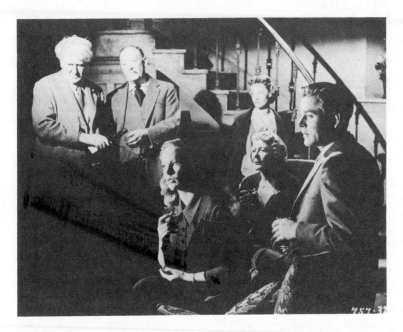

13 The domestic audience as it probably is (*Meet Mr Lucifer*)

working, the mother running the home, together with two children of school age. This conception is clearly seen in much advertising material; in the way in which statistics are interpreted on news bulletins ('for the average family, this means . . .'); in 'families' selected for quiz programmes; in 'families' shown in fictional representations of all kinds. The prevalence of this conception of the family is all the more remarkable since only a minority of the population of Britain currently live like this. Only a third of households currently consist of man, woman and dependent children, according to government statistics. In most of these units, the woman also has a regular job. In some cases, she is the only 'bread-winner'. In all, the supposedly classic nuclear family unit, of working father, housewife mother and dependent school-age children accounts for less than 5 per cent of the population. Yet social policies of all kinds assume this to be the norm, and so does broadcast TV. For many people living in ways that differ from this supposed norm, these ways of living are experienced as exceptions or temporary departures from the norm. The presence of a grandparent, of other relatives, the single-parent family, the childless household, all of these common and by no means 'radical' forms are taken as a passing phase rather than as a real way of living. Such is the power of the conception of the nuclear family in its particular form.

Broadcast TV assumes this norm as do most of the major institutions of British society. For broadcast TV, it has certain specific effects because TV tends to orient its programmes towards its presumed audience, to try to include the audience's own conception of themselves into the texture of its programmes. Hence broadcast TV gives central place to the series of cultural preoccupations that accompany the nuclear family: to heterosexual romance, to the stability of marriage, to the notions of masculine careers and feminine domesticity, to the conception of the innocence of childhood, to the division of the world in public and private spheres. In addition, this conception of the family-as-audience determines a series of attitudes to what is legitimate material for broadcast TV. Any specialised interests are avoided, especially those which divide across generations. 'Youth' as a specific audience is not catered for by broadcast TV to any appreciable extent; neither, for that matter, are those over sixty. Such categories of audience are normally deployed only as the reasons for prohibitions: no sexually explicit programmes before 9 p.m. because children will be watching; no disturbing programmes about death because old people may be watching on their own. TV programmes are addressed to a generalised audience which is conceived in a very specific way: as isolated nuclear families in their domestic settings.

The particular ideological notion of the nuclear family in its domestic setting provides the overarching conception within which broadcast TV operates. Given this setting, and the multiple distractions that it can offer, broadcast TV cannot assume the same level of attention from its viewers that cinema can from its spectators. So broadcast TV has developed specific forms of narration, and specific

forms of organisation of its material. The basic organisation
of material is that of the segment, a coherent group of sounds
and images, of relatively short duration that needs to be
accompanied by other similar such segments. The segment
as the basic unit according to a short burst of attention is
matched by the serial and series form. These provide a
particular kind of repetition and novelty that differs
markedly from that found in the narrational patterns of
classic cinema. In turn, the series and serial imply a third
term: scheduling. Scheduling is the means by which a day's
broadcasting is arranged so that particular programmes
coincide with particular supposed events in the life of the
family. Scheduling provides a regular, week by week, slot
in which the repetition of particular series formats can take
place. This aspect of broadcast TV's arrangements is dealt
with in Part III.

Within the context of the segment and series, broadcast
TV can, at particular moments, adopt a form that corresponds much more closely to that of cinema. Broadcast TV
can present a single work that has a high degree of internal
coherence and patterns of repetition and innovation. Broadcast TV does use the model of the Hollywood film. It does
so in two ways. First, it transmits films, which provide it with
a convenient form of raw material. Second, it produces 'TV
films' or 'special presentations' or 'single plays'. These are
the area of broadcast TV which aims most directly towards
cultural respectability. The 'single play' on British TV has
always been the area of greatest ideological and aesthetic
risk, and the area of the greatest artistic reputation for
writers and directors alike. However, it is significant that
these productions are increasingly cinema films in all but
name; they rely upon cinematic techniques, and they invite
their audiences to try to view them with the attitudes and
intensity of concentration that is more characteristic of
cinema. For broadcast TV, the culturally respectable is
increasingly equated with the cinematic.

However, the vast quantity of broadcast TV's output,
usually the critically neglected part, conforms to a different
model. Its basic unit is the segment, with segments following
on from each other with no necessary connection between

them. This definition of TV's commodity as a programmed series of meaningful segments used in a domestic context owes much to Raymond Williams's definition of broadcast TV as 'flow'. The notion of 'flow' is a much misused one, and its openness to misuse is the result of the way in which Williams defines the idea. He argues that TV cannot be conceived of as unitary programmes which are 'interrupted' by advertisements and suchlike material. 'Yet it may be even more important to see the true process as flow: the replacement of a programme series of timed sequential units by a flow series of differently related units in which the timing, though real, is undeclared, and in which the real internal organisation is something other than the declared organisation' (*Television* p. 93). 'There has been a significant shift from the concept of sequence as *programming* to the concept of sequence as *flow*. Yet this is difficult to see because the older concept of programming — the temporal sequence within which mix and proportion and balance operate — is still active and still to some extent real' (*ibid.*, p. 89). In arguing against two assumptions (that programmes are interrupted; that TV is a series of separate coherent programme items), Williams describes flow as a liquid and even confusing process by which broadcast TV tends to average out the various programme forms that its formal organisations of production claim to keep separate. According to Williams's model of flow, then, everything becomes rather like everything else, units are not organised into coherent single texts like cinema films, but form a kind of montage without overall meaning: 'like having read two plays, three newspapers, three or four magazines, on the same day that one has been to a variety show and a lecture and a football match. And yet it is not like that at all, for though the items may be various the television experience has in some important ways unified them' (*ibid.*, p. 95). Here both the strength and weakness of Williams's argument becomes clear. Flow assembles disparate items, placing them within the same experience, but does not organise them to produce an overall meaning. This is a valuable insight; however, the problem lies in Williams's definition of 'items'. 'Items' are still separate texts, independent works like a

cinema film. Finally, for Williams, flow is a feature of TV
that severely compromises and alters the separate texts that
TV has manufactured. His model is of cinema-style texts
which appear in a context that reduces their separation one
from another. In doing so, he underestimates the complexity
of broadcast TV's particular commodity form, which has
very little to do with the single text.

The 'spot' advertisement is in many ways the quintessence
of TV. It is a segment of about thirty seconds, comprising
a large number of images and sounds which are tightly organised amongst themselves. This segment is found accompanied
by other similar segments: coherent within themselves, they
have no particular connection with each other. Meanings
are discrete and separate; their interrelation lies in the fact
that they belong to a similar class of segments, or, occasionally, in the way that they proudly produce puns upon each
other. Watching advertisements is often an exhilarating
experience because of their short span and their intensity
of meaning: they are expensive (more expensive than the
programmes they come with) and precisely calculated (often
better than TV drama). They are sparklingly diverse, the
shiny surface wrapping of a domestically oriented consum-
erist society. They are also the supremely televisual product:
hence another part of their exhilaration, that of seeing a
medium used for itself, and not weighed down by cultural
presumptions that are not its own.

Yet, being a segment, each advertisement does not stand
on its own. The experience of watching advertisements is
that of seeing segments cluster together, inciting each other.
Their specific meanings have relatively little to do with each
other; their generalised generic meaning (a domestic con-
sumerist relation to objects) gives them a certain common
thematic; but their organisation together is something new to
Western representations. Advertisements on TV cannot be
scanned or ignored like the page of a newspaper: they
demand short bursts of attention, producing an understanding that rests at the level of the particular segment involved
and is not forced to go further, is not made to combine as
a montage fragment into a larger organisation of meaning.
Thirty seconds by thirty seconds, the 'spot' advertisement

expands but does not combine: it is the furthest development of broadcast TV's segmental commodity.

The segmental commodity is found right across TV's output, and even inflects its use of material originating from the cinema. TV news and current affairs programmes have adopted this segmentalisation: in a news bulletin the standard approach is for each item to be separated from all others. It is a rare event for two items to be related together, the sure sign of an important ideological operation at work: the emergence of a common-sense view of affairs. One such event was the yoking-together of reports of 'industrial strife' on British TV during the winter of 1978. Newspaper journalism generated the term 'The Winter of Discontent': TV's persistent combination and foregrounding of reports of industrial disputes nightly consolidated this definition. Yet such an occasion is rare, and can be subject to complaints of 'over-interpretation' on TV's part. The news segment is characteristically isolated within a context of its likenesses: each a particular report, discursively organised to present a totalising view, yet no overall meanings emerging from the juxtaposition of segments.

In some sense, advertisements, news, and current affairs magazine programmes provide the most obvious examples of the segmental aspect of TV. However, this procedure extends very much further across virtually the whole of TV's output. It is not only a characteristic of those TV channels that carry advertisements: it has also become the standard form of TV construction for the BBC as well. First, it can be argued, as Raymond Williams has, that a significant proportion of broadcast TV consists of small segments that fill the gaps between substantial programme units: the announcer sitting in a studio providing a link; the trailer for a programme coming some time in the future; the show-casing extracts of the evening's entertainment, then tomorrow's, the weekend's and so on. The BBC does this just as much as ITV. This segmentation extends to programmes themselves, especially the title sequences. The title sequence is in effect a commercial for the programme itself, and it has all the features of a commercial. It is considerably more expensive per second than the programme it fronts; it is

highly organised and synoptic, providing a kind of narrative
image for its programme. Every programme has a title
sequence, whether a news bulletin or a documentary or chat
show or police drama, and their manufacture is a long-
established practice. There is a high degree of autonomy for
the title sequence, since it is repeated every time the programme format is used and usually provides a highly generalised, gestural conception of the programme it advertises,
unlike the material used to showcase individual programmes.
A strategy increasingly used with American series is to
combine the two forms, so that the standard title sequence
integrates shots from the individual programme in a highly
enigmatic or incoherent way. This is the closest that TV has
come to constructing a narrative image in the cinematic
mode. The main difference from cinema's narrative image is
that broadcast TV's title sequences invariably come with the
programme: there is an immediacy of realisation of the
narrative image which marks it out from the cinematic
practice. The practice of manufacturing title sequences (for
which cinema has no real equivalent) is another obvious
example of segmentalisation: this time occurring within
the bounds of what is conventionally designated 'a programme'.

Further, programmes which have a high degree of coherence compared to news, advertisements, promotion material
and title sequences can themselves be regarded as being
composed of segments. Any fiction series or serial is prone to
segmentalisation, and the series and serial form the vast bulk
of broadcast TV material almost everywhere. This segmentalisation takes the form of a rapid alternation between scenes
and a frequent return to habitual locations and situations
rather than any sustained progression through sequential
logic of events. In the series and the serial alike, these segments tend never to coalesce into an overall totalising
account. The form that tends to be adopted by TV fiction,
in this sense, is the same as TV news, with a continuous
updating on the latest concatenation of events rather than a
final ending or explanation. Even though events are frequently intercut in the series and serial, there is habitually
no parallelism implied between the events beyond a simple

one of simultaneous occurrence and general connection between the characters.

This segmentalisation is TV's own creation, and is not traceable directly to the effects of 'spot' advertisements being scattered at various moments through the TV fiction. One of the classic moments of the development of this process in British TV was the police series *Z-Cars* produced by the BBC. *Z-Cars* was renowned (among other things) for the fact that it had more scenes than it had minutes, an effect achieved by the intercutting of slightly related events. The segment in this sense is not essentially different from the segment that is found in advertisements. Each scene is coherent in itself, delivering a particular meaning, an event, a relation between characters. Its characteristic effect, however, depends upon its placing in relation to other discrete segments that are also relatively coherent in themselves. This internal coherence in effect prevents the generation of effects of parallelism, contrast or irony between sequences except in special moments.

Hence, to take a slightly unpredictable example, the episode of the series *Telford's Change* transmitted on 25 February 1979. This series was characterised by a series of rather filmic concerns: the naturalistic performances of Peter Barkworth and Hannah Gordon, a tendency towards long takes with fluid camerawork rather than a multiple camera shooting style characteristic of studio-based TV series. Yet, for all its upmarket (i.e. cinematic) pretensions, the series was profoundly of TV. Its basic structuring division was between a semi-separated married couple, Peter Barkworth as Dover bank manager, Hannah Gordon as producer of a play in Brighton. The 50-minute programme alternated between these two basic segments, with a vague parallel being implied: both getting on 'on their own', both being experimentally flirtatious. The programme (the series) gave more weight to Barkworth (the Telford who changed a high-level international bank job for a humble one), and consequently he was involved in a long series of relatively short self-contained segments, organised around bank employees (senior and junior) and around bank clients: a garage owner on the brink of disaster (dispatched to file for bankruptcy);

a woman owner (rejuvenated by an affair); a woman wanting to expand her sauna business (Barkworth's socio-sexual attitudes explored). Each segment delivered its meaning and its cameo performance. The demarcation between segments was so great that any one could have been dropped out of the episode without material damage to the overall impression. At one moment only did the two major series of segments (Barkworth/Gordon) come together, a phone call between the two whose cautiously reconciliatory purpose was thwarted by the pressures of their respective immediate situations. Perhaps the only segment that could not have been eliminated (as it was the only moment of narrative progression), it was marked by a rapid alternation between the two major segmental series. *Telford's Change* is a series whose pretensions are towards cinema (for TV, the locus of artistic respectability and of authorial recognition), yet it still displays TV's characteristic segmentalisation.

Any single programme taken as an example of segmentation reveals only the way in which this characteristic procedure has 'invaded' what is characteristically taken to be an independent textual entity: the programme. However, broadcast TV does not consist of programmes in the way that they are listed in programme guides in newspapers or magazines. Here Williams's notion of flow is important: it indicates the way in which TV presents segments in larger or smaller conglomerations. Broadcast TV is characterised by a succession of segments, of internally coherent pieces of dramatic, instructional, exhortatory, fictional, or documentary material. The major difference between the BBC TV service without advertising and ITV with advertising lies only in the size of the conglomeration of segments. BBC is capable at certain points of presenting a fairly coherent set of segments, perhaps a whole narrative. But, feature films apart, this is a comparatively rare occurrence, the long documentary or the single play. BBC as much as any other broadcasting institution has adopted the characteristic commodity form of TV, the segment, and its complementary aspect, the series form.

The segment form implies repetition: TV's characteristic form of repetition is the series or the serial, a form of continuity-with-difference that TV has perfected. This form fosters the segmental approach, the generation of large numbers of diverse coherent and relatively self-contained elements. The serial implies a certain narrative progression and a conclusion; the series does not: whether documentary, drama or everlasting soap opera, it has no end in view. The series always envisages its own return. The series itself divides into two types: fictional series that are centred around a particular situation and set of characters, and non-fictional series that are characterised by a recurring format and known set of routines.

The series and serial both provide a means of generating many segments from basic narrative or expository techniques, and from basic thematic material. The serial aims towards a conclusion which is a number of weeks distant. Like the massive three-decker novels of the nineteenth century, the TV serial multiplies incident along the way. It uses its characters, plays around with the possible permutations of relationships and situations. Its span is often that of generations. It implies a certain knowledge accumulated over the span of its broadcasting, but this itself causes worries within the broadcasting institutions, because it is quite conceivable that a large proportion of the audience will miss one or other episode, or will not be hooked on the expository first episode. Hence a number of techniques: the title sequence that introduces characters (faces connoting a characteristic) and even their relationships; the repetition of material from the end of one episode at the beginning of the next; carefully placed references to events in the conversations of characters. Again, there is the generation of segments which have a purely broadcast function, and an attempt to compensate for the effect of narrative progression and accumulation. A popular serial will tend to generate a semi-news status for itself, with commentaries on its latest enigmas being provided in the television pages that form a substantial part of popular newspapers. The enigma to be resolved 'tonight' is restated and ruminated over: the next day, not a word in the newspaper. This is another isolated example of construction of a narrative image, but again distinctive from the cinematic process.

Serial construction presents problems for broadcast TV, those of ensuring a large enough constant audience. Increasingly, the series form is becoming standard. Here, each episode is more or less self-sufficient, and very little if any narrative progression is implied from episode to episode. *Telford's Change* represents a compromise between serial and series that is becoming increasingly popular. Each episode is coherent enough for the casual viewer, packed with varied and satisfying segments; the serial aspect is provided by the continuing enigmas of whether Telford's change will be a success, and whether his marriage will break up.

The series itself provides a stable situation in which various incidents take place week by week. The incidents usually form a complete group each week (except in the case of soap opera). Such a definition of the series extends over most of TV's output: news programmes, investigatory documentaries, situation comedies, variety shows, chat shows, sports programmes. A fundamental stability and return to zero at the end of each programme or programme section is implied by the series. The news, current affairs, documentary and chat show series provide a stable format in which events from the world beyond TV can appear. The series format ensures that they can appear at all by providing them with a set of known expository procedures. Hence it is expected that the news series will consist of segments that have absolutely no connection between them, whereas the segmentalisation of an investigatory programme will tend to construct an overall strategy of relation between segments. Of course, the series format is by no means a neutral means: it constructs segments according to quite precise routines which create the events portrayed as meaningful and as coherent within their segments. The sheer repetition of the series format enables this process to go ahead, as it provides a framework of expectancy, intelligibility and evaluation. 'Now, back to the studio . . .' is a cue for a different form of discourse (presentation, overview v. witness account), not for a neutral geographic shift.

The format series is matched by the fictional series, which operates across all the modalities of fiction from farce to tragedy. It is characterised by the constant repetition of basic narrative situations and characters: a family, a business enterprise, a hospital, etc. Each week the characters encounter a new situation which has no permanent effect upon them: the following week they will be in the same relation one to another. The repetitions are very marked, to the extent of some series (from USA chiefly) ending their weekly narrative with a kind of coda in which the basic relations between characters are reaffirmed outside of any narrative context. Subordinates joke with boss; children outwit their parents over some domestic chore. The formula, the basic situation, receives a final statement in a segment that tends to echo the title sequence. This has the effect of reaffirming the stasis from which the next episode will depart: a stasis that is more a basic contradiction or power relation than a zero degree. The series, then, relies on repeating a basic problematic which is worked through on each occasion without a final resolution. In a police series, the police catch the criminals in each individual instance of the series, but two things still remain: criminality itself (the episode ends with another call, a trivial assignment, etc.) and the particular relationship between the police involved (*Starsky and Hutch*'s spiky mutual dependency; *The Sweeney*'s blend of antagonism to authority and respect for justice). The series is based upon the notion 'what will happen to them this week?', known elements are repeated with no discernible development from one episode to the next.

The series is very widespread in TV, and complements the construction of TV output into segments. Segments gain their mutual organisation and some of their coherence from the complicated series patterns which generate them. The series ensures that each segment will be classified into a particular class of segments because of the repeated elements (character, mode of address, etc.) that play through them. Programming, the art of scheduling, appears in this context as the deliberate policy of TV organisations of ensuring that segmentation does take place. Scheduling determines the way in which an evening's TV will be organised so that one class of segments does not dominate, yet the series will find a permanent 'slot', a place where its particular pattern of repetition can take place. Scheduling

effectively provides a supra-segmentation of broadcast TV.
The characteristic broadcast TV experience is a domestic consumption of a succession of segments organised according to the logic of the series. The characteristic entertainment cinema experience is public and collective, an experience of a single text which performs and completes the narrative image circulated for it. Broadcasting has not developed the institution of the narrative image; instead the series provides the necessary expectancy and anticipation, which is distinct from that of the cinema. TV's process of segmentalisation of its flow contrasts again with cinema's emphasis on the single unitary film. This also has effects which mean that in their common area of narrative fiction, cinema and TV tend to develop different forms and approaches. It also has effects in that each medium tends to concentrate on different procedures of signification of events.

8 Broadcast TV as sound and image

TV offers a radically different image from cinema, and a different relation between sound and image. The TV image is of a lower quality than the cinematic image in terms of its resolution of detail. It is far more apparent that the broadcast TV picture is composed of lines than it is that the cinema image is composed of particles of silver compounds. Not only this, but the TV image is virtually always substantially smaller than the cinema image. Characteristically, the size of TV sets ranges from the 12 inch portable to the 24 inch or sometimes 30 inch model: all these measurements refer to the distance across the screen diagonally. The TV image shows things smaller than they are, unless it is a close-up of a small object, or of a person in head and shoulders only, when they appear more or less their real size. Such simple observations have profound effects on the kind of representations and spectator attitudes that broadcast TV creates for itself.

First, it is a characteristic of broadcast TV that the viewer is larger than the image: the opposite of cinema. It seems to be a convention also that the TV image is looked down on, rather than up to as in cinema. TV sets that are produced with stands are about two feet off the floor, which gives the effect of being almost but not quite level with the eyes of an individual lounging in an easy chair (as indeed we are meant to watch TV according to the advertisements it screens for itself). TV takes place in domestic surroundings, and is usually viewed in normal light conditions, though direct sunlight reflects off the screen to an unacceptable degree. The regime of viewing TV is thus very different from the cinema: TV does not encourage the same degree of spectator concentration. There is no surrounding darkness, no anonymity of the fellow viewers, no large image, no lack of movement amongst the spectators, no rapt attention. TV is not usually the only thing going on, sometimes it is not even the principal thing. TV is treated casually rather than concentratedly. It is something of a last resort ('What's on TV tonight, then?') rather than a special event. It has a lower degree of sustained concentration from its viewers, but a more extended period of watching and more frequent use than cinema.

This has two major effects on the kind of regime of representation that has developed for TV. First, the role that sound plays in TV is extremely important. Second, it engages the look and the glance rather than the gaze, and thus has a different relation to voyeurism from cinema's. Sound on TV is a strange paradox; although it is manifestly important, the manufacturers of TV sets provide speakers of dismal quality, even though the broadcast sound signal in many places has a wide tonal range. TV sets come with speakers that are massively geared towards the acceptable reproduction of speech. Music, especially rock music, does not reproduce at all well. This provides an alibi for broadcast TV to provide a minimum of rock music, and to provide the wasteful simultaneous stereo radio and TV transmissions of classical music on occasions.

The role played by sound stems from the fact that it radiates in all directions, whereas view of the TV image is sometimes restricted. Direct eye contact is needed with the TV screen. Sound can be heard where the screen cannot be seen. So sound is used to ensure a certain level of attention, to drag viewers back to looking at the set. Hence the importance of programme announcements and signature tunes and, to some extent, of music in various kinds of series. Sound holds attention more consistently than image, and provides a continuity that holds across momentary lapses of attention. The result is a slightly different balance between sound and image from that which is characteristic of cinema. Cinema is guaranteed a centred viewer by the physical arrangement of cinema seats and customs of film viewing. Sound therefore follows the image or diverges from it. The image is the central reference in cinema. But for TV, sound has a more centrally defining role. Sound carries the fiction or the documentary; the image has a more illustrative function. The TV image tends to be simple and straightforward, stripped of detail and excess of meanings. Sound tends to carry the details (background noises, music). This is a tendency towards a different sound/image balance than in cinema, rather than a marked and consistent difference. Broadcast TV has areas which tend towards the cinematic, especially the areas of serious drama or of various kinds of TV film. But many of TV's characteristic broadcast forms rely upon sound as the major carrier of information and the major means of ensuring continuity of attention. The news broadcast, the documentary with voice-over commentary, the bulk of TV comedy shows, all display a greater reliance on sound than any form that cinema has developed for itself. The image becomes illustration, and only occasionally provides material that is not covered by the sound-track (e.g. comedy sight-gags, news actuality footage). Sound tends to anchor meaning on TV, where the image tends to anchor it with cinema. In both, these are a matter of emphasis rather than any simple reliance one upon another. Sound and image exist in relation to each other in each medium rather than acting as separate entities. However, the difference of emphasis does exist between the two. It gives rise to two critical attitudes that are fundamental to the way in which newspaper critics and practitioners alike tend to conceive of the two media. Any film that contains a large amount of dialogue is open to the criticism that 'it could have been a radio play', as was Bergman's *From the Life of Marionettes* (*Aus dem Leben der Marionetten*, 1980). A similar accusation is never hurled at a TV play, however wordy. Instead, there are unwritten rules that govern the image for TV. Especially in British broadcast TV (possibly the most hide-bound in the world), the image is to be kept literal for almost all the time. There are licensed exceptions (science fiction, rock music programmes) where experimentation with the physical composition of the video image can take place; but the rule is that the image must show whatever is before the camera with the minimum

of fuss and conscious technique. The image is to be kept in
its place. Both these attitudes refer to occasions in which
the subservient partner in the sound/image relationship tends
to assert itself too much: for cinema, it is sound; for TV it is
the image.

TV's lower level of sustained concentration on the image
has had another effect upon its characteristic regime of
representation. The image on broadcast TV, being a lower
grade image than cinema's, has developed in a particular way.
Contrasting with cinema's profusion (and sometimes excess)
of detail, broadcast TV's image is stripped-down, lacking in
detail. The visual effects of this are immediately apparent:
the fussy detail of a film shown on TV compared to the
visual bareness of a TV cop series, where cars chase each
other through endless urban wastes of bare walls and near-
deserted streets. The broadcast TV image has to be certain
that its meaning is obvious: the streets are almost empty so
that the movement of the car is all the more obvious. The
walls are bare so that no writing distracts attention from the
segmental event. This is not an effect of parsimony of
production investment (rather, it enables it to happen). It
is a more fundamental aspect of the broadcast TV image
coming to terms with itself. Being small, low definition,
subject to attention that will not be sustained, the TV
image becomes jealous of its meaning. It is unwilling to
waste it on details and inessentials. So background and
context tend to be sketched rather than brought forward
and subject to a certain fetishism of details that often occurs
in cinema, especially art cinema. The narratively important
detail is stressed by this lack of other detail. Sometimes, it is
also stressed by music, producing an emphasis that seems
entirely acceptable on TV, yet would seem ludicrously heavy-
handed in cinema. This is particularly so with American
crime series, where speed of action and transition from one
segment to another dictates the concentration of resources
on to single meanings. Where detail and background are used
in TV programmes, for example the BBC historical serials,
action tends to slow down as a result. The screen displays
historical detail in and for itself; characters are inserted
around it, carrying on their lengthy conversations as best

they can. Segments are drawn out, their meanings unfolding gradually. For historical dramas, especially of the Victorian and Edwardian era, this tends to lend greater authenticity to the fiction: these are assumed to have been the decades of leisure and grace.

The stripped-down image that broadcast TV uses is a central feature of TV production. Its most characteristic result is the TV emphasis on close-ups of people, which are finely graded into types. The dramatic close-up is of face virtually filling the screen; the current affairs close-up is more distant, head-and-shoulders are shown, providing a certain distance, even reticence. Close-ups are regularly used in TV, to a much greater extent than in cinema. They even have their own generic name: talking heads. The effect is very different from the cinema close-up. Whereas the cinema close-up accentuates the difference between screen-figure and any attainable human figure by drastically increasing its size, the broadcast TV close-up produces a face that approximates to normal size. Instead of an effect of distance and unattainability, the TV close-up generates an equality and even intimacy.

The broadcast TV image is gestural rather than detailed; variety and interest are provided by the rapid change of images rather than richness within one image. TV compensates for the simplicity of its single images by the techniques of rapid cutting. Again, the organisation of studios is designed for this style of work. The use of several cameras and the possibility of alternation between them produces a style of shooting that is specific to TV: the fragmentation of events that keeps strictly to the continuity of their performance. There is much less condensation of events in TV than in cinema. Events are shown in real time from a multiple of different points of camera view (all, normally, from the same side of the action). Cinema events are shot already fragmented and matched together in editing. Still today, video editing is expensive, and the use of the studio set-up (in which much is already invested: capital and skills alike) provides instantaneous editing as the images are being transferred to tape for later transmission. This enables a rapid alternation of images, a practice which also affects the

editing of TV programmes made on film. The standard
attitude is that an image should be held on screen only until
its information value is exhausted. Since the information
value of the TV image is deliberately honed-down, it is
quickly exhausted. Variation is provided by changing the
image shown rather than by introducing a complexity of elements into a single image. Hence the material nature of the
broadcast TV image has two profound effects on the regime
of representation and working practices that TV has adopted.
It produces an emphasis on sound as the carrier of continuity
of attention and therefore of meaning; it produces a lack of
detail in the individual image that reduces the image to its
information value and produces an aesthetic that emphasises
the close-up and fast cutting with strict time continuity.

However, this is to compare the broadcast TV image with
the cinema image. The TV image has further distinct qualities
of its own, no doubt the result of a tenacious ideological
operation, that mark it decisively as different from the
cinema image with its photo effect. The broadcast TV image
has the effect of immediacy. It is as though the TV image is a
'live' image, transmitted and received in the same moment
that it is produced. For British broadcast TV, with its tight
schedules and fear of controversy, this has not been true for
a decade. Only news and sport are routinely live transmissions. However, the notion that broadcast TV is live still
haunts the medium; even more so does the sense of immediacy of the image. The immediacy of the broadcast TV image
does not just lie in the presumption that it is live, it lies
more in the relations that the image sets up for itself. Immediacy is the effect of the directness of the TV image, the way
in which it constitutes itself and its viewers as held in a
relationship of co-present intimacy. Broadcast TV very
often uses forms of direct address from individual in close-
up to individuals gathered around the set. This is very different from cinema's historic mode of narration, where events
do not betray a knowledge that they are being watched.
Broadcast TV is forever buttonholing, addressing its viewers
as though holding a conversation with them. Announcers and
newsreaders speak directly from the screen, simulating the
eye-contact of everyday conversation by looking directly

14 Even Gilbert Harding's direct address failed sometimes (*Meet Mr Lucifer*)

out of the screen and occasionally looking down (a learned and constructed technique). Advertisements contain elements of direct address: questions, exhortations, warnings. Sometimes they go further, providing riddles and jokes that assume that their viewers share a common frame of reference with them. Hence advertisements for various staple commodities, beer for example, tend to make oblique and punning references to each other's advertising campaigns. The audience is expected to understand these references. This also is an operation of direct address: an ephemeral and immediate knowledge is assumed in the viewer, who otherwise would have no understanding of the reference or the joke. Hence these advertisements are addressing a viewer as an equal: 'we both know what we are talking about'.

Direct address is recognised as a powerful effect of TV. Its most obvious form, that of an individual speaking directly (saying 'I' and 'you'), is reserved for specific kinds of people. It can be used by those who are designated as politically neutral by TV itself (newsmen and women), or by those who have ultimate political power: heads of state. Otherwise, direct address is denied to individuals who appear on TV. Important personalities are interviewed in three-quarter face. Other strategies of address are open to them, that of recruiting the audience against the interviewer by appealing to a common sense that media persons do not share, for instance. Interviewers in their turn tend to construct themselves as asking questions on behalf of the viewers: 'what the public/ the viewers/ordinary people *really* want to know is . . .'. This is also a form of highly motivated direct address. Again, it assumes an audience who is there simultaneously, for whom events are being played out.

Direct address is not the only form of construction of broadcast TV's effect of immediacy. Broadcast TV's own perpetual presence (there every night of the year), and its series formats, breed a sense of the perpetual present. Broadcast TV declares itself as being in the present tense, denying recording as effectively as cinema uses it. TV fictions take place to a very large extent as though they were transmitted directly from the place in which they were really happening. The soap opera is the most obvious example of this, where events in a particular milieu are everlastingly updated. Broadcast TV has a very marked sense of presence to its images and sounds which far outweighs any counterbalancing sense of absence, any sense of recording. The technical operation of the medium in its broadcast form strengthens this feeling. The tight scheduling that is favoured by most large broadcast operations means that an audience wanting to see a particular programme has to be present at a very precise time, or they miss it. This increases the sense that broadcast TV is of the specific present moment. In addition, unlike cinema, the signal comes from elsewhere, and can be sent live. The technical origin of the signal is not immediately apparent to the viewer, but all the apparatus of direct address and of contemporaneity of broadcast TV messages is very present. The broadcast signal is always available during almost all normal waking hours. It is ever-present.

The favoured dramatic forms of broadcast TV work within this framework of presence and immediacy. Besides the obvious forms of soap opera, entirely cast in a continuous present, the series format tends towards the creation of immediacy and presence. The open-ended series format of the situation comedy or the dramatic series tends to produce the sense of immediacy by the fact that it presents itself as having no definite end. Unlike the cinema narrative, the end of the episode and the end of the series alike leave events unresolved. They are presented as on-going, part of the texture of life. This sense even extends to the historical reconstruction dramas beloved of the BBC, through the operation of a further mechanism that produces the effect of immediacy.

Immediacy is also produced by the logical extension of the direct address form: by echoing the presumed form of the TV audience within the material of the TV fiction itself. The institution of broadcast TV assumes its audience to be the family; it massively centres its fictional representations around the question of the family. Hence TV produces its effect of immediacy even within dramas of historically remote periods by reproducing the audience's view of itself within its fictions. Hence TV dramas are concerned with romance and the family, both conceived of within certain basic kinds of definition. Broadcast TV's view of the family is one which is at variance with the domestic practices of the majority of domestic units and of individuals in Britain at the moment. Yet broadcast TV's definition has a strength in that it participates in the construction of an idea of the normal family/domestic unit, from which other forms are experienced and remembered as temporary aberrations.

Broadcast TV dramas are constructed around the heterosexual romance in its normal and perverse forms, and the perpetual construction of standard families: wage-earning husband, housekeeping wife, two children. Situation comedies play on the discrepancies between this assumed norm and other forms of existence: male and female students sharing a flat (*Man About the House*), the childless, woman-dominated couple (*George and Mildred*), the landlord and his variegated bedsit tenants (*Rising Damp*), the rejuvenated divorced father (*Father Dear Father*). Historical dramas found their sense of the historical on the never-changing patterns of romance and family life: Edward VIII's *amour fou* (*Edward and Mrs Simpson*), the problems of the powerful career woman (*Elizabeth R*), the problems of male lust breaking the confines of the family (*The Six Wives of Henry VIII*), the consequences of one sexual transgression repercussing down the centuries (*The Forsyte Saga*, *Poldark*, etc.).

The centring of all kinds of broadcast TV drama upon the family (much as direct address assumes a family unit as its audience) produces a sense of intimacy, a bond between the viewers' conception of themselves (or how they ought to be) and the programme's central concerns. So a relationship of humanist sympathy is set up, along the lines of seeing how everyone is normal really, how much they really do desire the norm that our society has created for itself. But the intimacy that broadcast TV sets up is more than just this form of sympathy. It is made qualitatively different by the sense that the TV image carries of being a live event, which is intensified by the habit of shooting events in real time within any one segment, the self-contained nature of each segment, and the use of close-up and sound continuity. All of these factors contribute to an overall impression, that the broadcast TV image is providing an intimacy with events between couples and within families, an intimacy that gives the impression that these events are somehow co-present with the viewer, shared rather than witnessed from outside. The domestic nature of the characteristic use of broadcast TV certainly contributes here, but more important is the particular way in which TV has internalised this in its own representations. Broadcast TV has ingested the domestic and bases its dramas upon it. When it does not address its audience directly, it creates a sense of familiarity between its fictions and its audience, a familiarity based on a notion of the familial which is assumed to be shared by all.

Broadcast TV has a particular regime of representation that stresses the immediacy and co-presence of the TV representation. Its particular physical and social characteristics have created a very particular mode of representation that includes the image centred upon the significant at the cost of detail, and sound as carrier of continuity. It gives its audience a particular sense of intimacy with the events it portrays. All of these features of broadcast TV create and foster a form of looking by the TV viewer that is different from the kind of voyeurism (with fetishistic undertow) that cinema presents for its spectators.

TV's regime of vision is less intense than cinema's: it is a regime of the glance rather than the gaze. The gaze implies a concentration of the spectator's activity into that of looking, the glance implies that no extraordinary effort is being invested in the activity of looking. The very terms we habitually use to designate the person who watches TV or the cinema screen tend to indicate this difference. The cinema-looker is a spectator: caught by the projection yet separate from its illusion. The TV-looker is a viewer, casting a lazy eye over proceedings, keeping an eye on events, or, as the slightly archaic designation had it, 'looking in'. In psychoanalytic terms, when compared to cinema, TV demonstrates a displacement from the invocatory drive of schopophilia (looking) to the closest related of the invocatory drives, that of hearing. Hence the crucial role of sound in ensuring continuity of attention and producing the utterances of direct address ('I' to 'you').

The different balance between the activities of looking and

listening produces a qualitatively different relation to the TV transmission. It is not that the experience is less intense than cinema; rather, it has a distinctive form of its own. In particular, there is far less separation between viewer and image than with cinema. Broadcast TV does not construct an image that is marked by present absence, its regime is one of co-presence of image and viewer. The image is therefore not an impossible one, defined by the separation of the viewer from it, but rather one that is familiar and intimate. The cost of this intimacy is that the voyeuristic mode cannot operate as intensely as in cinema. In particular, the broadcast TV viewer's look is not a controlling look in the same sense as that which operates in cinema. The cinema spectator is secure in the separation from the image that allows events to take place as though they were not watched. The broadcast TV image is quite often directly addressed to the viewer, in a simulation of everyday eye contact. In addition, the sense of cinema's consent to the act of being watched (implied in the event of the projection of a film for spectators) is radically absent from broadcast TV. TV continues whether a particular set is turned on or not. In this sense, it is not for the viewer in the way that the cinema projection is for the spectator. If no one turns up to a film screening, it can be cancelled, but if no one is watching a TV programme, it will be transmitted anyway in blithe ignorance of its lack of reception. The broadcast TV event is just there, it carries no sense with it of being for anyone as the cinema projection is for a definite group. This implies a lack of the consent by the representation to being watched that is vital to the construction of a regime of the voyeuristic gaze in cinema.

Broadcast TV can be left on with no one watching it, playing in the background of other activities in the home. This is perhaps a frequent event; certainly, it also makes impossible the construction of a voyeuristic contract between looker and representation. Instead, broadcast TV uses sound to appeal to its audience, using a large degree of direct address whose function is to attract the look and attention of the viewer, and to hold it. The separation that this practice implies is different from that of cinematic voyeurism. It makes explicit a relationship between viewer and broadcast TV image, designating a TV first person singular or plural ('I', 'we') and a viewing second person ('you', beautifully flexible in its lack of singular/plural difference). Together these first and second person designations can observe and speculate about third persons: 'he', 'she', 'they'. The practice of segmentalising TV broadcasting means that direct address is present regularly to reaffirm this relationship. It surrounds the segments of dramatic material and comic material so that they become constituted as 'they': the people whom we *and television* both look in upon. But drama's characters are not constituted as a totally separate 'they'. TV drama is constructed around the presumed self-image of the audience: the family. The mobilisation of this sense of intimacy, together with TV's effect of co-presence both tend to push even dramatic material into this sense of first and second person togetherness. Characters in drama series on broadcast TV tend to become familiar figures, loved, or excused with a tolerance that is quite remarkable: it is more than is normally extended to members of the family or to neighbours. The construction of a 'real monster' in a TV series is a difficult process: this is perhaps why J.R. Ewing in *Dallas* excited such attention.

The community of address that broadcast TV is able to set up excludes a fully developed regime of voyeurism as found in cinema. This is perhaps why films screened on TV do not quite achieve the same intensity of experience as they would in the cinema, and why broadcast TV's adoption of the cinematic mode has not been more widespread. The community of address sets up a different relation between viewer and representation. The distance between viewer and image is reduced; but a compensatory distance is constructed and separation/between the 'I' and 'you' of the community of address and the third person outside that it constructs. The 'they' that is always implied and often stated in direct address forms becomes an other, a grouping outside the consensus that confirms the consensus. Certain characteristic attitudes are taken towards these outsiders: patronisation, hate, wilful ignorance, pity, generalised concern, indifference. These are encouraged by the complicity that broadcast TV sets up between itself and its viewers; a series of categories of 'they' has begun to appear, often creating curious dislocations in the operation of TV representations when they are used in news and current affairs. The most obviously dislocating is that of 'housewives'. Housewives suffer from inflation, they worry about their families, they rush out and 'panic buy' when threatened with shortages. 'Housewives' are designated as a 'they' whose actions are scrutinised by the TV institution and its viewers together. This effectively prevents the recognition by women in that audience of themselves as 'housewives'. If they do identify with that term in its use in a news bulletin, they cast themselves outside the consensus of the direct address mode. The effect is that the 'housewife' is presumed to be everywhere, blindly devoted to the maintenance of her little family, but no one recognises themselves in that designation. Rather, individual women look on at the scene of these strange beings acting in their pitiful ways, rather than recognising themselves there, even if they would otherwise claim to be ('only') a housewife. The 'they' of a TV direct address news bulletin or announcement is always elsewhere, always outside the consensus between viewer and TV.

Broadcast TV's designation of race has more unilateral consequences in Britain. The 'black community' or 'immigrants' (often and wrongly equated) appear in a news and current affairs context only as problems. The amount of non-current affairs material that appears regularly including coloured people is minimal. There is no continuity of representation of any ethnic minority in British entertainment TV. 'They' are always the exceptions, the cause for concern. A few remarkable (and short-lived) attempts to create such representations have occurred, like BBC 2's *Empire Road*; otherwise, ethnic minorities only appear in their own minority programmes, broadcast at marginal hours of the day like early on Sunday morning. Individuals who are coloured sometimes appear in TV fictions: as a rule, they come weighed down by their colour, supporting a whole invisible culture on their backs. Their colour becomes an obsessive point of dramatic interest, or the butt of jokes in comedy. Perhaps Britain's new Fourth Channel will begin to produce representations that are not so demeaning, but the work has hardly begun on the other three channels. Even the American policy of positive discrimination would be an improvement, producing as it does at least regular appearances of coloured people. On British TV, coloured people are excluded from the world of TV, the world of the familiar and everyday in representations. 'They' appear as a problem or an object of concern only, and are therefore constructed as such for most of the viewing public. Outside the community of TV and viewers, the 'natural' tendency is to conceive of Britain's coloured populations as an 'unnatural' feature of society. Such is the insidious way in which British TV participates in the construction of casual racism. Broadcast TV's particular version of this pervasive attitude is based on its ability to construct a community of address between viewer and TV institution that is capable of excluding any group designated as 'they'.

These examples of casual racism and of the dislocations produced by the designation 'housewife' are both taken from news and current affairs. This is one area in which the construction of the direct address form is most prevalent. Dramatic forms of various kinds occur regularly within TV's direct address context, and are inflected by it to some extent. Dramatic forms are not constructed in broadcast TV for the voyeuristic gaze in the same way as cinematic forms. There is a sense of complicity of the institution of TV in the process of looking at dramatic events which increases their sense of co-presence with the viewer. The effects of immediacy, of segmentation and of the series rather than strong narrative development, and the concentration of TV drama on the family (as presumed reflection of its audience) all intensify this sense of TV drama as part of the consensus between broadcast TV and its audience. Hence drama is crucial in revising and altering the effects of news and current affairs' rather more brutal division of its world into a series of 'theys' beyond the consensus of viewer and TV first persons. The dislocation produced by the designation 'housewife' as beyond the consensus in TV news is made innocuous by the persistent dramatic and advertising use of housewife-figures.

The final effects of TV's low emphasis on the construction of the voyeuristic position lie in the representation of the female body and of female sexuality, and in its characteristic forms of narration of events. Cinematic voyeurism, with its fetishistic counterpart, is centrally concerned with the representation of the female body and of female sexuality as a problem, constructed from the security of a definition of the masculine as positive. TV's concerns are not so heavily centred towards the investigation of the female. This is not only the result of the different mechanisms of self-censorship and imposed censorship that prevail in the two media, nor only of the different sense of the viewing conditions that the two media have of themselves. After all, Hollywood's relentless investigation of the female was carried out under codes of censorship in the 1940s that were every bit as vigilant as those operating in broadcast TV today. TV does not have its equivalents of the *film noir* or of the 'love interest'. Different conditions prevail. Broadcast TV's lack of an intense voyeuristic appeal produces a lack of the strong investigatory drive that is needed alike for tightly organised narration and for intense concern with the 'problem' of the female. Similarly, the regime of broadcast TV does not demonstrate a particular drift towards a fetishistic activity of viewing. Its forms of narration are not particularly repetitive in the fetishistic manner of obsessive replaying of events. The series and the segmental form construct a different pattern of repetition that has much more to do with constructing a pattern of familiarity (as the next chapter demonstrates). The fetishistic regime does operate to some extent, however, as does voyeurism. Its characteristic attention in broadcast TV is not directed towards the whole body, but to the face. The display of the female body on TV, in dance sequences or in a series like *Charlie's Angels*, is gestural rather than fascinating. The techniques of rapid cutting prevent the access of the gaze at the body being displayed. Instead, TV's displays of the female body, frequent and depressing enough as they are, provide material for the glance only. Details and complete bodies are both presented only to the extent that they can be registered as 'a bit of a body/a whole body'. The exception to this is the face, and specifically the female face. In some sense, the female body is hidden, made obscure, by the heavy emphasis that broadcast TV gives to various kinds of close-up. This is particularly so with newsreaders. Newsreaders are on the screen in close-up for long periods of time, but their bodies are never revealed. The face becomes a distraction from the message of the voice for some viewers a lot of the time, and for most viewers some of the time. The fetishistic regime is encouraged by two additional factors: the use of direct address by newsreaders, radically reducing any separation between viewer and image, and the fact that the image of the newsreader is held for a long period (in broadcast TV's terms), with very little alteration. Newsreaders thus can become obsessive objects; when women newsreaders were introduced in Britain, in the mid-1970s, they became the targets of a national fetishism. Speculation about their 'private life' was rife in the popular press and in ordinary conversation: a speculation amply rewarded by Anna Ford. The close-up of the face is the one moment where the average TV image is more or less life-sized rather than less than life-size, and the equality of scale between image and viewer contributes to a dramatic reduction of separation between image and viewer that is one aspect of the fetishistic regime. The fetishism is still concentrated upon women, because of the generalised culture of sexual difference under which we suffer.

Broadcast TV's level of investment in voyeuristic activity is generally not intense enough to produce the investigatory and forward-moving narratives that are characteristic of entertainment cinema. Instead, the form of narration that corresponds with the activity of the glance rather than the gaze is one of providing variety. Broadcast TV provides a variety of segments rather than the progressive accumulation of sequences that characterises cinematic narration. The segment form corresponds to the regime of the glance. It is relatively coherent and assumes an attention span of relatively limited duration. Broadcast TV's characteristic form of multi-camera editing tends to give the segment the strong coherence of proceeding in real time; TV's characteristic use of a small number of actors in any one situation also increases the coherence of individual segments. Segmentation has been developed in broadcast TV towards the provision of variety: segments of different kinds follow each other for most of TV's output. Hence the TV cop series will present successively the dramatic face-to-face confrontation, the comic routine, the chase sequence, the scene of pathos. Soap operas tend to present a variety of different moods across each episode by alternating between different kinds of segment. Broadcast TV's whole attitude to scheduling is nothing other than the provision of this variety on a grand scale. Scheduling ensures that programmes of the same kind are not bunched together, that a spread of different forms will be found over an evening's output. Such a conception has virtually disappeared from the entertainment cinema, which is more and more intent on presenting one film-text only.

Broadcast TV characteristically offers an image that is stripped down, with no unnecessary details. Cutting produces forms of variation of visual information, and sound has an important role in drawing the viewer's attention back to the screen. The image and sound both tend to create a sense of immediacy, which produces a kind of complicity between the viewer and the TV institution. This can provide a powerful form of consensus, since it tends to define the domestic place of the TV set as a kind of norm, against which the 'outside world' represented on TV can be measured. This regime of image and sound, together with the segment and series forms, has created a distinct form of narration in broadcast TV.

9 Broadcast TV narration

Commercial entertainment cinema is overwhelmingly a narrative fiction medium. Non-fiction films have always had a precarious place in the commercial cinema, and nowadays they are practically non-existent. Broadcast TV on the other hand carries large amounts of non-fiction: news, documentaries, announcements, weather forecasts, various kinds of segments that are purely televisual in their characteristic forms. It could be argued, therefore, that any model of televisual narration would have to give pride of place to this division of TV products between fiction and non-fiction. Whereas the classical narrative model, basically a fiction model, still underlies our assumptions about the entertainment film, it would seem that no such generalised conception of TV narration would be possible. In fact, this does not seem to be the case. Quite the reverse, the non-fiction and fiction modes of exposition of meanings seem to have converged within TV, under the impulsion of the characteristic broadcast TV forms of the segment and the series, and the pervasive sense of the TV image as live. This has produced a distinctive regime of fictional narration on TV which owes much to its non-fictional modes. After all, the first true use of the open-ended series format would seem to be the news bulletin, endlessly updating events and never synthesising them.

The mode of narration on TV does not have to be divided into two distinct models, one appropriate to fiction, the other to non-fiction. Instead, one model seems to be enough, a model that is capable of inflection by fictional or non-fictional concerns. This explains the ease that TV has long since had of producing programmes that are ambiguous in their status: the documentary-drama, or the drama-documentary, forms that seem to have existed in the late 1950s at least on the BBC. The divisions between fiction and non-fiction exist at another level to that of narration; they are chiefly concerned with the origin of material used in the programme.

Any model of narration on broadcast TV therefore has to be based on the particular institutional and material nature of that TV as we now know it. It depends on the conception of the broadcast output as that of segment following segment, segments which by no means always have any connection between them. It depends on the counterpart to this segmental process, the programme series with its distinctive forms of repetition and favoured forms of problematic. It depends on the conception of TV as a casual, domestic form, watched without great intensity or continuity of attention. It assumes the ideology of TV as a medium which transmits events as they happen, even though (especially in Britain) this is virtually never the case. It is worth repeating in this connection that, although the overwhelming mass of TV output is recorded, it still carries a different sense of immediacy from the cinematic image. Broadcast TV is capable of adopting a filmic mode of narration as a kind of borrowing from an already established medium. This will almost always be announced as such: by the form of the TV movie (often a 'pilot' for a series), or by the designation of a programme as a prestigious cultural event. This tends to mean that the programme will not so much have been made on film as made within a cinematic mode of narration. In this sense, TV acknowledges a certain inferiority to cinema. Cinema, for TV, means the culturally respectable, the artistic text. The designation 'film' for a TV transmission indicates that this transmission is to be viewed despite TV; it is not to be segmented, interruptions in terms of advertisements breaks or viewer attention 'at home' are to be kept to a minimum. The 'film' transmission on TV will then proceed to construct a more cinematic narration. The vast majority of such events, indeed, are cinema films which have already been exhibited in a cinematic context. Cinema is currently not capable of a similar borrowing of broadcast TV forms, however: the collective exhibition of TV material is still a novelty or an aberration.

Cinema narration has a strong internal dynamic, a movement from an initial equilibrium that is disrupted towards a new harmony that is the end of the fiction. Broadcast TV narration has a more dispersed narrational form: it is extensive rather than sequential. Its characteristic mode is not one of final closure or totalising vision; rather, it offers a continuous refiguration of events. Like the news bulletin series, the broadcast TV narrative (fiction and non-fiction) is open-ended, providing a continuous update, a perpetual return to the present. Since closure and finality is not a central feature of TV narration (though it does occur in specific major ways), it follows that the hermetic nature of the cinema narrative, with its patterns of repetition and novelty, is also absent. Repetition in the TV narrative occurs at the level of the series: formats are repeated, situations return week after week. Each time there is novelty. The characters of the situation comedy encounter a new dilemma; the documentary reveals a new problem; the news gives us a fresh strike, a new government, another earthquake, the first panda born in captivity. This form of repetition is different from that offered by the classic cinema narrative, as it provides a kind of groundbase, a constant basis for events, rather than an economy of reuse directed towards a final totalisation.

The series is composed of segments. The recognition of the series format tends to hold segments together and to provide them with an element of continuity and narrative progression from one to the next. The segment form itself has a strong internal coherence. Certain forms of segments are free-standing: the spot advertisement and the item in the news bulletin are both examples. They occur alongside similar segments which have no connection with them except a similarity of class. Other segments, those in a documentary exposition of a particular situation, or a fictional depiction of characters, will have definite connections of a narrative kind. But again, the movement from event to event is not as concentrated and causal as it tends to be in classic cinema narration. Broadcast TV's fictional segments tend to explore states and incidents in real time, avoiding the abbreviation that is characteristic of cinema. Hence a certain sense of intimacy in TV drama, a different pace and attention from entertainment cinema.

The segment is self-contained in TV production partly because of the fragmentary nature of much broadcast TV (especially if it carries spot advertising), but also because of the attention span that TV assumes of its audience, and the fact that memory of the particular series in all its detail cannot be assumed. People switch on in the middle and get hooked; they miss an episode or two; someone phones up in the middle. The TV production cannot be hermetic in the way that the film text is, otherwise the audience for a long-running soap opera like *Coronation Street* would now consist of half a dozen ageing addicts. The segment and the series are the repository of memory, and thus of the possibility of repetition and coherence.

The segment is a relatively self-contained scene which conveys an incident, a mood or a particular meaning. Coherence is provided by a continuity of character through the segment, or, more occasionally, a continuity of place. Hence many fictional segments consist of conversations between two or three characters, an encounter which produces a particular mood (embarrassment, relief, anger, love-at-first-sight, insults, anxiety) and tends to deliver a particular meaning which is often encapsulated in a final line. The segment ends and, in conventional TV fiction, is succeeded by another which deals with a different set of (related) characters in a different place, or the same characters at a different time. There is a marked break between segments. The aspect of break, of end and beginning, tends to outweigh the aspect of continuity and consequence. The non-fiction segment tends to operate in the same way, though in the expository or investigatory documentary it is a series of fragments (interviews, stills, captions, studio presenters, reporter-to-camera in locations) which are held together as a segment by the fact that they all combine to deliver a particular message. Each segment then represents a 'move' in the argument of the overall programme. In both drama and investigatory documentary, the segment is relatively self-contained and usually does not last longer than five minutes. Being self-contained, the segment tends to exhaust its material, providing its own climax which is the culmination of the material of the segment. It is a characteristic of soap operas that they withhold the climactic revelation or action to the end of the segment and the end of the episode. This reaches a purely formal perfection with a series like *Crossroads* where the climactic revelation is followed directly by the credits (entering, emblematically, from every possible direction), and is then repeated as a kind of coda: two characters in frozen face-to-face confrontation with one delivering a line that summarises the previous segment. This process of climaxing directly followed by a break to other forms of segments (title sequences, advertisements, programme announcements, etc.) generates a series of segments in the next episode which effectively chart the repercussions of the climactic event. A series of conversations and actions exhaustively explores and, in the process, recapitulates the climactic action or revelation. The discovery of a husband's affair is followed by a rush of disconnected segments, adverts and so on; a week's wait produces a series of conversations: wife to friend, children, neighbours; husband to lover, colleague; and perhaps even The Couple themselves. Each depicts a certain attitude and mood, produces subsidiary revelations and mulls over the situation. These segments are self-exhausting: enough is said, done and shown to convey a particular meaning. This completion and internal coherence means that movement from one segment to the next is a matter of succession rather than consequence.

This effect of the self-containedness of the segment is intensified, especially in fiction and observational documentary work, by the use of real time. Where cinema elides actions within a scene by cutting out 'dead time' (a character's movement across a room that has no directly narrative function, for example), TV tends to leave this 'dead time' in. This stems directly from the studio multiple camera technique, where events are staged in temporal sequence and picked up by a number of cameras one of whose images is selected at any one moment by the director. Where cinema stages events in a very fragmentary way (sometimes just a gesture, a look), TV will stage much more like a theatrical scene. The result is that events unroll in real time for the audience, in the time that they took. A segment will tend to hold to temporal unity, especially if it is a conversation. This produces a sense of intimacy within the segment, and a sharp break between segments.

Not all segments hold to temporal unity, not all segments are so isolated from each other. It is quite simple for a segment to be organised around two locations and the journey between them made by a couple of characters. This will involve a great deal of compression and elision. It is also possible to produce effects of alternation and contrast between segments: the contrasting pastimes of two connected characters, or an anticipatory alternation between the tranquil life of one character and the arrival of another who will cause an upset. However, such effects do have to be marked, to be stressed so that they are visibly and audibly different from the normal neutral transition between segments. Hence the anticipatory alternation will be marked by a repeated and rapid movement between the two scenes together with a marked contrast on the level of the soundtrack. So it is with the beginning of the first episode of *A Bouquet of Barbed Wire*. Peaceful scenes of Frank Finlay walking through the sunlit park back to his office are intercut with scenes of arrival at Victoria Station, crowds, train noises, doors slamming, station announcements. Discontinuity on the soundtrack indicates that this alternation is meaningful, that the arrival constitutes a disturbance. From the same series, examples abound of the segment structured around two locations and the journey between them. Here again, the soundtrack ensures that the continuity of the segment is recognised over its discontinuities of space and time. Dialogue overlaps: it is as though one conversation continues, with the same train of thought running through the segment.

These examples mark TV's difficulty with connecting segments too closely. The normal movement between segments is one of vague simultaneity (meanwhile . . . meanwhile . . . a bit later . . .). Where an event with narrative consequences does take place, several segments are required to work through those consequences and to recapitulate the event itself. There is far less concentration on the cumulative repetition and innovation of meanings than in the classic cinematic narration. The segment is coherent within itself, and may well contain its own echoes of dialogue and gesture. Apart from isolated examples of almost emblematic repetitions across TV narratives (a significant line of dialogue, for instance), this repetition is not characteristic of broadcast TV programmes.

The narrative movement between segments does not follow the cinematic pattern of a relatively rapid transition from event to event in causal sequence. The movement from event to event is more circumspect. This circumspection shows itself in two ways. The first is the multiplication of incidents whose consequences and conclusion are suspended. This is a characteristic of the TV action series like the cop saga *Starsky and Hutch*. Our heroes perpetually encounter fresh incidents, and equally often find themselves suspended in an ambiguous position at the end of a segment (cue for commercial break). The second form of circumspect movement from event to event is that characterised by the soap opera and the drama alike. Events are at a premium: when they occur they generate tidal waves of verbiage, of gossip, discussion, speculation, recrimination. Guilt, jealousy, worry and an immense curiosity about people is generated by this form. The action series tends to generate car journeys, car chases, interrogations and the segment that reveals the furtive goings-on that the action-heroes will head off.

In each form, the events that take place are anticipated. For the soap opera/drama, the deliciousness of the anticipation is worth in many instances more than the event itself. Speculation abounds; the event is perfunctory; the mulling over of the repercussions is extended. But it is a characteristic of the action series too that it carries few surprises. Its form of suspense is more incidental. Rather than proposing a central 'whodunnit' problem, it is more characteristic to find the central mystery revealed fairly early in the programme. Suspense then becomes a serial affair: the heroes and villains become entangled in a series of different situations, each of which involves escape, chase, shoot-out, etc. Narration in the cinematic sense is relatively perfunctory. Little play is made with the fact that the solution to the 'whodunnit' has been revealed to audience before it has to the heroes. This differential knowledge and analytic attitude to the actions of the heroes, characteristic of a cinema director like Fritz Lang (who usually reveals the narrative enigma to the audience), is relatively absent. Instead, the narrative enigma (the aim of the heroes' quest) is incidental. It provides the ground for a series of relatively self-contained segments that deal with particular actions. These segments could be called 'clinches': a struggle at close quarters (and also the standard term for an embrace between lovers in the entertainment cinema that thought mostly of such encounters as the male conquest of the female). The action series, then, breaks down into a series of clinches whose motivation is provided by a narrative enigma (a mystery) which more often than not is purely perfunctory. Some very elegant and accomplished uses of this form have been made, alongside the more automatic uses exemplified by a series like *Hawaii Five-O*. *The Rockford Files* produced a liberal-intellectual variant of the clinch. It became the encounter between the amiable Jim Rockford and a series of off-beat eccentrics, where the aspects of performance, milieu and sparring conversation became the real pleasure of the series. Here, the cinematic genre of the *film noir* and private eye film provided a partial reference point. Another very cultish use of the clinch was *The Prisoner*, with Patrick McGoohan trapped within a series format from which he perpetually tried to escape. The essence of the series was that it was the same each week: the frustrated escape attempt and the frustrated search for some kind of explanation for the series format: who was keeping him prisoner and why. This generated a high degree of independence for each clinch action: it became the only comprehensible and explicable aspect of each episode. Whereas in cinema this procedure would be intensely frustrating and ultimately pointless, the balance between enigma and clinch-incident in TV is different. Clinches can carry the programme when the enigma is never resolved. It was enough to see McGoohan's attempts to enlist fellow inmates to help him escape and to see the doomed escape attempt. It was enough to see McGoohan's attempts to find the identity of 'Number One', and to resist the intimidation of various sophisticated brainwashing techniques.

Broadcast TV characteristically has a slighter stress on the causal narrative chain of events than entertainment cinema. Instead, a more extensive mode operates: segments which are relatively self-contained, exploring a particular exchange between individuals, a conversation or an action-clinch. Movement from event to event is slower than in cinema, and particular incidents tend to proliferate and be explored in more detail. This tends to produce an emphasis on groups rather than individuals, on communities rather than couples. The core of a TV series is more often a family, a street or a workplace than it is an individual. The kind of exploration of a relatively large group and their interrelations which the entertainment film rarely handles (*Written on the Wind* (1956) or *The Cobweb* (1955) being rare examples), is a common phenomenon on TV. Similarly, the assurance with which a TV documentary is able to draw together, place and relativise very disparate views is something that film documentaries produced before the era of TV hardly dared attempt.

Groups of characters rarely appear all together in one segment. Arguments in expository documentaries are made by a series of relatively self-contained segmental 'moves'. The unifying principle behind these programmes is not as it is in cinema (significant patterns of repetition and innovation of meanings; narrative sequence; central problematic); it is the series which provides coherence between segments. The series provides the unity of a particular programme, pulling together segments into a sense of connection which enables a level of narrative progression to take place between them. The series is the major point of repetition in TV, matching the innovation that takes place within each segment. This pattern of repetition and innovation is very different from the cinematic model. Where the cinematic form is a closed system which aims to reuse as much material as possible and to balance kinds of repetition and innovation against each

other, the TV form is more open-ended. It is a pattern of
repetition that is far more centred on the narrative problematic than in cinema. Cinema's single texts tend to inaugur-
ate a novel problematic, a new story subject, for each film.
The TV series repeats a problematic. It therefore provides no
resolution of the problematic at the end of each episode,
nor, often, even at the end of the run of a series. Hence
again the reduction of onward narrative progression. The
TV series proposes a problematic that is not resolved; narrative resolution takes place at a less fundamental level, at the
level of the particular incidents (clinches, confrontations,
conversations) that are offered each week (in the case of
situation comedies) or between one week and the next
(with the cliff-hanger serial ending). Fundamentally, the
series implies the form of the dilemma rather than that of
resolution and closure. This perhaps is the central contribution that broadcast TV has made to the long history of
narrative forms and narrativised perception of the world.

The series is based on the repetition of a problematic.
It repeats a situation, a situation which can be fictional or
non-fictional. Hence the news series and the current affairs
series both present a certain inquiring, fact-finding vision:
the situation of reporters observing and collating information, then organising it for presentation to an uninformed
public. This is as much a situation as a father and son running
a scrap business with a totter's horse and cart and a crowded
London yard (*Steptoe and Son*). The news and current
affairs series present a problematic of vision and of explanation. Specific characters encounter a specific set of circumstances every week. But across the specificity of the week's
circumstances runs the generality of the same problematic:
that of how to see, how to understand. The terms of the
understanding are always specified by the programme format. It will be 'we go behind the scenes' (*Panorama*), 'we
ask the awkward questions' (*World in Action*), 'we update
and see how this affects London' (*The London Programme*),
'we glance around' (*Nationwide*). In addition to these specific
forms of understanding, there are the terms in which these
understandings are cast: 'moderate/extremist', 'the housewife', 'But surely you don't think that. . . ?' The role of

presenter is fundamental to these operations. The characters who investigate and explain for us are a loose group remarkably similar to the cast of a soap opera: some are central, long-running figures (presenters, anchor-persons); others come and go (reporters). In some areas of current affairs, the soap opera aspect becomes more or less explicit. *Nationwide* and *That's Life* are specific examples. The series format constitutes a stable basis of repetition in the programme format, its cast of characters, and its particular kind of reporting attention. Novelty each edition is provided by the specific circumstances that these characters and their vision run up against. It is often explicit that the particular focus of attention for the characters is provided by outside forces over which they have no control, the world of current events. This world tends to be constituted as a place where problems occur. The political actions that the current events series is constituted to explain thus become a particular modality of action: they are problems, troubles, disturbances. The current events series provides a security against these disturbances. The result is that the political arena tends to be given the same status as the emotional problems encountered by soap opera characters. This is one effect of the series format, and one aspect of it.

The fictional series, too, repeats a basic problematic or situation week after week. Like the news and current affairs series, the situation comedy, the crime drama and the hospital series all return to the stability of the basic dilemma at the end of the week's episode. There is no development at all across the series. The serial marks a long slow narrative movement towards a conclusion, but often that conclusion is tentative (allowing a second series) or incidental (the dispersion of the characters). The situation that provides the steady core is a state of permanent or semi-permanent relationships between a stable but antagonistic group of characters. This is most fully developed in the situation comedy. *Steptoe and Son* may well hate each other, but they also love each other, and Harold's repeated threats to leave his father were never serious. This is exactly the dilemma that situation comedy deals with: it presents conflicting forces or emotions that can never be resolved. Hence

the series situation is highly suited to present a particular
static vision of the family and of work relations. What is
particularly marked about the situation series is that the
characters lose all memory of the previous weeks' incidents.
They never learn.

A kind of cross between the serial and the series has
become increasingly popular on British TV. In a light drama
or a situation comedy like *Agony* a particular event is passed
on from episode to episode, whilst the rest of the events are
specific to one episode. Hence in *Agony* Maureen Lipmann's
agony columnist is pregnant, and her pregnancy increases
until the last episode is concerned with giving birth. However, everything else that occurs, the week's catastrophes
and comic turns, take place within one episode which
presents their resolution or expulsion from the programme.
No memory remains of them next week.

Repetition across the series is one of problematic, of both
characters and the situation (or dilemma) in which they find
themselves. These situations provide a steady state to which
audience and fiction return each week. Specific incidents are
fed into this steady state, to provide fresh ammunition for
our embattled family to fire at each other and the world,
or for our reporters to look into and arrange for our inspec-
tion and concern. The incidental problems are solved, but the
series format provides no real place for its own resolution.
There is no final closure to the series' own recurring problematic. The run of a series ends without resolving its basic
dilemma. This marks a basic difference between the cinema
narrative and the TV series narrative. The film text aims
for a final coherent totalising vision, which sets everything
back into order. The series does not share this movement
from stable state to stable state. The basic problematic
of the series, with all its conflicts, is itself a stable state.
The series works on a sense of perpetual tension between
individuals, whose causes it routinely does not care to
examine. These individuals encounter different incidents
that do receive some kind of resolution each episode. Week
by week, we choose to forget, as do the characters, the incidents of the week before. With the serial drama, the flow of
events is much less: the serial works over its small ration

of incidents; the series proposes more incidents but at the cost of forgetting them week by week. The soap opera comes between these two forms. It moves forward, a slow history always in the immediate present; characters remember, events are cumulative. The programme is ever-present, broadcast regularly throughout almost the whole year. It is massively composed of talk; conversation, speculation, confrontation, chat.

The TV series and serial form gathers together segments (both 'fiction' and 'non-fiction') to form patterns of repetition. These patterns of repetition pull segments together to constitute programmes. The repetition is of format or situation (of a basic problematic), and of characters (reporters, presenters, families, workmates). This particular series form of narration has a particular modality on TV. Since TV itself presents an immediacy at the level of the image and the experience of viewing, then the series tends to present itself as a kind of continuous update. This is explicit with the news and current affairs series. They bring us up to date with events here and there around the globe. Their movement is one of beginning in the immediate past and returning to the present. The current affairs presenter will tend to pose some rhetorical questions at the end of the programme: 'Will the two sides sit down and talk through their differences?' (implication: they'd bloody well better ...). The soap opera does the same: an update on events followed by the cliff-hanging question. The series tends to do so too. The announcer's ritual before a situation comedy acknowledges this: 'What are our [or your] favourite characters up to this week?'. The same announcement could precede a news bulletin, or current affairs programme.

Perhaps exactly this remark couldn't precede news; the news bulletin and the current affairs programme are filled with infuriating characters. Their regular cast is composed of stubborn individuals often beyond the TV consensus, acting without discernible motive, who should see reason. This feeling is the result of the series format working to create a continuous update. The updating takes place within a stable format of characters and reporting routines. This stable news reportage format comes to constitute normality, exactly as the family squabbles of *Till Death Us Do Part* or its imitator *All in the Family* constitute a normality. The routines are constant: particular events intrude episode by episode. These intrusions are incidental upsets. They are incidental because the basic problematic of the series (the situation, the news investigation procedure) remains unchanged by the episode-by-episode events. The series format therefore sets up a pattern of the normal or the everyday, which recurs more or less unaltered. This everyday is a dilemma between characters in the case of a fictional series, or a set of journalistic procedures in the case of news and current affairs. This normality then constitutes particular incidents as intrusions, upsets or worries. In fiction, this tends to produce a view of family and work structures as unchanging and unchangeable, a stable core buffeted by outside forces. In news, this constitutes current events as bad news, as intrusions upon the peaceful life of the viewers at home and their surrogates, the reporters.

This, then, is the characteristic form of broadcast TV narration. The movement from event to event characteristic of cinematic narration is radically reduced in favour of the multiplication of incident, of action-clinch and of conversation. These take place in relatively self-contained segments. Segments are bound together into programmes by the repetition device of the series. This constitutes a basic on-going problematic, which rarely receives a final resolution. This problematic has laid over it an episode-by-episode incident, often in the case of a fiction series an enigma whose solution is revealed very early to the audience. These incidents tend to constitute intrusions to the stable normality that is the series format. The characteristic form of series narration is that of the continuous update, returning to the present and leaving a question or a cliff-hanger for the future. Overall, it is a form of narration that lends itself to the exploration of incidents and their repercussions in terms of inter-personal psychology. It habitually deals with a larger number of characters than the cinematic narration, and can concern itself more with their interaction and nuances of behaviour. It is an extensive form rather than a consecutive one. Similar narrational forms can be found at the levels of fiction and of non-fiction. There is no real difference in narrational form between news and soap opera. The distinction is at another level: that of source of material.

This broadcast TV form of narration proposes itself to a particular kind of viewer, a viewer relaxing at home. It makes certain assumptions, more or less unwarranted, about this viewer, and proposes a particular kind of position of viewing for that viewer. This form of viewing attitude has the effect of sealing the consensus nature of broadcast TV.

10 The broadcast TV viewer

Broadcast TV proposes itself a very different spectator from that of cinema. The viewer for TV is very far from being in a position of producing a totalising vision of the truth from an initial stance of curiosity. For broadcast TV, the regime of viewing is rather one of complicity with TV's own look at the passing pageant of life. TV's regime is not one of enigma and solution of enigma, but rather one of continuous variety, a perpetual introduction of novelty on the basis of repetition which never reaches a final conclusion. Broadcast TV's viewer is therefore a bystander, but a bystander in very specific circumstances, those of the home.

Broadcast TV does not solicit its audiences in the way that cinema has to. Even though specific programmes are advertised in the press and even on posters and the new season's schedules are given wide coverage, TV can always rely upon having some kind of audience. The presence of TV in most domestic units is now an established habit. The TV and its use has become a normal part of domestic life, and nightly TV viewing has become an established part of the evening's activity for most Western countries. Up to half the population can be counted upon to be watching TV at some point during most evenings. So broadcast TV is extensive, attracting spectators in numbers that cinema has rarely achieved. But the cost of this coverage is TV's normality: TV belongs to the everyday, to the normal backdrop of expectations and mundane pleasures. Broadcast TV is perpetually present in the home, always available as an experience even if specific items appear at fixed times during the evening. TV viewing

15 The TV set is mute witness to every domestic drama (*Expresso Bongo*)

is typically a casual experience rather than an intensive one. The consumption of TV is often described as 'relaxation', indicating a process that demands little concentrated attention, and is concerned with variety and diversion rather than enlightenment and excitement.

The broadcast TV viewer is not engaged by TV representations to any great degree: broadcast TV has not so far produced a group of telephiles to match the cinephiles who have seen everything and know the least inconsequential detail about the most obscure actors and directors. Broadcast TV does not habitually offer any great incentives to start watching TV; instead, it offers them to people already watching TV: trailers, promotion material, announcements. The incitement to watch is part of TV's own internal activity. Where cinema solicits its spectators outside the screening of a specific film by the construction of a narrative image, TV draws the interest of its viewers through its own operations of broadcasting. The viewer is cast as someone who has the TV switched on, but is giving it very little attention: a casual viewer relaxing at home in the midst of the family group. Attention has to be solicited and grasped segment by segment. Hence both the amount of self-promotion that each broadcast TV channel does for itself, the amount of direct address that occurs, and the centrality given to sound in TV broadcasting. Sound draws the attention of the look when it has wandered away. So TV's use of music often serves to underline and mimic actions in adventure series, announcing excitement or particularly significant details. Laughter runs through comedy programmes to ensure a continued attention rather than to incite laughter from the domestic viewer. Often, the laughter is not that of an audience (members of which might have rather too individual laughter-sounds or off-beat senses of humour), but 'canned laughter', recorded and dubbed where judged necessary. Both laughter and music serve to solicit the attention of a viewer who already has their TV turned on. Signature tunes have a similar function.

The TV viewer is therefore constructed as an individual who is prone to consume TV broadcasts, but needs to have attention drawn back to them. The means of attracting attention are much more instant than those which cinema uses. Broadcast TV assumes that its viewer will need to be drawn back to each successive segment, except in the most prestigious drama based on filmic or theatric modes of attention. Such broadcasts always run the risk of obtaining substantially smaller audiences than those obtained at other times by their channel, but they are justified by their claims to cultural respectability. Normally, the TV spectator is assumed to have competing claims for his or her attention: the other individuals in the home, other kinds of pastime. So TV cannot assume that its viewers have given it their attention in advance. The position given to the TV viewer is that of someone whose interest has to be courted over a short attention span: a viewer who is seeking diversion moment by moment, and accords little importance to this diversion.

Broadcast TV recruits the interest of its viewers by creating a complicity of viewing: the TV look at the world becomes a surrogate look for the viewers. TV presents the events of the world, both documented and imagined, to an audience that is secure at home, relaxing and seeking diversion. Broadcast TV creates a community of address in which viewer and TV institution both look at a world that exists beyond them both. So TV is a relay, a kind of scanning apparatus that offers to present the world beyond the familiar and the familial, but to present them in a familiar and familial guise. Hence the lack of a truly voyeuristic position for the TV viewer. It is not the TV viewer's gaze that is engaged, but his or her glance, a look without power. It is not the viewer's look that is at stake in the process, but the look of TV itself on to a world beyond. There is no voyeuristic separation for the TV viewer as there is for the cinema viewer. Events are not played so much for the viewer as they are in cinema. Certainly, news and current affairs events do not perform themselves for the TV viewer; they are presented through the medium, the look, of TV, but they happen largely irrespective of the TV look. They are not centrally directed towards that look. Dramatic performance, too, is less centrally for the audience because of the way that the norm of the familial and domestic is central to the operation of TV dramas. The more successful a TV drama, the more it generates the sense that it presents life continuing, or rather specific segments from that life in what is more or less real time. Performance for a viewer certainly enters into the construction of TV drama, but the form of performance that is striven for in broadcast TV is exactly that form of performance that disappears as such. The characters in a soap opera (the most obvious example) tend to become confused with the people who play them. The casting for a TV series demands types rather than performers, actors who can live their particular phantasy-selves through the parts that they play. Performance, too, enters into TV documentaries rather more than TV would like to admit, but the element of performance by the subjects (objects?) of documentary programmes tends to be read as the reality of those subjects. Just like the actors in TV drama, the subjects of documentary do not seem to be acting: they are simply being. Implicit in this general assumption is that the people involved are not directly participating in a voyeuristic contract, since they are not performing for the TV viewer.

The power and separation of seer and things seen that are central characteristics of the voyeuristic state are not activities typical of the TV viewer. Instead, it could be said that the separation and power are invested in the mechanism of TV itself. It is TV that looks at the world; the TV viewer glances across TV as it looks. This delegation of the look to TV and consequent loss of intensity in the viewer's own activity of viewing has several consequences. First, TV has to hold the attention of the viewer by various means; second, TV constructs a general sense of complicity between itself and its viewers in order to continue this sense of delegation of the look to it; third, TV has to seek to investigate the world outside. The title *TV Eye* given to a current affairs programme sums up this state: TV is the eye that sees; it is also the 'I' that is constructed as voyeur, investigating from a position of security. The viewer is at one remove from the process, glancing over it.

The problem faced by broadcast TV is that the two aims of investigation and construction of a complicity between TV look and viewer at home tend to become mutually contradictory. The position from which TV's investigations of the

world, both fictional and factual, can take place is determined by the creation of complicity. TV assumes that it has
certain kinds of viewers, and that it speaks for them and
looks for them. Interviewers base their questions on 'what
the viewers at home want to know', drama bases itself on
the notion of the family. Both notions have much that is
purely mythical about them. Nevertheless, the effect of such
an address to viewer from TV is that viewers will tend to see
themselves in the terms used by TV. Viewers will tend to see
themselves in the places addressed by TV's notion of 'family',
in the position of 'you, the viewer', 'you at home'. The
viewer is able to see him- or herself in such positions only in
so far as these positions are already generally in circulation
as common-sense definitions of life; TV takes them up, re-
fashions them and launches them anew into the world. The
TV viewer is placed by TV's system of direct address complicity as a particular kind of being, even if TV's assumptions
about the nature of its audience do not strictly accord with
how particular viewers live their lives. This placing of the
viewer weighs largely on the terms in which the investigatory
look of TV goes about interrogating the world and constructing representations of the world.

The effect for the viewer of this process of delegation of
the look to TV is rather unexpected. TV tends to assume
that this delegation enables it to function as the surrogate of
its viewers, seeing for them, seeing into them to provide both
information and entertainment. However, the process is
rather less certain. The process of delegation of the look
leaves the TV viewer in a position of isolation rather than
separation from the events shown. The sense of complicity
with the audience presented by broadcast TV tends to
intensify this isolation. The viewer is at home; TV presents
things that come from outside the home. This sense of
isolation has been succinctly expressed and exploited by the
right-wing vigilantes like Mary Whitehouse (who see nothing
wrong with domestic isolation), who ask whether we want
such and such an obscene thing brought into our homes. This
question fastens upon one aspect of the position constructed
for the TV viewer: the sense of isolation from the events
portrayed, and the consequent sense that they somehow

invade the domestic space of the viewer. The isolation of the viewer implies a lack of involvement with the events portrayed. This lack of involvement is intensified by the voyeuristic activity of TV itself, and its recruitment of the viewer to a complicity with it. TV's separation from the events at which it looks becomes the viewer's isolation or insulation from them. For this reason, it is unnerving to return home from a demonstration and see it reported on TV: the position to which you are recruited as TV viewer, one of sceptical non-involvement, does not fit with the position of having been a participant in the event. The language of broadcast TV reporting subtly reinforces the detachment and isolation of the TV viewer, inviting dismissal of the event as less important than it considered itself to be.

The experience of watching TV is therefore an experience of confirmation for the TV viewer. TV confirms the domestic isolation of the viewer, and invites the viewer to regard the world from that position. The viewer is therefore confirmed in a basic division of the world between the 'inside' of the home, the family and the domestic, and the 'outside' of work, politics, public life, the city, the crowd. This accords with the basic ideological division of life in our society, to which other distinctions can then accrue. The 'inside' becomes the area of safety, of confirmation of identity, of power; the 'outside' that of risk, of challenge to identity, of helplessness. In another version, the 'inside' is that of the mundane, the everyday, that which can be taken for granted; the 'outside' that of adventure, of the exceptional, the area of the novel and unpredictable. In yet another, the 'inside' is the area of happiness, stability, mutual respect and equality; the 'outside' that of misery, turbulence, inequality and subordination. All of these different designations stem from the same conceptual differentiation of the world into the domestic and the outside world. Broadcast TV participates in each of them, and several others, more or less as suits the particular moment. But this continuity of the division and the opposition between the two sides of the division continues in the operation of TV.

The effect of this division for the broadcast TV viewer is to confirm the normality of the domestic and the abnormality of the world upon which TV's look is turned. The viewer is brought the weird and wonderful, the transient and the unstable, the eccentric and the bizarre. The viewer glances over these as TV looks at them. They all pass by. But the viewer in a domestic setting still remains, along with the TV set, as an integral part of that setting. TV drama presents a gallery of characters in their own domestic settings, or quasi-domestic settings, all of whom are in some way abnormal (hence their comic or dramatic interest). Their abnormality confirms the normality of both the viewer and the viewer's presumed setting. The TV viewer is thus a viewer who is confirmed as isolated, even insulated, from the events of an outside world which is defined in opposition to the domestic and familial setting in which TV viewing is assumed to take place. Broadcast TV is thus in a position to be disturbing for its viewers when it represents something that is repressed in most domestic situations. The largest scandals about TV broadcasts have occurred in Britain when a few TV programmes have dared to represent activities which are censured or go unrepresented in many families. Thus scandals erupted about representations of sexuality, violence and the use of censored words, swear-words. In producing representations of such often-repressed elements, TV came closest to upsetting the confirmation of the viewer's position. It broke with the definition of 'inside'/'outside' by refusing conventional definitions of the domestic and familial. The usual opposition of meanings which accrued to the central 'inside'/'outside' oppositions was disrupted, and the complicity between viewer and broadcast TV was momentarily broken. British TV soon retreated from such a perilous activity, and has continued to do so throughout the last decade, as is witnessed by several 'controversial' plays cancelled whilst in production.

Broadcast TV confirms the normality and safety of the viewer's presumed domestic situation. The viewer delegates the activity of investigatory looking to TV itself. TV returns a particular overall sense of the outside world to the viewer, against which the normality of the domestic is confirmed. The outside world is posed by TV in a different way from that of cinema, which is always concerned with specific enigmas, and ignores wide areas of human experience. TV takes the whole world, the whole of human experience, as its potential material. But it does not totalise its views of that world into any coherent overall viewpoint: that would be to become partisan, to sacrifice the generalised domestic address for a specific politicised address in which only a certain section of the audience could recognise themselves.

Instead, broadcast TV presents the world as variety, and contents itself with producing an endless updating on the state of the variety. The typical form which the variety of the world is made to take is that of the dilemma. In both news and series drama, no resolution is met: instead, forces continue to confront each other and the same conflicts continue. The outside world is constituted as a series of continuing dilemmas whose individual rationales can sometimes be glimpsed, but no overall sense of meaning ever emerges. British TV is quite remarkable in the way that it allows virtually no explanatory framework to emerge for the activities it presents. Virtually the only areas of popular programming in which general explanations are attempted are those which deal with the 'apolitical' world of nature. Even here, explanatory frameworks have their vogues that are not unrelated to general political developments. The philosophy of the self-regulating eco-system fashionable in the mid-1970s has now given way to the intense determinism of sociobiology. Elsewhere, TV presents a variety which refuses any resolution. It is a variety composed as much of kinds of segment as anything else. Broadcast TV does not present the same kind of segment continuously over a long period of time: its typical mode of functioning is one of pulling together several different kinds of segment to follow each other without any particular links being drawn between them other than those of similarity (a group of advertisements, the various dilemmas of a group of characters, etc.).

Broadcast TV proposes itself to its viewers as a diversion; the TV viewer is assumed to be in a state of being diverted. Diversion applies to the state of the viewer in several ways. First, the TV viewer's look is diverted through the apparatus of TV, so that TV operates as the delegate of the viewer who remains at one remove from the active process of looking.

Second, a diversity of attractions is offered to the viewer. TV produces variety, diversity, as its typical means of covering the world with its gaze. Diversity ensures that no connections need be made between various kinds of segment, since differences usually outweigh significant similarities. This diversity is composed of diversions, a particular modality of entertainment that depends upon familiarity, upon being known in advance. TV's diversions depend upon repeated formats and on the series and serial form in order to retain their familiarity for their viewers. The diversion is a pastime rather than an activity which is accorded a great deal of importance, meriting special attention or rituals like cinema attendance. It serves to divert attention away from other concerns, which can at any time attract attention back to them. TV is well aware of this aspect of diversion: it regularly uses strategies to pull back the attention of the viewer.

Broadcast TV places its viewers in a particular kind of position. TV viewers are assumed to be seeking diversion, to be watching in domestic surroundings, to be part of some family grouping. The TV viewer is given a certain position by these assumptions: the viewer is constituted as the normal citizen. This is the position constituted for the TV viewer by the processes of broadcast TV; many viewers occupy the very position which TV addresses, even if they would never consider themselves to be such a strange being as a 'normal citizen'. Normality is constituted as a constituent of the viewer's position by the intensive use of the familial and the domestic as point of reference for TV, both in direct address and in fiction; and by the constitution of the opposition 'inside'/'outside', which insulates the viewer from events seen by TV. Normality, too, comes through the sense of TV as the ever-present, there whenever the set is turned on during normal waking hours; and the sense of the TV image as ever in the present, always broadcasting live rather than something already past as with cinema. Broadcast TV comes to the viewer as something familiar, habitual and of the present moment.

Broadcast TV positions its viewers as citizens through the double distance from events that it installs by complicity with the viewer and delegation of the look. The viewer-as-

citizen is uninvolved in the events portrayed, yet can mani-
fest (as a result) a generalised concern and vague sense of
scandal by turns. Citizenship is a position from which the
outside, the 'theys' of various kinds that TV constitutes, are
recognised 'as problems. Citizenship recognises problems
outside the self, outside the immediate realm of responsibility and power of the individual citizen. The citizen is at
ease with the world, but is not in the world. Citizenship
therefore constitutes the TV viewer as someone powerless
to do anything about the events portrayed other than sympathise or become angry. The whole domestic arrangement
of broadcast TV and the aesthetic forms that it has evolved
to come to terms with this domestic arrangement provide
broadcast TV with the capability to do this and no more.
The citizenship that it provides as the position for its viewers
is a position of impotence: TV viewers are able to see 'life's
parade at their fingertips', but at the cost of exempting themselves from that parade for the duration of their TV viewing.
    Broadcast TV can thus be seen as having a distinctive
aesthetic, different from that of cinema. It offers relatively
discrete and short segments organised according to the
patterns of repetition and innovation offered by the series
and serial form, or merely into an agglomeration like a
group of advertisements. These series forms are oriented
towards the repetition of a basic dilemma rather than the
resolution of an onward narrative movement. Often, the
problematic that the series offers is that of vision itself:
news and current affairs anchor themselves around the
conception of the programme format as an eye roving across
the world's events. The viewer tends to delegate his or her
own look to the institution of TV. This delegation is made
possible by the immediacy that the broadcast image claims
for itself, despite the fact that almost all broadcasts are pre-
recorded. This immediacy, with its major form of direct
address, and its dramas overwhelmingly concerned with
notions of the domestic, can create a sense of complicity
between TV viewer and institution. Both are in the home;
the TV functions as a safe means of scanning the world
outside.
    This characterisation of a general aesthetic of broadcast

TV as distinct from the characteristic aesthetic of cinema needs to be complemented by a sense of the institutions that produce these representations. Both have generated forms of production of representations that preserve, develop and promote their particular aesthetics. Broadcast TV, in its comparatively short history, has usually developed into centralised institutions, charged with both the production and the broadcasting of programmes, though sometimes legally separate 'client' institutions undertake some of these functions. Cinema has had a longer history, in which it developed as a medium of mass entertainment. Broadcast TV has taken over this role from cinema, which has moved to produce rather different kinds of representations. However, the basic notion of what constitutes a film (the 'Hollywood film') still predominates, both in popular conceptions of the cinema, and in the vast majority of current cinematic practices. This conception tends to play down some of the aspects of cinema which could have a vital social role in changing the way in which our society conceives of and produces representations. The new forms of independent cinema being developed in Britain are considered at the end of this book, together with some of the possible lines of development for new video technologies.

Part III

The institutions of cinema and broadcast TV

11 The current situation

Cinema and broadcast TV may have different characteristics in their predominant usages, but they are still generally recognised as occupying a similar area of human experience. They are recognised as somehow in competition with each other: in competition for people's attention, and in competition for commercial and critical attention. A series of similarities between cinema and TV has been registered here, even whilst indicating their dissimilarities. Both are media which combine sounds and images, and are predominantly used to provide narrative fiction, and to a lesser degree forms of information; in their public images both occupy the positions of entertainment, leisure and pleasure, rather than of work, duty and repression. Their particular products are to some extent interchangeable: cinema films are shown on TV, some material made for TV surfaces in the cinema. Ideas circulate freely between the two media. Films give rise to TV series; shooting techniques are transposed from one medium to the other; TV often appears as the implied polemical adversary of many films.

All of this indicates that cinema and TV occupy the same space: they are similar social activities, and are used in similar ways. Yet they continue to co-exist, however precariously. TV has not superseded cinema; cinema has not rendered TV redundant by providing infinitely superior and more sophisticated spectacles. The notion of the 'decline of cinema' that has somehow infiltrated everywhere as an established fact is far more complex than a simple decline from a position of pre-eminence to a subordinate position, or even towards extinction. The space of representations opened up by cinema, and vastly expanded by the advent of TV, contains both cinema and TV in a series of mutually defining, and mutually dependent relationships. TV needs cinema, cinema needs TV. Each medium has defined the space and possibilities for the other in each context in which they exist. In Britain cinema has almost ceased to exist because of the reactions of the major companies to what they perceived as a 'decline of cinema'. Cinema nevertheless continues to provide forms of entertainment and spectacle that are not found on TV, from the pornographic to the radical and collective. In France, TV has until recently been tied to the will of the ruling right-wing factions. Here, cinema with appropriate forms of aid, has functioned as both a creative and a left-wing arena, as well as providing a refuge for High Culture in the face of what it perceives as TV's relentless petit-bourgeois trivia. In the United States, cinema is able to provide entertainment for a series of minorities who define themselves away from the massive consensus that TV conceives of itself as serving: minorities which are urban-based and range from teenagers to gays, intellectuals and left-wingers. In each situation, the mutual relation between the two media is different. Each has defined a slightly different place for the other. Nevertheless, certain common features emerge: TV occupies a particular centre ground in each political situation, and cinema exists in a series of different roles in relation to the central fact of TV. Cinema is marginal, it is divergent, it is specialised, it is more intense than TV.

The division cannot be seen as a simple agreement to differ, or a treaty dividing up separate territories. Each medium needs the other. Cinema needs TV to provide a certain general basis from which its particular creations can be understood. Many films made nowadays presuppose a sophistication in dealing with the medium which can only be gained from a familiarity with broadcast TV. TV needs cinema to provide it with prototypes, to incite new kinds of work. The industrial production of TV tends towards repetition at the expense of innovation. One of the roles that cinema plays in relation to TV is thus one of providing indications of possible forms of innovation, as well as simply providing kinds of material that TV cannot or will not provide. The relationship between the two media is one of exchange, a relationship of mutual dependence whose terms are constantly shifting.

If TV and cinema are in some sense complementary rather than adversaries, then the myth of the 'decline of cinema' needs to be explained. This myth has dominated not only the general conception of cinema that circulates in our culture, but also the conception that cinema has had of itself. This myth has interpreted the facts of a change in cinema's role in the general space of representations as a process of shrinking which will eventually lead to the disappearance of cinema. All the surface signs are there, and exist in their most extreme form in Britain. The large cinemas which provided entertainment for two generations have mostly closed and been demolished or converted to other uses, not all of them forms of entertainment (cinemas make good supermarkets). Many large centres of population now have no cinema at all and cinema is increasingly becoming an activity exclusive to London. Fewer films are being produced globally, and 'British' production has all but disappeared; studios are closing or radically reducing their facilities. Distribution companies are merging their operations; marginal distributors of 'art' films are in danger of collapse. Many of the cinemas that do continue to exist have a decidedly seedy air about them, compounded by their reliance on the exhibition of pornography. Yet still, even in the dire circumstances of Britain, this cannot be interpreted as a 'decline of cinema' in the absolute sense.

It is the decline of a particular kind of cinema, the kind of cinema that has dominated both popular conceptions of cinema and the economics of film-making and exhibition. It is the decline of the commercial entertainment cinema. The central market for commercial entertainment is now the TV screen, and the commercial entertainment cinema has since the 1950s been trying to find the means to co-exist with this fact. Largely, it has been unsuccessful in this attempt. It still continues to exist, to produce films and to produce vast profits from time to time, but it is this cinema which is in decline. The effects of this decline have been felt particularly strongly in Britain because the British commercial entertainment cinema has long been dominated to a larger degree than any other European cinema (except that of post-war Germany) by American interests. Since the late 1940s at least, the predominant British commercial interests (Rank and ABC) have been more concerned to act as exhibitors of American films than they have as producers themselves. Successive governments have offered no satisfactory form of support for film production that would yield films that differed markedly from those of Hollywood, as most European countries have tended to do. So British cinema, being a client cinema in both its production and its exhibition, had no distinctive forms to develop once the commercial entertainment cinema began to contract. And being a client cinema, the force of this contraction has been felt much more directly than it has in the USA, which has maintained its position as the global centre for entertainment cinema finance.

Commercial entertainment cinema is contracting, and that contraction has been extreme in Britain because of British cinema's close client relationship with the United States. Commercial entertainment cinema still provides the culturally predominant image of what cinema is (and can be), and it is for this reason that the contraction of the commercial entertainment cinema is confused with the decline of the whole of cinema. 'Cinema' for most people means the kind of film produced principally in Hollywood between the years 1915 and 1955. This form of cinema provided a model that was imitated to a greater or lesser degree by most European countries, and has had wider effects as well. This model has had effects also in the conception of the financial, technical and human scale on which film production can and should take place. It has also dominated the conception of film exhibition that has become standard throughout the world. However, underneath and despite this blanket conception of cinema, the kinds of films made, their modes of exhibition, the kinds of audience they expect and attract, all of these have been changing and diversifying under the impact of TV. It is not so much a case of the 'decline of cinema'; rather it is the creation of different cinemas where

16 An event that ceased with the coming of sound: the Whitechapel Rivoli shows a German film, Fritz Lang's *Die Spione*, London, 1928

once one form of cinema (the commercial entertainment cinema) had an almost absolute predominance. The emergence of these new forms of cinema has taken place alongside the continued existence of commercial entertainment cinema (which may have contracted, but still is far from disappearing), and has often made use of this cinema, though perhaps to a lesser degree in Britain than elsewhere.

It is not so much that cinema, in its Hollywood sense, has diversified as that the cinematic institution in its widest sense has found a variety of representational roles in relation to TV. Cinema finds itself on the borders of representation, producing material that has a highly equivocal social acceptance, like pornography; producing material that is rather too aesthetically daring for TV, like some areas of art cinema and independent cinema in Britain; producing spectacles that are financially too extravagant for TV, and that exploit to the full the cinematic image, like the recent round of science-

17 Hollywood film or art cinema? *Letter From an Unknown Woman*

fiction films (*Star Wars* (1977), *Close Encounters of the Third Kind* (1977 and 1979)); producing films whose politics are profoundly at variance with those prevailing on TV (Ron Peck and Paul Hallam's *Nighthawks*, 1978), or which are not particularly suited to viewing without the presence of a live audience (e.g. some work on Cinema Action in Britain); or simply providing a place in which to exhibit work initially financed by TV but then refused transmission (*Le Chagrin et la Pitié* (1970) in France, *The War Game* (1965) in Britain). These varied activities can be called 'cinema' only when the word is stripped of its usual connotation 'Hollywood'. They use a common form of projection of the image in public, but not necessarily in specially constructed halls. They use celluloid as the basis for that image, but work under very different forms of financing and scales of labour.

However, the very relationships that cinema has entered into with broadcast TV have ensured the continued dominance of the public conception of cinema as precisely *Holly-*

wood cinema. The conception of a film as an entertainment fiction of about two hours length, comprehensible to all without specialised knowledge, and self-sufficient as an experience, is still a predominant conception, partly because it suits broadcast TV's demands for a particular type of material. This conception was definitively developed in Hollywood during and after the First World War. Arguably, it does not take full advantage of the public nature of the cinema screening event, nor of the intensity of concentration that is possible within it. This argument is explored more fully in Chapter 16, by examining some of the directions adumbrated by new independent cinema practices in Britain.

Before this, cinema and broadcast TV's production forms are examined. Cinema production is a less industrialised form than that of broadcast TV since it is devoted to the production of single works rather than serial works. Broadcast TV's institutions have developed methods of production suited to the creation of serials and series. Cinema, on the other hand, even in its phase as a mass entertainment medium, has tended to produce only one version of a narrative problematic at any one time. These different products have engendered different production methods. It can be said, without forcing the issue too far, that broadcast TV has a more industrialised production than that of cinema. Cinema is a more craft-based production procedure, producing prototypes on a one-off basis. These prototypes, marketed through the creation of narrative images, can become the bases for TV series, which repeat their basic problematics over a large number of episodes. It is always difficult to apply models of production of commodities (like sweets or cars) to the production of fictions, because of the very different demands that are put upon fictions: they can be used many times over without 'wearing out'. However, a certain set of comparisons concerning the organisation of labour in particular can be drawn. The consequence of broadcast TV's more industrial mode is that labour is more automatised than it is in cinema. It is quite possible for more than one individual to take a key role like camera person or director on a TV production without any noticeable unevenness in the finished product. This interchangeability of labour is possible because of the development of a particular set way of carrying out tasks; a kind of 'house style' develops as a result. Cinema's prototype production means that profitability is calculated on a film-by-film basis. The division between production and exhibition (classically involving entrepreneurs of rather different temperaments) reinforces the need for such a calculation. However, broadcast TV does not habitually make calculations on this basis. Profitability is calculated on the basis of the income for the whole broadcasting institution (whether the source be advertising or some form of taxation of viewers), measured against the operating costs of that institution. The pressures of profitability are different in the two media, and the forms of decision-making and planning differ as well. A series for TV broadcast has a budget finely calculated in advance, and the decision to make it at all is based on an overall calculation of the balance of types of programmes wanted by the broadcasting institution. In entertainment cinema, however, the situation is rather more chaotic, even though there is a fairly precise limit on the number of films that could be profitably exhibited in any one year. The ceiling of possible cinema attendances is limited by the number of available seats. Cinema films are therefore financed on a far more speculative basis than TV productions, and a tendency towards overproduction within cinema is checked only by the centralisation of power in the hands of a relatively small number of film distributors.

Cinema and broadcast TV therefore diverge in their typical forms of production organisation as well as in their typical aesthetics. In practice, aesthetics and production organisation are interconnected: the production organisations continue to call into being the kinds of products that incited them in the first place. In addition, each medium is profoundly affected by the other, and each uses the other to a greater or lesser degree. The current nature of these interrelations is therefore examined in Chapter 15.

12 The organisation of film production

Cinema once performed a similar function to that of broadcast TV: it provided forms of entertainment and information to a large proportion of the population of a number of Western countries and many other nations as well. A form of industrial production was developed to service this large market, but it never became as organised and subdivided as that of broadcast TV. In particular, the series form always remained marginal to cinema production. Series like the newsreel *March of Time* (1935-51) or the serial *Flash Gordon* (1936) were not the main attractions of the programmes in which they appeared. Series production is rather more characteristic of the earlier period of film production, before American dominance of the market was assured, with series like *The Perils of Pauline* (1914) or Feuillade's *Fantomas* (1913), *Les Vampires* (1915-16) and *Judex* (1917). The characteristic form of film production is that of the single film, highly differentiated from the other films which surround it. In this sense, film production can be described as craft production rather than industrial production. Cinema's typical production is the single film rather than the series, a prototype rather than a group of similar products. Cinema has often directly provided TV with prototypes for series: *M*A*S*H*, *The Ghost and Mrs Muir*, *Flamingo Road*. This is one aspect of the co-existence of cinema and TV which has developed over the last thirty years. But before the 1950s, cinema existed as an entertainment medium which had no direct competitors in the home other than radio. During this period, film's craft production of prototypes

183

was organised into a form of industrial production (loosely
called 'the studio system') which no longer exists except in
isolated instances (China, Hong Kong). This system has,
however, left a powerful legacy. Its conception of the film
commodity still dominates current conceptions of what 'a
film' is, at all levels of industry and criticism. So besides the
general conception of the film commodity that springs from
the particular conditions of the current cinema, there is the
continued dominance of a conception that springs from a
rather different form of cinema production. In this sense,
the cinema commodity is a rather more difficult form to
describe, because there are different tendencies within it.

Cinema as an institution is characterised by a separation
between the moments of production and exhibition. Whereas
for TV, the same broadcasting institution encompasses both
production and dissemination of programmes, cinema production and exhibition are separate activities. They are geo-
graphically separate (production is centralised, exhibition
is far-flung), they are separated in time (exhibition occurs
over a period of weeks and sometimes even years), and they
are often separated as financial activities. Film production
and film exhibition have usually been the realms of different
kinds of entrepreneurs, with film production as a far more
risky financial activity than exhibition. There are straightforward reasons why cinema developed in this way. First,
because the construction of exhibition sites (cinemas or
picture palaces) was a large financial investment; and because cinema exhibition in each place on the obvious model
of theatre or music hall needs individuals who are responsible for the running of the theatre and decisions about the
local market conditions. This historically defined separation
between exhibition and production throws most of the
financial risks involved in cinema on to the area of film
production, because of the forms of investment and profit
calculation that it involves. The major case (other than
Japan) of a large-scale integration of production and exhibition into single corporations is that of the USA, where
such an integration was effected immediately after the First
World War, and lasted until its outlawing in 1948 (the 'Paramount Decrees'). This form of organisation of the world's

largest single domestic market for a film industry consolidated the American dominance of the world film market. It provided a security that allowed the risks of film production for each corporation to be underwritten by the more secure income from the exhibition of large numbers of films. From this secure basis, the American cinema was able to define the popular conception of 'a film'. It is still this conception, or developments of it, that dominates conceptions of 'a film' today.

The separation between exhibition and production, together with the characteristic form of exhibition, leads to a pattern of financial calculation in the film industry. This is the calculation of profit and loss for each individual film produced, rather than for a programme of films or for a part of a film. This calculation is based on the amount collected at each cinema's box-office: so to some extent at least it is a result of the drawing power of the film's narrative image together with the attractiveness of the particular cinemas in which it is shown. The cinema shows a particular film (or films) for a particular length of time. It is responsible for advertising the particular showings itself, usually profiting from the distributor's prior publicity activities. An agreed proportion of the total box-office income, known as the rental, is remitted to the film's distributor. This amount is characteristically calculated on a sliding scale, with a guaranteed minimum amount, and a gradation of percentage rising as the total ticket sales increase. The average percentage remitted to the distributor is about 35 to 40. The distributor then deducts a series of amounts from the income collected from the various exhibition sites. This includes the costs incurred in the initial publicity and in the production of a large number of prints from the negative supplied by the film's producer. After this amount has been deducted, the distributor divides the remaining amount, remitting an agreed percentage to the film's producer, and keeping the balance as profit. Information on the figures at this point is very difficult to establish: it depends on the relative bargaining power of distributor and producer and the kind of relationship they have. Often the distributor has a large investment in the film's production. Often, distributors adopt a rather creative approach to accountancy at this point, which involves the diversion of amounts to cope with various 'unforeseen circumstances'. The whole process is far more complex than this simple sketch because it takes place across time. Exhibitors are remitting money each week (sometimes even each day for several weeks and months on any one film); the distributor is therefore the central point of cash flow within this structure. The distributor amasses money and redistributes it. The speed of this cash flow has often been a contentious subject in all areas of film production.

A relatively small proportion of the box-office takings finds its way back to the production enterprise: often it is as little as 15 per cent. This in itself is not too much of a handicap for film production; it is the periods of time that are involved that produce many more difficulties. Film production characteristically involves a large investment at the moment of shooting; smaller amounts are involved in the pre-production stage of scripting and production organisation; and less is involved in the post-production activities of editing, effects production and production of the final negative. Yet this second stage often produces delays; usually it takes a period of months. During this time, the investment involved in the shooting stage is tied up in fragile footage unusable until post-production is completed. If that money was borrowed, as it usually is, the interest charges are accruing during those months. If this delay is compounded by other factors (difficulty in finding an early release opening; slowness of payments from the distributor), then the potential profits from the film can easily be consumed by interest charges on the original loans.

The atomised nature of film exhibition and the necessarily centralised method of production of each film has produced the development of a mediating agency, the distributor. The historical separation of interests in production and exhibition, and the fiercely defended independence of many exhibition outlets has produced the individual film as the accounting basis for cinema. Payments are geared to each separate film. Payments are collected by the distributor, and the balance after deduction of expenses, etc. is made over to the producer.

Film production is the most risky part of the process. This is because production is remote institutionally from the point of initial exchange of money for the right to see a particular film. It is also because the risks in film exhibition are spread over a large number of films (usually at least fifty a year), whereas film production is undertaken by entrepreneurs involved in small numbers of films. Very few production enterprises outside the vertically integrated combines of Hollywood 1920-48 or Rank 1942-9 have been able to undertake a large-scale programme of production in which risks can be spread over a wide range of differing productions. More usually, modern film production is undertaken by companies which exist solely to produce a particular film, or by companies characterised by one single production commodity, like Clint Eastwood's Malpaso company which has produced a series of films all starring Clint Eastwood. Film production, in the twenty years since the decline of studio-based production, has been characterised by this film-by-film enterprise. Film production is highly risky and profitability is profoundly uncertain.

However, there are certain controlling factors within film production which prevent a total anarchic situation. The main form is the power that is concentrated in the hands of the film distribution companies. Distributors act as financial institutions and as marketing institutions. Distributors are responsible for the advertising and promotion of the films they distribute. As is clear from the importance of the 'narrative image' in the cinema, this marketing function is crucial to the success of a film. Distributors control marketing and they control cash flow in the film industry. Hence they are in a position to regulate the film production sector both by providing loans to production companies, and by guaranteeing to distribute (and hence market) films. It is remarkable how the same companies that dominated the film production of the USA in the early 1950s still dominate international entertainment cinema finance and distribution today: United Artists, Columbia, Paramount, Universal, Twentieth Century-Fox, MGM, Warner Brothers, Disney/ Buena Vista. The key to these companies' continued success lies in their continued dominance of the American domestic market, with the cash flow that this dominance generates for them. In 1977, the American market alone provided 59 per cent of the income for these majors, and Canada 2.7 per cent more. Britain is nowadays little more than a section of this domestic market separated by an inconveniently large stretch of water (increasingly, prints from American distribution are subsequently sent to Britain for release there). In 1977 it provided the majors with only 0.78 per cent of their income. The scale of the money involved enables the companies to spread their risks across the whole range of film production, exactly as the studios of the classic Hollywood era tended to do (Disney, in those days, excepted). Each of the majors has had a success in the lucrative 'block-buster' category within the last ten years. These majors constitute a tight group controlling the finance for major feature films. The tightness of their organisation is indicated by the way in which they were able to merge their overseas distribution operations into mutually owned organisations (e.g. CIC, now UIP, owned by United Artists and Universal, also distributing for MGM). This enables them in effect to limit in practice the number of feature films that are made per year to something near the number that are theoretically needed to sustain the cinema market, limiting the tendency to over-production that exists in the international cinema market.

There is a tendency at certain times for speculative capital to pour into film production from a number of financial institutions. This occurs, for example, in times of rapid economic expansion, or in reaction to various tax legislation (film accountancy being a flexible form). This can lead to an over-production of films for the cinema, as there is only a limited number needed to fill the premiere release circuits of Europe and America's entertainment cinema. Distribution companies are in a position to limit the number of films produced and to curb any tendency towards over-production within the restricted international entertainment market. Distribution guarantees perform this function. However, since the market is fairly competitive, the balancing of the system occasionally goes wrong. There was, for instance, an over-production of cinema films in the early 1970s which led to some films, usually those seeking a more specialised audience, being denied widespread exhibition. This is particularly true of films produced in Britain immediately before the massive and speedy withdrawal of the American distributor finance that had underwritten British production in the 1960s. The films concerned are 'cult' successes like *Performance* as well as more dubious enterprises like *Leo the Last* and *Ned Kelly*.

The market for international entertainment films is limited. Within it, a distinctive form of film production has been evolved. The characteristic form of the entertainment film demands that it should have a high degree of differentiation from the other films that surround it. The characteristic form of finance makes film production into the most risky part of the cinema. So film production has become a form of craft production, producing prototypes with little continuity of personnel or experience from production to production. The characteristic mode of film production has a small group of entrepreneurs, often director alone or director with producer, aiming to assemble a 'package'. This package consists of an idea worked into a script (classically a dialogue script), together with commitments from key personnel such as stars, camerapersons, editors, composers. This package is then touted around to various possible sources of production funding, always including distributors. If a distribution guarantee and enough money is raised, then the production goes ahead. More often than not, the whole process is a waste of time. No money, or too little, is forthcoming; another idea, another package has to be assembled. This version of the process sees the initial momentum as generated by one or more of the chief creative personnel within the established division of labour of the industry. Another variant has the package assembled by a special kind of cultural entrepreneur, the agent. The role of the agent is to represent various forms of creative talent in the marketplace: to find work of particular kinds for actors, writers, directors, etc. Quite often, it is the agent or the agency that initiates a package to further the career of one client or because of the fortuitous combination of talents represented by one agency.

Film production is intensely entrepreneurial, and as a result has developed a number of job functions which merely consist of putting people in contact with each other. The task of the agent is one such; that of casting director is another. In broadcast TV these functions are carried out by a central management along the lines of management in any other branch of industry. However, in film production these functions are themselves 'freelance'. They are carried out by personnel who are not employed by a central organisation, but are self-employed, or employed by an enterprise devoted to a single function (e.g. an agency). Film production thus represents an extraordinary spectacle: a complex management structure existing separately from any corporation. The reason for this is that the controlling corporate structures (those of the distributors) demand that film production should be established on recognisable lines, with a division of responsibilities, a hierarchy of tasks, and a separation between the roles of 'creation' and 'administration'.

Effectively, all levels of film production work have become casualised. The situation that held up to the early 1950s in most countries with regular production was one of centralised studios. The studio was either owned by a production enterprise that had almost exclusive use of it, or hired out as a going concern to producers of particular films. In both cases, the studio provided a large workforce to carry out the less prestigious activities: carpentry, electrical work, film cutting, security and maintenance. Also included in the studio would be specialised staff engaged in models and special effects work, costume, music, etc. Since the decline of studio production, during and since the late 1950s, such labour has also been casualised. In the process, many skills have been lost or eroded (particularly those of models work and set construction) so that they are now relatively rare. This casualisation has affected all levels of the industry. There are some directors whose careers flourished in the atmosphere of the regular work they could find under regular studio contracts, but who have found the situation of casualised freelance work unconducive. Some of the directors associated with Ealing Studios between 1945 and 1955 are a clear example. Others have thrived, like Stanley Kubrick.

The result of this system is that the name attached to a piece of work becomes important. The film industry attaches great importance to the notion of 'track record', since a person's most recent work is the only guarantee that she or he could perform the particular tasks that they might be called upon to perform. Reputation is everything: hence the continued importance of publicity agents. Once employed to avoid scandal, nowadays they are more intent on preserving the professional reputations of their clients. The importance of 'names' has produced a situation where films are increasingly seen by the public as well as within the industry as the product of particular individuals. There is a considerable cultural prestige that accrues to being star, director, producer, script-writer or cameraperson on a feature film. The inevitable result is that film's pretensions to being considered an 'artistic activity' along with the more traditional, less collaborative arts of writing, painting and composing have been fully exploited. A film director like Woody Allen or Federico Fellini will build a reputation and a style on the basis of a series of personality traits and a calculated campaign of self-aggrandisement. An activity like broadcast TV production, more industrialised and less dependent on named labour, resists being labelled as 'artistic'; film production, more craft-like and centrally dependent on named labour, has become the realm of the artistic amongst the audio-visual media. This definition then rebounds upon film production, accentuating the tendency, encouraging various forms of artistic production of cinema. The major problem with this tendency occurs when the notion of artistic production is identified exclusively with the notion of 'personal genius'. In the atmosphere of intensely insecure employment for film personnel (the 'natural' consequence of casualisation), this leads to a very damaging cult of the personality, with directors like Francis Ford Coppola and Stephen Spielberg becoming increasingly locked into their image as creative geniuses, and increasingly unable to create anything of any relevance.

The notion of individual genius is rapidly becoming a standard marketing device in cinema: it guarantees both a degree of familiarity (the 'vision' of the named artist) and

18 The film director as tortured artist: Woody Allen in *Annie Hall*

novelty ('what will he come up with next?'). It is equally a notion that requires a huge amount of self-confidence and perhaps of self-overestimation. For every Coppola or Lucas there are hundreds of aspiring talents chasing this particular form of acclaim. And such is the personality structure needed, such is the power of the myth of the artist, that all but a very few of these aspiring artists are men. The growth of this particular vision of the creative genius within cinema, where almost any production is a collective activity, is peculiar. Yet films are increasingly known by the real or supposed identity of their creators, usually their directors. This reaction, in marketing and in popular consciousness, is the result of the particular conditions of film production and dissemination, which differ markedly from those of broadcast TV and to some extent from those of classic Hollywood. Film production is geared to the manufacture of quite highly differentiated products: it is prototype rather than series production. Production organisation has become casualised, with one-off organisations mirroring the one-off nature of films. Within this arena where novelty is at a premium, the limits of novelty have to be established so that some familiar elements are present to establish a film as a particular form of attraction. There is little marketing sense in calling a film 'totally different from all others'. First, the claim is highly dubious (after all, the film is working within the technical and ideological limitations of its moment); second, this claim will attract a relatively small audience. The more common marketing strategy is to establish a difference-within-similarity: 'Fellini's best yet'; 'From the creator of *Jaws* ...'. The notion of the individual as creative genius provides this similarity that allows for a high degree of novelty. It is a response to the situation of film production, providing a means of creating and selling packages within the industry, as it is a response to the new status that film has in relation to TV. TV is industrial, anonymous series work; cinema is the area of creativity, of the single work created under conditions of craft labour rather than industrial organisation. Hence 'genius' enters as a criterion, where it does not for TV.

The whole organisation of commercial cinema, and its subsidised variants in 'art cinema', still depends to a very great degree upon the conception of 'a film' developed in an earlier period of cinema's history. This conception is the notion of 'a film' as a single work of about an hour and a half to two hours which is self-contained, and can be understood within itself without requiring any particular knowledges on the part of its audience. This conception has undergone revisions within commercial cinema, some of them radical, but it still holds. It is the terrain upon which individual genius works. It is the terrain upon which film financing and the film-by-film accountancy system still work. The historical genesis of this conception of 'a film' and the economic basis which secured it are the subject of the next chapter.

13 The dominance of the Hollywood film

The conception of a film, according to anyone's common-sense definition, corresponds to that which was developed in Hollywood by the middle of the First World War. It organises both film production and film exhibition into a unit: both at the level of economic organisation, and at the level of the experience of film viewing and the construction of film texts. From the particular and powerful basis of the American market, this conception of film and of cinema was spread to dominate the whole of the Western world, and to a greater or lesser extent other markets with strong traditions of cinematic representation of their own, like India and Japan.

The Hollywood film proposes a text that is comprehensible in principle to everyone: it is a mass entertainment form in this sense, rather than in the sense that it assumes that everyone will want to see the same film. It proposes conditions under which these films can be consumed: the conditions of the narrative image, of the rapt attention to the image projected to isolated and individualised spectators. It also assumes particular organisations of production of those films, and is based upon, in the classical period, the direct control of the crucial, pacemaking, 'first run' cinemas. Hence, an explanation of the dominance of the Hollywood film in the world market begins by an examination of the forms of power developed within the American industry by 1922, little after a quarter of a century since the first public film projection.

Film production and film exhibition involve different

financial perspectives. Film production is a high-risk business, where the whole investment is lost if a film is not shown to a paying audience. Exhibition involves an initial investment (in a building and its equipment) that foresees a slow and steady return on it, through the regular exhibition of many different films, all of which are hoped to be income-generating to a greater or lesser degree. These two modes of operation have tended to attract rather different kinds of businessmen, with a rather less adventurous type perhaps gravitating towards exhibition. Certainly, the two were largely separate in the early years of the cinema, and varying levels of financial return accrued to each sector at different times. This is one tendency within the American film industry: it is countered by two others. First, there is a tendency within expanding capitalist areas of business for large integrated corporations to appear. This happened in America towards the end of the First World War. The investment involved on the part of the production companies who bought or built a large number of cinemas meant that those production companies had to sell shares on the stock market. Up to that point, the film industry had expanded to being a major American industry simply on the capital it generated from its own internal operations. There is also a tendency for the integrated corporations in any American business to begin to extend their sphere of influence across the whole globe. This the American production companies did, using their secure and efficient exploitation of their domestic market as a basis.

Film exhibition and film production had been organised separately until about 1918 because the production companies had been concerned with organising production so as to take best advantage of an ever-expanding market, both at home and abroad. The disruption to the major export market of Europe that was caused by the First World War was more than compensated for by the almost total collapse of fiction film production in European countries. Thanks to the war (which, unlike the war of 1939-45 did not devastate cities and their cinemas) the American industry found itself without its French, Danish and Italian competitors, virtually unrivalled as purveyors of fiction film to the world. Production had been organised along factory lines: Thomas Ince perhaps going furthest in his highly centralised and planned production factory of 1911-1915. A producer's and equipment manufacturer's cartel had attempted to control exhibition (and hence rake off some of the huge profits made in this sector between 1903 and 1910), but had been broken largely because of their aesthetic conservatism and poor business practices. Production was increasingly organised after the First World War into a series of large corporations (Paramount, First National, Loew's (MGM), Fox), who produced a determinate number of films of a roughly similar length (80-90 minutes). Production organisation had established a division of labour whose broad outlines are not fundamentally changed even today, except by the addition of the function of production supervisor (producer/associate producer), a development of the later 1920s. Production took place within factories (studios) in which functions as diverse as script-writing and costume design were centralised, and a large proportion of the staff worked in full-time waged or salaried posts.

Production investment remained a fairly risky business, even with the increasing tailoring of the number of 'feature' films produced to the scale of the market, and the number of regulatory devices being developed, like the star and generic systems. A certain degree of competition and mutual suspicion reigned between the corporations, whose autocratic executives had grown up in some of the most savage sectors of late nineteenth-century American capitalism. There was a constant jostling for the attention of the exhibitors, whether independent cinema-owners, or the chains that had developed in large cities. Film sales became increasingly aggressive, and various restrictive practices developed, especially that of block blind booking ('To get our big star picture, you'll have to take our productions numbers 105-118, whose subjects we'll think of when we come to make them'). A more ruthlessly elegant way of handling exhibition was therefore developed by Adolph Zukor at Paramount, already the largest producing corporation. His solution was to integrate production and the most important, 'first run' sector of exhibition into one corporation, both conceiving of and exhibiting films to the public. This would have several advantages. First, it would guarantee a market for Paramount products, and enable a large degree of control over the market; it would enable a certain level of return on all films made, good or bad; it would enable distribution to concentrate on selling films to the national public rather than having to sell first of all to exhibitors. Integration of production and exhibition, in short, would alleviate the risks inherent in production by balancing them with the steady return from exhibition.

Quite apart from the strong-arm tactics used to encourage independent exhibitors to sell out, Paramount needed a large amount of capital to buy and build cinemas, hence the stock-market flotation. The immediate consequences were that the other corporations followed suit, also buying and building first run cinemas across the United States. The result was a series of vertically integrated corporations which, after the adjustments occasioned by the introduction of sound at the end of the 1920s, consisted of the famous names: the 'big five' corporations, all having substantial cinema chains (Paramount, Warner Brothers, Twentieth Century-Fox, RKO and MGM) and the 'little three' who had no large cinema chains and provided specific kinds of films to the major's chains and to independent cinemas (Columbia, Universal and United Artists). The longer-term consequences come as a surprise only to those who have a belief in American capitalism as a system based on competition. For the long-term result of the creation of a series of vertically integrated corporations was the effective elimination of any real level of competition between those corporations. They arrived at a system of mutual co-existence and support that lasted a remarkably long time: until the beginning of the 1950s. The system was one of an informal division of the market within the United States, which enabled a concerted drive to maintain domination of the world market, through diplomatic and other means. The major studios tended to specialise in particular genres: Warners in crime pictures, MGM in musicals. Other studios also made such pictures, but to a lesser degree. Allied to this, a certain level of number of films (varying dependent on the changing practices in exhibition) was reached as being the optimum for the market as controlled by the majors. Finally, exhibition was structured so that a close co-operation could take place. The rush to buy and build cinemas had resulted in a regional pattern of power, with Paramount strong in the south, MGM's controlling company, Loew's Inc., in the eastern seaboard cities like New York and Philadelphia. None of the majors produced enough films to provide full programmes for these cinemas by themselves. Hence in effect, a successful production of one company would be shown in cinemas belonging to the others: every company sharing through its exhibition interests in the success of one. It is reasonably certain that production losses (frequent through the earlier 1930s) were underwritten by profits from exhibition. The system from the mid-1920s, through to the early 1950s was one of a 'mature oligopoly' whose stability crucially rested upon the pattern of film exhibition.

The American domestic market was large enough to sustain a volume and scale of film production that enabled those films to dominate the world market. From the late 1930s through to the end of the 1940s, the American domestic market alone was enough to cover the costs of the majors. Through those years, income from elsewhere was pure profit. As an index of the American attitude, it should be noted that the 'domestic' market included Canada. American production set both the terms of the 'classic style' during this period, and the terms on which a film should be constructed as an economic entity if it was to be recognised as a film by the mass entertainment audience. American production provided the definition of 'a film' in terms of the level of investment visible to the audience; in terms of the forms of technology to be used in film manufacture; in terms of the forms of promotion of films and exhibition of them. It defined the genres into which production fell so that audience recognition could be assumed; it defined the star system and poached stars from Europe; it kept an eye out for intellectual trends of all kinds, not only in cinema, offering contracts to figures as diverse as Sergei Eisenstein, Sigmund Freud and Gracie Fields.

After the initial large profits from cinema had been reaped, the American cinema settled to a system by which risky film production was offset within the same organisation by the more dependable profits from exhibition. This cinema, economically dominant in the world market from the end of the First World War, effectively provided a definition of cinema. This definition of cinema is still with us today: it provides the natural assumption of what cinema is, natural so long as it is not thought about. American entertainment cinema defined a particular commodity: a fiction film, composed of a coherent narrative, that runs for about an hour and a half. Significant variations can be allowed to this in certain cases. There are 'B' features from the 1930s onwards that last an hour or a little over; there are prestige or super productions which can last two hours or more. There are very occasional non-fiction films, usually produced by extraordinary circumstances, like war. But as a general definition, the ninety-minute narrative fiction defines the common conception of 'a film'. Within this basic commodity definition, the American industry set further definitions. It developed the 'mass market' form in a particular direction. The American industry did not assume that everybody would or should want to see all its products: it always recognised divisions within the mass market. The twin institutions of genres and stars provided a basic subdivision of the mass market into types of film (and therefore of audience taste) and types of performer (and of audience self-image). This process of subdivision of the market is a tentative yet marked process through the 1920s and early 1930s. There seems to be a tendency when a genre is being established towards inserting comedy if the genre's internal coherence or audience acceptability is at risk. Hence an early sound horror film like the *Mystery of the Wax Museum* (1933) provides a major sub-plot of a go-ahead woman reporter and her boss, slightly reminiscent of *The Front Page* (1931) and even more of *His Girl Friday* (1939). The generic identification of films is present very early in the ways in which films are identified in studio production plans and information for exhibitors. In a less explicit form, it is signalled through publicity to the audience, through the titles of films, their slogans and review synopses, their stars and the images on posters and in papers and magazines. Stars are a better known and more immediate means of identifying films; often stars are identified with genres, like Jane Wyman with melo-dramas, Bob Hope with comedy.

The mass market that American cinema acquired was never conceived of as totally homogeneous, lacking any differentia-tions within itself. The American industry did not assume that everybody (or even every cinema-goer) would go to see any one film. However, it did ensure that its films were comprehensible to the whole of the potential audience. The American industry defined the regime of comprehensibility of the narrative entertainment film. The 'mass cinema' does not refer to an averaging out of films so that their subjects are uniform so much as an averaging out of their means of expression so that they are uniform. The filmic narrative was defined as a tight, self-referential field, where all the terms necessary for the understanding of the film could be found within the film itself, unless they could be assumed to be a part of the 'common knowledge' of the whole American nation. Seeing films from the 1930s fifty years after they were made gives some indication of the amounts of informa-tion that could be assumed to be known by the audience, from films or from wider culture. The form of the narration was defined so that a limited complexity (flashback, montage sequence) could be permitted within a framework that called for scenes based upon action and dialogue. Dialogue itself, when sound was introduced in the late 1920s, presented severe problems for this regime of comprehensibility. Speech patterns vary enormously within one language, and it is quite possible for two native speakers of the same language to be unable to understand each other. Hollywood cinema had to find, and train its actors in, modes of speech that would be comprehensible across the United States and in Britain, its largest other English-language market. Some of the groundwork had been done by radio, present through-out the 1920s across America. But much more needed to be done before the acceptable standard American and its possible versions of regional variants was established. The resultant regime of comprehensibility of speech was based quite directly in the early 1930s on British models, mediated by the West Coast theatre.

The regime of comprehensibility of the mass market film (assumed knowledge, standards of speech and narration) and the divisions of the mass market into areas of generic and star interest are all creations of the American industry. The American industry also set the pace in defining the budgetary levels of what would constitute 'a film' for cinema audiences. These levels vary over time, but have a tendency towards gradual growth. The effects of the Depression on the film industry, felt definitively in 1932, led to a decrease in the amount spent on any one film, partly because the number of films needed increased dramatically. The exhibitors' response to the decline in cinema attendances was to offer two films per programme where before there had been only one: the 'double bill'. The costs of individual films were therefore kept in check as much as possible, and this had results in the number and scale of sets that were used, amounts and extravagance of costume, complexity of camera movements and photographic effects, size of cast, use of locations, and many other aesthetic effects. Even so, studios seem to have made a fairly consistent loss on production during the 1930s, their parent companies staying in business only because of exhibition profits. A dramatic increase in the amounts available for investment in any one film arrived with the Second World War. The resultant reflation of the economy meant a large increase in consumer spending at the same time as a large decrease in consumer goods to satisfy that spending. An increase in movie-going was one of the few available ways of spending money. As a result, films were held over in cinemas for more than one week, the practice of offering double bills was discontinued in major cinemas. As a result, more finance was available and less films were needed. Hence an increase in spending on each film, and the resultant aesthetic effects: lavish sets and costumes; the possibility of photographic experiments like deep focus and long takes; lengthier production schedules.

The investment levels set by the American film industry carry with them quite precise definitions of what the film should look like, and how it should be made. There is a reasonable historical continuity through the vicissitudes of the film industry which has maintained this definition of the

19 The myth of film production: Jerry Lewis in *The Errand Boy*

level of desirable investment. It means, quite simply, that a film made for £20,000 in Britain in 1981 (a considerable sum) will not be recognised as a legitimate pretender to the title 'film' by a large fraction of its audience. Either it will attempt to reproduce the aesthetic of commercial films made for at least forty times that amount (and will fail), or it will produce an aesthetic appropriate to its production costs, and will not be recognised as belonging to the cinema. Such is the hold of the common-sense definition of what constitutes a film that even the film critics of the national press will fail to recognise such a production.

The level of investment set by the American industry (first by Hollywood, now by the international distributors) needs a mass market. The American film industry has always dealt in audiences numbered in millions. As one contemporary film producer put it, 'If less than ten million people come to see our film, then we're in trouble.' This mass conception entails a certain conception of a film: the ninety-minute fiction constructed within a particular regime of comprehensibility, directed towards one or more of the recognised subdivisions of the cinema market. The exact contours of this conception have altered over the cinema's history, but they have continued to provide the basic, common-sense idea of 'a film'.

A series of circumstances made it possible for the American industry to gain a very large share of the world cinema market. Films being easily transported commodities, the film production of any one place could seek widespread export markets quite easily. This is so with the cinema before the First World War, with several major production centres serving a global market. Chief amongst these seem to have been France, Britain (until about 1906), Denmark, Italy and the USA. However, certain economic developments favoured the USA. The first was the large-scale disruption of the European market and of European producers wrought by the First World War. The second was the large size of the American domestic market compared to any other single market. The third was the greater concentration of American production capital and resources into a comparatively small number of large companies. This last began to tell even before the First World War with a trend towards the production of longer and more lavish films.

With the disruption of the European market by the First World War, both the economic and the aesthetic initiative in film production were ceded to the American industry. The two are interdependent. Without economic dominance, it is doubtful whether the American aesthetic would have held such a tight hold on the definition of entertainment film; it is doubtful, too, whether it would have remained such an exclusively American means of constructing a film for so long. Without the aesthetic initiative of constructing an internally subdivided mass cinema, it is doubtful whether the American dominance of the market could have continued through the 1920s.

The film industries of Europe, including Soviet Russia, found that their domestic markets after the First World War were dominated by films imported from America. Diverse initiatives in production in different countries had different results. One of the chief problems was that cinema exhibition was crucially underdeveloped in Europe. During the years 1914-17, many picture palaces had been constructed in the USA; no building had taken place in many European countries apart from that associated directly with the war effort. Much of the capital available to the film industries of Europe went towards the construction of splendid exhibition outlets (which were guaranteed a supply of equally splendid Hollywood films) rather than towards production, a much more risky business. The tendency towards vertical integration could be discerned in some countries, but it took place much more haltingly and much later than in the USA. In both France and Germany the emergent large production companies crucially failed to gain a large stake in exhibition simply because of its intensely chaotic, individualised and localised nature. For UFA in Germany and Gaumont in France there was no opportunity to institute the kind of relationship that American companies developed between exhibition and production.

Two vertically integrated combines did emerge in Britain, the chief one, Rank, during the dark days of the Second World War by a series of mergers which left an organisation of formidable complexity. Both Rank and its junior partner in control of the British cinema, ABC, integrated production and exhibition in organisations that were able to use exhibition profits to undertake a planned programme of production. For a few years, 1943-9, this did indeed happen. Towards the end of this period, it was becoming evident that one sector of Rank's production was running into serious problems. This was the sector aimed at producing prestige large budget films aimed at breaking into the American mass market. Evidence was accumulating of the failure of this attempt (doomed from the start, as some remarked) at the same time as it was becoming clear that a particular emerging sector of the American market was open to different kinds of British films: Olivier's films of Shakespeare, the Ealing films, the productions of Lean, Asquith, Powell and Pressburger, Launder and Gilliat found a market in the growing 'art circuit' in America, which dealt in imported European films for cultured audiences. But before this growing realisation had time to affect future policy, a series of government fiscal measures in August 1947 aimed at protecting sterling brought about an American boycott of the British film market. No new films were to be imported until the import taxes were lifted. Rank, along with other producers, entered into a large-scale and sudden expansion of production designed to provide the bulk of the film needs of their cinemas. Many ill-considered decisions were taken, and many productions eventually written off when the American boycott was called off in May 1948, after negotiations with the government. The amount written off as absolute loss on these productions is disguised in Rank's published accounts (through changes in accounting practice), but appears to be between £4 and £6 million. This huge loss coincides with the beginning of the drastic decline in cinema attendances brought about by diversification of leisure expenditure after the war, and chiefly by the introduction of television. Rank had no hope of reconstructing a large production programme after this. But rather more surprising is the economy programme introduced by the accountant John Davis who was promoted to clear up the mess. He discontinued exactly those more experimental and lower-budget productions which were beginning to have some success in the American market.

Rank's is a relatively isolated European experiment in vertical integration. Effectively, it was using the relatively safe income from the exhibition of predominantly American films (never less than half the number of features shown in Britain) to finance an expansion of British-based production. Rank's vertical integration was on the same pattern as that of the American Big Five. The one difference was that though the Big Five had access to Rank's cinemas to show their products, they did not return the compliment. The major American circuits did not need Rank's films, as the American production already provided sufficient films, as a result of the system of vertical integration in the USA. For the American market, Rank's expansion and the allied increase in British production represented an unwanted surplus that could only find a home in the rather different and specialised market of art cinema.

Rank's expansion was based on a sound economic principle,

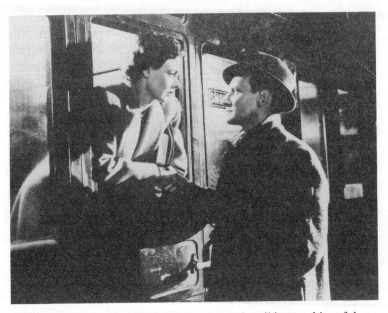

20 Rank's art cinema: the *Brief Encounter* that did not achieve fulfilment

that of using the relatively dependable income from exhibition to underwrite the much more risky investment in film
production. The British market at the end of the Second
World War was large enough to allow this to happen, to
permit the financing of films on a level of production
expenditure that ensured that they would conform to the
American-defined conception of 'a film'. Production in other
European countries had no such financial basis. French
production in the 1930s is typified by a large number of
small production companies which lurched from film to film
and were wiped out by any one failure. In Germany and
Italy, however, Fascist and pre-Fascist legislation brought
a degree of protection to the market that promoted a certain
amount of domestic production. By setting various kinds
of quotas for Italian or German cinemas to show a certain
proportion of Italian or German films, a space was created
for domestic production. The quotas were effective in
Germany (unlike those in France or Britain, also dating

from the late 1920s) because they correctly identified the real locus of power in their film industries. Quotas in Britain and France merely decreed that exhibitors had to show a certain proportion of domestically produced films. The exhibitor was fined for not doing so. However, many exhibitors were quite willing to risk fines because they found that American films were infinitely more profitable than domestically produced ones. The German quota system in the late 1920s set quotas both for exhibitors and distributors. So the powerful American distributors had to offer as many German-produced films as they did American-produced ones. Of course, they adopted various strategies to avoid this legislation, but its effect, nevertheless, was to provide a rather more secure basis for risky production investment than existed in either Britain or France at the beginning of the 1930s.

Quota legislation was the first form of protection adopted by the European film industries, and was argued through various parliaments using basically cultural arguments about protection of the native language and way of life rather than economic ones about setting a secure financial basis for film production. At the beginning of the 1950s, at the time of the break-up of the oligopolistic American industry and the shift towards television as the mass entertainment medium, European governments and film industries began to adopt a series of measures designed to institutionalise the subsidy of film production by film exhibition. European film industries began to try to achieve by legislation the effects that economic organisation alone had achieved in the USA since the 1920s, and Britain briefly in the 1940s.

The system adopted in Britain in September 1950 was that of the so-called 'Eady money'; in France, that of the 'advance on receipts'. In both systems, a central state-sponsored agency levies a tax on the box-office receipts of all films shown, and the resulting fund is shared amongst domestically produced films. The funds are distributed differently in each country and so have had differing effects. In Britain, the fund is conceived of merely as a means of alleviating the cash flow problems that domestic producers may have: it pays money immediately that a film is released, so eliminating the time that producers have to wait for payments from distributors. The money is paid out on an 'objective' basis, that is, the films that are earning the most at the box-office get the largest share of the Eady fund each month. Conversely, those films which earn the least get the least, so the Eady fund is of little support to producers who are taking risks, and most support to those who are backing certainties. The French system is weighted towards the risk-takers. The French fund is used as production investment rather than an easer of cash flow problems. Projects are selected on their artistic merit and a share of the fund is invested as an advance against the expected receipts of the finished film. Sometimes the advance is returned, often not. In practice, the French system has favoured the creation of an 'art cinema' production; the British has sustained the James Bond cycle and American-dominated international production.

Alone of European countries, Britain has been unsure of the possible role for domestic film production. Since the isolated success of Korda's *The Private Life of Henry VIII* (1933) in the American market (a success due more to an unexpected demand for more films in America because of the widespread adoption of the practice of providing double bills) British production always had an eye on the possibility of making films for the American market. British scripts were. cleared with the Hay's Office, the American industry's censorship body. Other European countries were clearer about the role of domestic production. Particularly after the coming of sound, the belief was that American films were eroding the cultural traditions of European countries, particularly amongst the urban working class. Domestic production was justified on the grounds that it would combat this growing Americanisation. In practice, however, there evolved a tendency to divide the market along class lines, with the working-class audience effectively abandoned to the American action-oriented cinema, and the more middle-class audience courted by films that appealed to a diffuse notion of 'the cultural'. This involved adaptions of 'classics' from other media, principally theatre and the novel; a range of references within the films which assumed particular cultural parameters in the audience; a sentimentalisation of the working class; the exploration of 'adult' relationships (in which sex is a part, in which individuals discuss their emotions); the use of certain 'non-standard' stylistic devices which are conspicuous yet do not detract from the central movement of the narrative; extremely precise geographic and/or social location for the action. This broad characterisation can be applied to most of the French production of the 1930s, including both Renoir's 'realism' and the pessimism of Duvivier; to Blasetti's work in Italy in the 1930s; and equally to the films of Leni Riefenstahl or G.W. Pabst. This represents the first phase of a European 'art cinema', sometimes intersecting with the mass audience within a particular country or language-group, more often aiming very precisely towards a particular section of that audience which would have a disdain for the majority of the products of Hollywood, particularly those which worked within well-defined genres. This 'art cinema' production was further consolidated in most European countries with the post-war reconstruction. The one major exception is that of Germany, where there seems to have been a deliberate attempt by the occupying powers to dismantle the centralised film production industry so that a bare minimum of German films would be made.

The European art cinema still depended on the definition of 'a film' which had been developed during the First World War in America, and continued to be defined by the Hollywood industry until the early 1950s. European art film production is marked by a series of tactical divergences from this model, rather than any fundamental differences. Those forms of film production that did develop on the basis of fundamental differences from this model, like the French *avant-garde* of film-makers like Epstein, Dulac and Buñuel, or the British documentary movement, could find little or no place within the orthodox cinematic market. The commercial cinema did not consider such films as legitimate objects for their audiences; they had to seek exhibition outlets elsewhere. The American definition of 'a film' (a narrative fiction of an hour and a half's duration, comprehensible to virtually anyone) dominated the world market's conception of 'a film' because American films dominated the world market. This is not to say that American film production was a safe economic prospect. The continued dominance of American production relied on the integration of the film industry, a system in which exhibition profits (spread over a wide number of films) could underwrite the possible losses on the production of a smaller number of films. Each film produced in this industry is a prototype, and hence a high financial risk. This particular close form of integration was furthest developed in America. It is the basis for the construction of the 'classic' period of American cinema style from about 1915 to 1955. The economic organisation was consolidated in the early 1920s and began to break up late in the 1940s. After this period, the inherent risks in film production began to be amortised in different ways, and the interdependence of television and cinema became increasingly developed.

14 The organisation of broadcast TV production

Broadcast TV adopted the studio production methods that were developed in the 'classic Hollywood cinema, and imitated by film industries elsewhere. However, it represents a considerable refinement of these methods towards a more industrialised kind of production, directed towards the production of series and serials rather than the single 'prototype' film that was typical of the classical cinema. Broadcast TV also involves a different form of production financing from cinema. Its financing is characteristically a concern of the broadcast institution as a whole, rather than that of any individual programme or series. TV's industrial production involves a detailed breakdown of work as far as possible into separate functions that require a reasonable amount of skill; a corresponding management structure to co-ordinate this divided labour; a production geared towards repetition; and a financing that is geared to the total output of a given period rather than running on a programme-by-programme basis. This makes television a relatively secure industry, able to produce profits consistently in its commercial sectors, however insecure it may be for those who work in it, especially at its more interesting fringes. As an industrial structure, broadcast TV is more developed and integrated than cinema ever was, even in its heyday of industrial production. This stability makes TV institutions even more prone to aesthetic conservatism than Hollywood cinema. This is markedly true of British TV which, until recently, provided hardly any areas for really adventurous work.

TV integrates programme production and dissemination

in one organisation. In Britain the same enterprises are responsible for providing programmes and for broadcasting them. In American TV, a more federal version of this system operates: local broadcasters provide a small amount of material themselves and affiliate to a major conglomerate (CBS, ABC, NBC) for the bulk of their material. The major conglomerates commission series from outside producers as well as producing material themselves. In this model, a certain distance between the programme suppliers and the programme transmitters does exist, but it is scarcely one that allows for speculative gambles in the way in which cinema production can. More typically, a close relationship exists between the networks, their clients and their suppliers. Suppliers of programmes to the networks are constantly gambling on ideas for new series, but these ideas exist as scripts and outlines (a fairly minimal financial investment) or as pilot films which can be sold as 'TV movies' even if the series idea is not accepted. Broadcast TV's voracious appetite for more transmittable material and its use of repetition and series production makes this relationship possible. The major difference between this form of contracted-out TV production and the production of cinema films is that the revenue in TV is far more predictable than that of cinema. Where the income from a film is determined directly by the number of tickets sold at the box-office (mediated by the often bizarre accountancy practices of film distributors), the income to the contracted producer of a TV series is set in advance. The TV broadcasting network can broadly predict what its income will be from whatever source (advertising, licences, central government), and can therefore budget each programme or series as a fraction of that predicted total. This element of planning enables TV production to become far more industrialised than film production, both in the American system, which relies on a series of client relationships, and in the British system, where, in the case of BBC and ITV, the broadcasting institutions produce the bulk of TV material themselves.

Broadcast TV institutions are financed in a variety of ways. Their income can be gained from the screening of advertisements (like ITV in Britain); from the sale of licences to use TV sets (like BBC in Britain); from direct government grants; by contributions from 'excess' profits in another sector of TV (like Channel 4 in Britain), or by a mixture of these means. All of these means have important common features. First, they present the TV institutions with a relatively predictable income for up to a year in advance. Second, this income is global, contributing to the whole output of the station, and not tied to a particular programme or programmes.

Increasingly, an additional source of income has been developed: the international sale of TV programmes. This has had the noticeable effect of generally increasing the production values of TV output (i.e. making programmes look more sumptuous), but has brought with it a tendency for the standard cost-per-minute of all kinds of TV programme to increase rather faster than inflation rates. TV is now more expensive than ten or twenty years ago. However, the near-monopoly position that virtually all TV institutions have in their own markets has produced a counterbalancing tendency. Production for broadcast TV has become increasingly internationalised. This counterbalances the international sale of TV programmes by ensuring that there is no general free market for TV products. The USA, with its huge domestic market, dominates the world TV market, selling its series at prices that make it difficult for entrepreneurial producers from other countries to match. Other national TV networks make particular contributions to this world market: the BBC and, increasingly ITV, providing high-budget middle-culture drama and historical series; the Eastern bloc providing children's fantasies. As programme costs have increased, there is a growing tendency for co-productions to be launched involving more than one national broadcast institution. This is widespread between French, Italian and German TV institutions, as it has long been the practice between the film industries of these countries. The BBC has developed a co-production strategy that looks suspiciously like pre-sale. In order to inflate budgets to the levels now required to make 'respectable' programmes, the BBC has produced both nature series (*Life on Earth*) and dramas (*The Borgias*, 1981) in conjunction with American, Australian or Canadian interests. Since the entire staffing of these productions is provided by the BBC, the term 'pre-sale' seems rather more apt. It signals a new initiative in the international TV market. Along with the American model of domestic production sold as cheap air-time fillers to other networks and the French-German-Italian model of co-production, the BBC is developing a form which could develop into a fully internalised form of production financing, based with one TV producer but calculated for an internationalised market.

The international TV market has two functions. For a very few countries, it provides a means of supplementing the production money available from their direct funding. For very many countries, it provides a means of obtaining expensive-looking material (and in some cases, cheap-looking material) that the particular broadcasting institution could not afford to produce for itself. The international market, then, is scarcely a speculative market. There is no real residue of unsold programmes, no entrepreneurs wandering around with sparkling and dubious packages of series. It is a means of spreading the TV products of a few strong domestic markets to institutions that have a modest financial base, and, of course, a means of drawing profit from these areas. Internationalisation of the TV market consolidates the power of a few large broadcasting institutions, but it does not alter the fundamental financial patterns of broadcast TV. Even the most modest broadcasting institution shares the two fundamental characteristics of the largest: its income is broadly predictable; it is not tied to particular programmes but is related to the whole of the station's output.

There is a relatively remote relationship between individual TV programmes and the calculation of profit and loss for their producers. For programmes produced directly by the broadcasting institution, calculations of profit and loss do not impinge upon the making of particular programmes. For the makers of programmes under contract, profitability for the enterprise becomes a question of matching the costs of production to the already negotiated price that the broadcasting institution will pay. It is not a gamble on unpredictable box-office returns as in cinema. TV programmes are therefore budgeted with reference to an overall financial policy and predicted income for the broadcasting institution. The total predicted income is matched with the range of programmes that the channel has to provide, or wants to provide. The programmes that a TV channel has to provide range from those required by legislation (news programmes) to those favoured by advertisers (spectacular entertainment); those required by the general cultural assumptions of the audience, themselves bred by TV's previous work; and those required to produce a general air of cultural respectability to the channel (chat shows with philosophers and coverage of the arts). The programmes that a channel wants to provide are more difficult to define: sometimes there is a felt need to innovate, to provide satirical programmes, as the BBC did in the early 1960s. Sometimes it is to widen the TV audience and to enfranchise a particular minority group (usually a vociferous one).

Out of such often conflicting pressures, a profile of the kind of programmes that the channel will provide is produced: its proposed schedule. Implicit in the balance of programmes in the schedule is the awareness that some programme forms cost far more than others: three people sitting in a studio is very cheap TV, especially if the broadcasting institution owns the studio in question; twenty actors in period costume in a foreign location is expensive. The business of budgeting each programme or each series is thus a matter of balancing the channel's income against the different costs of the different kinds of programmes, knowing in advance both the probable income of the channel's operation and the probable costs involved. Many of the costs of making studio-based programmes (chat shows, quiz shows, small-scale drama, soap operas, a proportion of current affairs) are directly controllable by the broadcasting institution, because except for a very few cases (Channel 4 in Britain being one), the channel owns the studios. In such cases, the institution also employs a large staff under contract. Much TV production is therefore studio-based and made by a permanent staff. This model of production is directly industrial, leading to a straightforward set of labour relations between a permanent management and a permanent workforce. It can lead to a straightforward dispute about the division of the often massive profits from TV production like that which blacked out ITV broadcasts in Britain between 10 August and 24 October 1979. ITV companies were attempting to hold down wage and salary payments at the same time as announcing record profits: not a clever tactic. Such disputes are common in TV, but are rare in the film industry because of the massive casualisation of labour. Studio production is the basis for almost all TV institutions. In small countries, modest studio production is almost all that the TV station can undertake; everything else is bought in from the international market (i.e. from the USA). For larger TV enterprises, studio production is the basis and model for productions that are made on various locations: such productions, on video or on film, utilise as much as possible the resources, permanent salaried staff and administrative structure of the institution. They too can be considered to be industrialised production.

Industrial TV production implies that the tasks involved in programme making are divided into a series of different, repeatable and limited tasks. It equally implies a hierarchy of authority within this division of labour and a differentiated management structure to combine these tasks and their practitioners. The automatisation of tasks has gone further in TV production than was possible in studio film-making. The first TV studios were developed before any means of video-recording video signals: hence studio production was virtually synonymous with live broadcasting until the early 1960s. This regime of work imposed a high degree of automatisation. In particular, the regime of alternating different camera positions during a scene (learnt from cinema and in that sense required by the audience) was created by having a series of cameras shooting a scene simultaneously. These were then selected by the 'director', seated in a gallery separate from the space of the performed scene. The director was able to communicate with the camerapersons to tell them to alter their camera positions or lenses. Hence the function of the director in television is distinct from that of the director in cinema. The TV director has some of the functions of the editor (selection and combination of shots),

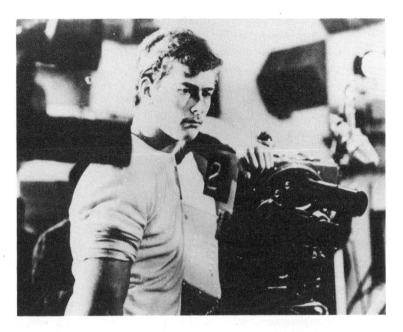

21 The turret lens of the studio camera: *Adieu Philippine*

and is deprived of some of the cinema director's functions, in particular that of controlling the action taking place in front of the camera(s). This function is delegated to a 'floor manager'. The director's control over the scene being shot is indirect, taking place through microphone-to-headphone links rather than directly. In particular, there is no chance of 'going again' in live TV: if a particular request from the director is ignored or executed in a way different from that conceived by the director, then the director just has to accept it as a *fait accompli*. *Adieu Philippine* (1962), directed by Jacques Rozier, an ex-TV director, contains several sequences illustrating forms of live TV broadcasting: a jazz band in outside broadcast, and a TV play, *Monserrat*, in live studio broadcast. It shows the director as a lonely and irascible figure, cut off from the activity of the stage, having very little control over the finished programme. It shows also the extraordinary organisation that went into the live broadcasting of a TV play: how sets were designed to abut on to each other according to the demands of scene transition, with the frantic behind-the-scenes rush to move equipment from one set to another to achieve the necessary continuity.

The exigencies of live TV are now almost a thing of the past: only news and sport come live. The personalities on a late-night chat show are either tucked up in bed when their show is broadcast, or watching themselves at home. However, the rigid division of labour and the automatisation of tasks is still a reality in TV production. Studios still divide labour into the floor staff (camerapersons and assistants, floor managers, performers) and the gallery staff (director, sound and vision technicians, script and administration personnel). In many areas of TV production, the division between floor and gallery has intensified. In current affairs programmes, it is possible to find studios which are deliberately designed so that the gallery does not have a direct view of the floor: all that can be seen is what the cameras are showing. This does not mean a shift of creative control from the director to the camerapersons; rather, it represents the total automatisation of the aesthetic level of the programme. There is no scope for the use of cameras in any out-of-the-ordinary way. The whole division of labour, here at its most extreme, only holds together because every task has been worked out into a series of known and predictable actions. Every person knows their role, and knows the actions that are expected of them. Only the director (and to some extent the other gallery staff) can see the finished pictures. The director's role is limited to that of selecting them: it is an editor's role rather than a co-ordinator's. Sometimes, the credit for direction is absent from such programmes: in such cases, the producer, whose role is paramount in co-ordinating everything that leads up to the actual shooting, has performed that role. In these extreme cases of automatisation, the principle of cost-effectiveness has played a role. The programme is allocated a certain amount of studio time that will allow only one or at most two run-throughs before the actual shooting and taping of the programme. The smooth co-ordination of automatised tasks is assumed in this calculation. There is simply not enough time to do anything different, even if it were dreamed up by the producer or director.

Such an extreme degree of division of labour and automatisation of tasks can only take place in programmes that treat TV in a purely utilitarian way: in current affairs discussion programmes, or programmes that insert snippets of filmed interviews or other filmed material. In other kinds of programme, like prestige drama, the amount of studio time allowed per programme minute is much larger. The automatisation still holds for low-budget soap-operas for the domestic market, like ATV/Central TV's *Crossroads*, where some scenes give the impression that the actors are having their first run-through rather than giving their worked-out performance.

This automatisation has several effects. First, it develops a very strong house style for each country's TV output. There has not been, to my knowledge, any systematic work done on this subject: the very national nature of broadcast TV makes it inward-looking at the level of research as well as that of programme production. So it is impossible to judge how much difference there is between the house styles of various TV networks. But a house style is necessary over a wide range of production so that the personnel at virtually all levels are interchangeable. Often, credits detail more than one cameraperson, sound crew, even editor without any perceptible difference between the various segments of the programme. Along with this house style goes a tendency towards the anonymity of labour. TV credits of twenty years ago in Britain detailed only the most visible of creative staff: actors of named roles, writer (often with the title), producer and director, and any special creative contribution such as music. A steady push has taken place towards naming more and more of the staff involved. This push seems to have come partly from those making programmes on film, by analogy with the long tradition of exhaustive cinema credits. Nowadays, a long list of credits will include such personnel as research assistants, dubbing mixers, etc., as well as the more obvious camera and sound crews. These credits eat into the amount of time available for the programme itself, but also provide a place for the creation behind the credits, of synoptic or emblematic images that provide a 'memory-image' of the programme.

American TV seems to have found a different solution: to run the credits so fast that they become illegible.

Automatisation equally goes with and promotes the use of complex management structures. In effect, TV management performs two roles. First, it organises and combines the various subdivided sections of the labour force. Second, it acts as a stratified structure for decision-making. Questions about the nature of TV's output, its characteristic forms, its outbursts of creativity, are not decisions which can be taken on the spot. They are planned at various levels of the management structure. At the top is the basic decision about scheduling, which classifies programme types, allocates them specific blocks of air time and specific sums of money. At this point, the decision is taken to provide a space for innovative work or to provide a completely automatised programme. This decision is taken on 'technical' grounds as well as direct aesthetic grounds: it is implied by the amount of money, of studio time, of film time, of provision to buy in material from outside suppliers. Once the parameters of this very material sort are set for a programme, the production team (whose size is dictated by these general budgetary considerations) are empowered to make basic decisions about the issues to be covered in the programmes, or about the precise direction of the fiction. These decisions can be taken in a variety of ways. Especially with fiction, they are to a large extent delegated to the writer, who has traditionally had a fairly privileged creative role in British TV. In documentary forms, these can be autocratically decided by the producer or executive producer of the series, or chosen by him or her from suggested projects. The finished programme is by this stage defined very highly: it has been decided when and where it will occur in an evening's viewing; whether its basic material will be film or video or both; what its budget will be; what its subject and the limits of that subject will be. TV management structures are therefore equally creative structures, if only in the sense that they take the major decisions that determine the general aesthetic features of a particular TV output. These decisions are the subject of intense political pressures. There are political pressures in the conventional sense that lobbying by interest groups and pressure from the state have results in the kinds of decisions that TV executives make and think they can make. There are political pressures in that intense lobbying takes place within the management structures of TV in order to secure or destroy particular interests. The history of TV is littered with examples of management decisions and their effects on programme possibilities. Let one example suffice. For several years until the end of 1981, BBC2 in Britain had a slot called *Omnibus*, which was nominally a programme about the arts, which, as everyone knows, is a term that does not include TV, at least as far as TV is concerned. *Omnibus* operated in a fairly unusual way, even if this mode seemed to generate no audience unease. It simply presented substantial programmes, often on film, about particular artistic activities. These were preceded by the standard *Omnibus* signature tune and logo, but it was up to the programme-makers concerned whether or not to use a presenter using direct address to camera. Often, they chose to dispense with this mode. Late in 1981, with the departure of the producer, Leslie Megahey, the opportunity was taken to reorganise the programme. *Omnibus* was redesigned as a magazine programme containing up to six separate items indiscriminately on video and film. This format produced the need for a presenter (or perhaps it was vice versa?); the presenter was found in the person of Barry Norman, well known for his frivolous coverage of cinema both in BBC1's *Film 79/Film 80/Film 81* . . . slot, and his gossipy documentaries about the lives of film stars. A series of simple management decisions had changed the programme entirely: no more substantial pieces, no more opportunity for interesting work in presenting the arts to a TV public. Instead, there reappeared the cult of the personality, and the presentation of easily digested segments of various disparate artistic activities.

The commodity produced by broadcast TV is a fully industrialised form. Its organisation of labour and decision-making is one side of this process. The other side is the typical production-form, the series. TV production can be highly divided into automatised tasks because TV arranges its output into series or serials. The need for a house style, for everyone to perform delimited and predictable tasks, comes with the series form of production that repeats week by week over a period of time and a set of segments. The most economical construction of a series demands that the various segments using one location should be shot at the same time, regardless of their place in the eventual series. Simply because of the amount of material necessary (compared to a ninety-minute feature film), a house style has to be adopted to ensure a stylistic continuity with material shot in other places, possibly by other people. This becomes especially important for series that mix filmed footage with studio video footage.

The series form is the basic unit of calculation for TV production, and the basic unit of programme scheduling. Increasingly, all TV broadcast output has been scheduled according to the model of the series: even one-off plays of radically different aesthetic aspirations have been flung together to form a series: *The Wednesday Play*, *Play for Today*, *Second City First*. The series is equally the basic unit of marketing for broadcast TV. Single programmes are not usually advertised (unless special events like a Royal Wedding), but series are. Single episodes can be accounted failures where a series can be a success according to whatever criteria are used. The series is the formal equivalent to industrialised production: it represents the repetition of tasks at the level of programme format, narrative problematic, character and location. The scale of production implied by the series form requires that almost all tasks involved can be performed indiscriminately by anyone of the required grade, except for those acknowledged 'creative' functions which are confined to writer and performer.

Broadcast TV is geared to producing a series commodity consisting of a number (which may be huge, e.g. *Panorama*, news bulletins, etc.) of individual programmes which have a high degree of similarity. The production of these commodities is organised on industrial lines. The tasks involved are specified and personnel are organised into various grades responsible for a particular task or tasks. The tasks involved are standardised as much as possible to provide the maximum interchangeability of labour. Series are produced within a defined hierarchy of labour which is itself subordinate to a management structure which plans production, including the overall scheduling of programmes, their budgetary levels and their general aesthetic and political limitations. This management planning can proceed with a high degree of knowledge of the probable income of the TV enterprise involved. Financing, from whatever source, is linked to the total output of the broadcasting institution rather than to any specific programme or series. Hence budgeting and the control over programmes that comes with it is a fairly precise and effective mechanism. The primary site of calculation of profitability is over the whole output of the institution rather than located with any particular programme. These features (industrial production/management planning/profitability not linked to particular programmes) make TV a characteristic commodity form and its production a very different activity from that of cinema.

15 Cinema and broadcast TV together

The conventionally accepted notion of what constitutes 'a film' is the product of a specific period of the history of cinema, lasting roughly from 1915 to 1950. This period was characterised by the dominance of American interests. The intervention of broadcast TV, which had become a mass medium in both North America and Europe by the late 1950s, radically changed cinema's methods of working. Cinema and broadcast TV have developed, over the last quarter century, both forms of co-existence and forms of divergence. TV has pioneered whole genres that had a primitive or fleeting existence in cinema like news and current affairs work. It has plundered cinema and literature for other genres, like melodrama. Within cinema, traditional mass entertainment forms have continued to operate, some with considerable financial success. Overall, however, cinema work has become more fragmentary, offering possibilities that broadcast TV cannot or will not provide. Sometimes, it is precisely because cinema has pioneered a means of representation that broadcast TV can then take it up. In this sense, cinema is rather more on the side of innovation than broadcast TV can be: this is one of the implications of cinema's production of prototypes rather than TV's industrial series production. Hence one of the most interesting relationships has grown up between cinema and TV. TV uses cinema to provide it with new ideas, new material, and, above all, to take its risks for it.

Since broadcast TV is a predominantly national phenomenon, the exact relationships between cinema and TV differ from one political situation to another. The strength of a particular state's TV operations, its popularity, its appeal to different sectors of the population, its distinctive aesthetic strengths and weaknesses, its openness or hostility to innovatory ideas, all of these factors affect the kind of cinema that is offered within a particular state. Platitudes abound on this topic, like the habitual assertion that British cinema (both in production and exhibition) is weak because British TV is so good. However, much of what cinema in other parts of Europe has produced is never seen either in British cinemas or on British TV. A whole dimension of work is virtually absent from the experience of most of the British population. In fact, the British situation is by no means accurately described by rather smug assertions about the supposed quality of British TV. Rather, the situation can be briefly characterised as one where cinema exhibition has been poorly managed by the conglomerates (Rank and Thorn/ EMI/ABC) that effectively control it. Popular cinema exhibition in Britain has been slavishly linked to the large American distributors, and has never looked towards alternative sources of alternative kinds of material, for instance the art cinema market. Art cinema production and exhibition has never received the level of subsidy that it has in Europe. British TV for its part can be characterised as being very good at a relatively narrow range of programme types: principally those of historical fiction and literary adaptation for which it has established its reputation in the international TV market. British TV has not entered into productive relationships with cinema in the way that other national TV institutions (Germany's ZDF, Italy's RAI) have done. British TV has a close relationship with British theatre: its prestige work is called 'drama' rather than 'film'; it lionises the writer rather than the director.

Certain generalisations can be made about cinema and TV and their relationship. Nowhere is cinema subject to more stringent censorship arrangements than broadcast TV: in some states, cinema is given a far wider freedom than broadcasting, in the USA for instance. In other states, like Britain, cinema is subject to different, less stringent, but still constricting forms of censorship. In yet other states, mostly right-wing dictatorships, cinema and TV are subject to exactly the same direct state intervention into their activities. These formal censorship mechanisms create an atmosphere where a pervasive self-censorship takes place: self-censorship being the result of the calculation that every film- or programme-maker makes about what subject and what approach to that subject are feasible in a particular circumstance. Self-censorship is in most states a far more restricting form in TV than it is in cinema: the judgments that are habitually made about what 'will be OK' for TV are notoriously more conservative. This is partly the result of TV's self-definition as a *mass* medium (and therefore needing to be intelligible to 'everyone'), partly because of the close relationship that national TV institutions have with controlling political elites, and partly because of the industrialised production form and the consequent difficulty of working in adventurous ways. Cinema no longer works with such a rigid sense of itself as a mass medium, although the pervasiveness of such a view of cinema in the general culture is still surprising. Cinema's characteristic commodity form makes it rather more open to introducing 'difference' at various levels: in the subject matter of a film, its formal construction, its method of exhibition and promotion, its production organisation, etc. Hence the broad distinction can be made between the current operations of the two media, that cinema is more prone to innovatory work.

Cinema work regularly appears on TV. Cinema films are consumed by TV, under a variety of financial and social arrangements that are usually rather more to TV's benefit than cinema's. Hence a major consideration in the interrelationship between the two media is what TV does with cinema, the way that it uses cinema to provide certain features to its outputs. TV tends to have contradictory relationships with the cinema films it shows. On the one hand, it looks to cinema to provide certain forms of innovation (which particular forms depends on the particular TV institution in question). On the other hand, its use of cinema films as broadcastable material elides one of the major features of cinema: the fact of cinema exhibition as a public exhibition of a high-grade image. One growing tendency in some cinema activity in recent years has been to emphasise the potential of the situation of public collective viewing. Any potential that lies in this aspect of cinema's work is denied in the way in which films are habitually broadcast; it is usually neglected in the coverage that TV gives to cinema as well.

Finally, TV has achieved a centrality in everyday life which outstrips anything that cinema could achieve. TV broadcasts have a particular kind of cultural visibility that is distinct from that still maintained by some of cinema's products. TV broadcasts are seen on one night by a huge number of people: they therefore create patterns of expectancy and publicity around that one exposure. Newspapers (themselves with a daily rhythm) are the privileged arena for creating notoriety around TV broadcasts. They either publicise the expectations of 'tonight's episode', or they pick up on 'last night's revelation by politician X'. The cultural visibility of particular TV broadcasts is thus one of a day or two's length; whereas that of a cinema film can last several months, depending on its pattern of distribution. Broadcast TV has an immediacy in the sense that its rhythm is that of everyday life. TV programmes are the stuff of small-talk, of 'did you see that thing last night where . . . ?' However, the centrality and familiarity of broadcast TV create definite ideological limitations to its work. TV is required to be predictable and timetabled; it is required to avoid offence and difficulty. This centrality that TV has is also responsible for creating a space of cinema, a space where everything that fits uneasily into TV's centrality can nevertheless take place.

The centrality of broadcast TV to everyday life combined with the resultant demands for timidity and predictability means that TV defines a kind of centre ground from which cinema, in a variety of ways, diverges. This centre ground is composed of TV's habitual attitudes and its habitual forms. TV's concentration on the domestic has already been explored as a pervasive representation resulting from the very conditions of use of TV in Western states as a private and domestic activity. This sense of the domestic is itself a representation rather than a reflection. It creates and mobilises notions of domestic life that are at variance with the actual conditions in which a large proportion of the population lives. The representation of the domestic is one aspect of TV's centre ground. Another aspect is the way in which TV (quite explicitly) seeks to speak from a central position. The current organising notion for news and current affairs in Britain is one of 'balance' between contesting official viewpoints, in which the TV institution holds a position of common sense. These two aspects of centrality are complemented by the spread of genres that TV uses. These genres define the levels of complexity and the characteristic forms of attention that are given to various areas of human life. Some forms of available social definition of the human body are used, for instance, and not others. There is the medical (*Your Life in Their Hands*), the sporting, the violent (the stuff of drama), but never the pornographic or the erotic. The domestic, the notion of balance and the habitual spread of genres constitute the core of TV's centrality in relation to cinema.

Broadcast TV displays its notions of the domestic in several ways. First, its own fictions are inclined to foreground 'family life' in all its complexities. Hence soap operas are constituted around families (*The Brothers, Dallas*), the street (*Coronation Street*), or the workplace conceived of as a kind of displaced domestic life (*Crossroads*). Serious drama deals with 'problems' which are usually those of a socio-sexual nature: domestic violence, the welfare state and its uneasy interaction with 'real people', interpersonal conflicts at work. Where life outside the family is shown (the sphere of public life, the workplace, boardroom struggles: all fit subjects for TV fiction), these aspects of life are interpreted in psychological terms which have their central basis in the vision of domestic life that TV presents. Characters form themselves into patterns of dependency and authority that often have as their implicit (sometimes explicit) psychological model the structures of family life. Hence the privileged representation of relations between employers and employees is that of fathers to their sons; and the range of relationships between workers takes notions of 'brotherhood' to sometimes ludicrous extremes. Of course, a range of TV productions go beyond these rather simple characterisations, to produce more acu⁺ᴳ analyses of the relations between those in authority an⁻. those who have to (or protest against having to) submit ᵗ ᴶ them. Yet even in these cases, the characters are assumed to have a family behind them, giving support, normalising their lives.

The appearance of notions of domesticity can be charted across the whole of TV fiction, reaching a level of pandemonium in situation comedy. It is equally present in the form of address of TV: whether it is the direct address of the announcer speaking to 'viewers at home' (or using them as an alibi for a certain line of questioning in an interview), and in the assumptions made about the patterns of programming. In Britain, programming presupposes certain audiences: weekday daytime TV assumes 'the housewife at home' until about 4.30 when children become the target audience (commercial TV advertisements register this shift very clearly). 5.45 is the homecoming of the breadwinner, eager to hear news of the world's affairs, followed by forms of domestic familial entertainment until 9.00. At this hour, children are deemed to have retired for the night (dreaming of the toys advertised between 4.30 and 5.45), and programming changes towards more adult programmes. After 10.30 only 'minorities' are deemed to be awake, and it is often around this time that the 'routine marginal' programmes are screened. These are as varied as the up-market American soap operas of *Lou Grant* (newspapers) or *Soap* (pushing the genre conventions to their limits); or programmes for racial minorities; or serious current affairs discussions like *Newsnight* (news/interviews/filmed reports) or *What the Papers Say* (sometimes astute comments on newspapers' coverage of a particular contemporary issue). A pattern of domestic life is assumed in the overall scheduling of the main channels of BBC1 and ITV. These patterns have a long and settled history. BBC2 presents a variant of this strategy, presenting its news for the late arrival (after 6.30) and its mid-evening entertainment for enthusiasts for particular activities (snooker, gardening, etc.) as well as the uncommitted family audience. The 9.00 p.m. embargo works for this channel as well. Scheduling assumes a certain domestic pattern: housewives at home; children in the late afternoon home from school; programmes to eat by between 6.00 and 7.00; an evening's entertainment to settle down with for the whole family until 9.00 when the children are packed off to bed and adults enjoy themselves alone. Most of the nation is assumed to switch off at about 10.30 or 11.00, unless a particular mania or insomnia holds them a little longer. This general cosy domestic vision itself determines the balance of kinds of programmes across the evening, with situation comedy, variety, made-for-TV films and police series gravitating towards the mid-evening peak hours.

The dominance of a particular image of domestic life over the whole of TV's output is only one feature defining its 'centrality' in relation to cinema. The notion of 'balance' that dominates the coverage of news and current affairs is another. 'Balance' does not mean that two sides of any question are shown, or are presented equally. Balance is rather more a matter of official political institutions, and ensuring that these institutions have a roughly equal access to air time. Balance is scrupulously operated when it concerns political parties; it is less so when it concerns other important political institutions like trade unions, professional bodies or employers' associations. There is no operational concept of balance in relation to ordinary people. The voice of those who have no institutionalised political power is heard very rarely. When 'pensioners', 'the self-employed' or 'housewives' are mentioned, they are used as a rhetorical point to bolster some argument about their supposed interests as presented by a politician, or by a TV interviewer or reporter. Indeed, it is difficult to see how things could be arranged otherwise, since TV's notion of current events is almost exclusively a passive one. TV claims to be reporting what is important at any one time, and the agenda of what is important is set by representative institutions or by acts of Nature. The actions of ordinary people only appear in TV's news-gaze when they are organised as 'newsworthy': picket lines, random acts of violence, spectacular protests. The 'newsworthy' is a particular definition that is put on to all actions so that a few can be selected to compose news bulletins and the subjects of current affairs. It is the product of the hundred years' history of popular journalism, not the product of TV itself. The 'newsworthy' is composed of two disparate functions. One is that of picking up on particular isolated and spectacular items, be they earthquakes or court cases; the other is that of informing the people of the intentions and actions of those in power. Sometimes, as in a strike or a war, the two come together. Most of the time, political actions are constructed according to the demands of the spectacular, so political parties 'split', they do not disagree; strikes are a 'confrontation' rather than a bargaining tactic. The most favoured form of spectacular model for political events is that of conflict between opposing institutions: government and opposition; trade unions and employers; trade unions and governments; Britain and the world; the West and Russia, etc. This adversarial pattern has suited the dominant representation of the world; it can ignore the Third World and China, parliamentary parties like the Liberals, the whole of extra-parliamentary political activity of both left and right and new political and social forces like the feminist movement. Such political factors do not make a routine appearance as 'news': their newsworthiness depends upon spectacular events: a military coup, a trade agreement with Britain, natural disasters, the disruption of a 'Miss World' competition.

The adversarial definition of political events has also constructed TV's notion of 'balance' in their coverage. If political events are constituted by two opposing forces, then TV's role as neutral observer, reporter and interrogator would seem to lie in the centre: holding the balance between the two sides. This is, indeed, how TV's role has been interpreted in the coverage of domestic affairs. In foreign affairs, TV has every right to be as chauvinistic and racist as it likes. There may be balance within the domestic political arena, but there is none in the coverage of international affairs. So the concept of balance effectively means occupying a central position in relation to domestic political events. This central position enables the TV institution to appear both unbiased (in the sense of not favouring one or other position) and common-sensical (in the sense of representing a 'possible compromise' between the two positions). This is TV's balancing act with balance. The concept of the newsworthy allied with the privileged access given to institutions of power creates the terrain upon which it can take place.

The complexities of politics are denied by this process, as are the areas of life beyond the orthodox institutions of power. Trade unions have a particularly uneasy relationship with this concept of balance. It is a concept that allows access to the trade union bureaucracy, but not to shop stewards, the base (and often 'unruly' base) of the trade union movement. The result is that the politics of the trade union movement itself tends to be travestied, and the nature of labour disputes is often misapprehended by TV news.

Balance is a concept that is central to the way in which that TV constructs its vision of domestic political events. Its current use in TV implies that TV is central, holding a neutral middle ground between opposing forces, seeking a compromise position or playing 'devil's advocate' by presenting the view of the right to the spokesperson of the left, and vice-versa. This has led to the elaboration of a specific TV rhetoric to describe political situations. There are 'moderates' and 'extremists'; 'moderates' are those who are nearer to the TV central position in any particular situation. It is quite possible for those who are moderates in one situation to become extremists in another: the so-called moderate candidate in an election for an important trade union post can become an extremist in a dispute with employers or government. The categories have no meaning except as derogatory or complimentary terms from the point of view of a centralist TV position.

However, the strenuous application of this centralist position under the banner of balance has finally produced effects within the political arena. It has made possible the conception of a political party whose self-presentation is that of being 'the party of the centre, the party of moderation'. Hence the recent emergence in British politics of the Social Democratic Party, whose rhetoric of centrality is in marked contrast to that of the other third party in British parliamentary politics, the Liberal Party. Where the Liberal Party's self-image was that of the party of mavericks, the party of ideas and originality, the Social Democratic Party has fastened on to the political rhetoric sanctioned by TV coverage of current political affairs. The SDP claims to be the party of centrality, of moderation, of compromise.

The emergence of a political party that claims the centre ground as its own is a serious challenge to TV's painstaking construction of balance from a position of centrality. The whole adversarial representation of the domestic political arena, the construction of TV as a neutral, centralist institution within this adversarial system, these are both challenged by the emergence of a political party which uses the very rhetoric that TV creates from its centralist position. The institution of balance from a position of centrality has reached the summit of its achievement in the creation of a political party which makes flesh the rhetoric of TV, but it also poses a serious problem for the operation and justification of the notion of 'balance'.

Balance, despite its current problems and its inherent fictional nature, still constructs the institution of TV as occupying a central position in the life of the nation. TV is central in its political position of compromise and moderation; it is central in that it is a privileged means of gaining political knowledge. These centralities are further reinforced by the spread of genres that TV uses, which effectively provide a kind of lexicon of human life and emotions. The TV salesman in Sirk's *All That Heaven Allows* (1955) describes the set as giving 'All the company you want:. drama, comedy, life's parade at your fingertips'. In the film, this is the moment of deepest hopelessness for the widow played by Jane Wyman. Appropriately enough, since TV does have an aura of presenting 'the whole of life', if only because of its ever-present nature. But this presentation of everything (or everything that counts) is always under the form of various genres. These split 'life's parade' into particular definitions, particular forms of attention. The spread of genres in TV defines the spread of definitions and attentions that are given to human life within the gaze of TV. Some aspects are emphasised, some disappear almost entirely; some combinations of ideas and experiences are ruled out. TV's generic system reinforces the centralist position that TV constructs for itself by the series of definitions (and consequent silences) that it involves.

The generic definition underpinning the whole of TV's broadcast output is the distinction between fact and fiction. A programme has to be one or the other: at limits it can be a fictionalisation based upon or using historical fact. But the corollary (a factualisation of a fiction) is an impossibility. The distinction is vitally important for TV because it defines two basic forms of attention and their consequent production techniques and audience expectations. A factual programme is one in which the concept of balance may well come into play (especially if it refers to a domestic political issue). It is one in which TV observes and reports the world beyond TV: the world of people or animals; of sport, model railway enthusiasts or doctors; of the conflict between man and nature, the co-existence of different species. Here the gaze of TV presents and interprets. It does not interfere, organise, construct or fictionalise events. The category of 'fact' is therefore an ethical position as well as a generic definition. It implies a particular relationship between broadcast TV and the raw material for its programmes. Factual programmes are those in which the activity of programme-making interferes to the least possible degree, aiming instead to preserve the truth and integrity of that which is presented to TV's gaze.

Fiction, on the other hand, is the area in which events are created for the gaze of TV. In fiction, the element of personal view is permitted to intrude to structure the material of the programme. Hence the privileged position given to the writer and, in some areas, to the director as the structuring consciousnesses of fictional output. Fiction is therefore the area in which particular interpretations of events can be produced without considering the formal demands of balance. However, this means that fiction is by and large kept away from the area of contentious political events, and from public controversy that has no clear moral position implied within it. It is by no means infrequent for a British broadcasting institution to replace an advertised fiction programme because its subject has become too contentious. Similarly, British TV institutions are unwilling to produce more than the isolated example of a militantly left-wing programme, even though there are numerous writers and directors within an orthodox TV aesthetic who could produce such material. Fiction implies a particular vision; but the range of possible visions is distinctly limited by the fear of political controversy and possible accusations of bias that is shared by senior TV executives.

The broad distinction between fact and fiction in TV output underpins the more flexible distinctions between different programme genres. These genres are defined in terms of content, for factual programmes (sport, news, current affairs discussion, interview, chat show, etc.), and in terms of formal definitions, for fiction (comedy, play, film, soap opera). These broad definitions of genre are steadily refined by the use of the series form: within each genre there are different series which are distinguished both by their content and by their form of attention to it. Thus *Nationwide* treats a range of domestic/political subjects (fit for the family feeding time) with an amount of amateurish humour mixed in; but *Panorama* (later on a Monday night on the same channel) consists of a filmed report from a particular political context, with a studio debate or interview. Each item is sustained, lasting up to thirty minutes. Thus *Panorama* tends to cast its gaze upon the world's trouble-spots, and to interview prominent political personalities, interrogating them about their current positions, if any. *Nationwide* is an intensely domestic arena, presenting consumer issues, short interviews with individuals who have achieved a temporary notoriety (local councillors who have banned a film from their cinemas), and even an 'eccentric' (someone carrying out research on toilet seats or slugs). Similarly, the various fiction series define different attentions to a particular topic: within police fictions there are those which concentrate on violence and the glamour of dealing with 'real villains' (*The Sweeney*); those which emphasise the caring, community aspects of police work (*The Gentle Touch*); those that highlight the problems of police corruption (*The Chinese Detective*). Each centres on particular definitions of power and character within the police force; each defines its own vision of the police force which obstinately cannot be reconciled with each other.

TV's centrality is defined by its insistence on the domestic; its conception of balance in its political coverage; and use of generically defined output to 'describe' the world. All of this is framed within a definition of intelligibility which is not unlike that which was developed by the American mass cinema in the classic period. Like the output of the classic mass entertainment cinema, the wide gamut of TV output is not meant to appeal to everyone indiscriminately; however, it is meant to be intelligible to everyone. Broadcast TV is the inheritor of mass cinema in this respect: it has inherited a belief in the universal intelligibility (within one nation-state) of particular sets of formal procedures. These underlie the planning of the industrial production procedure, which is designed to yield this easily intelligible set of standard forms. The rules of intelligibility encompass forms of transition and classification of material (the news transition from neutral newsreader to 'subjective' on-the-spot witness reporting to 'our own correspondent' producing comment, analysis and prediction). It instrumentalises the TV image (so that one image is held until it has been used as information, then cut to another image), and uses conventions of sound/image relations (the voice-over, and synchronised dialogue both with ascribed sources). The construction of a form of intelligibility (some would call it 'transparency') by TV is the final and founding component of its construction of a central position for itself: it is central to the informational and entertainment lives of its huge audiences; it is centralist in its attitudes; it is central to the culture of the moving image because it defines a norm of intelligibility against which other procedures (film or video) are implicitly judged.

However, this ideological centrality, allied with an industrial mode of programme production, produces a powerful tendency towards conservatism within broadcast TV institutions. In these circumstances, TV looks towards cinema as one of the main sources for innovation. Not only does TV use cinema as a source of entertainment material, but it also looks to it as a source of new ideas, because it is very difficult to generate new ideas within the structures of TV institutions. Cinema is seen as an area in which new styles of shooting and editing can be pioneered; and equally new forms of subject matter. It was up to cinema rather than TV in the USA to develop ways of approaching the ideological problem that Vietnam represents. Hence a spate of films about Vietnam, dealing with the war itself as an incomprehensible event on to which American soldiers can project their fantasies or inadequacies (*Go Tell the Spartans*, 1978); or as an act of collective insanity (*Apocalypse Now*, 1979); or showing the problems of veterans returning to a society hostile to them as reminders of what is 'best forgotten' (*Coming Home*, 1978); as well as standard forms of oblique reference to veteran as a social problem (providing motivation for dramatically interesting social misfits like muggers or bank robbers). Broadcast TV was subsequently able to ingest these approaches to the topic.

Some broadcast TV institutions acknowledge this relationship between cinema and TV. Some few of them straightforwardly subsidise radical forms of cinema production (albeit on minimal budgets), and regard the broadcasting of the resultant films as distinctly secondary to their life in the cinema. An example is the German ZDF's weekly *Das Kleine Fernsehspiel* slot, which has subsidised the work of such film-makers as Rosa von Praunheim, Stephen Dwoskin and Helka Sander. Channel Four in Britain has institutionalised a relationship with a cinematic form of production by purchasing its production from independent producers rather than adopting an industrial production model. Whilst half of its programmes come from the existing industrial giants that dominate the ITV channel, other material is produced in a way that closely resembles film production with its film-by-film pattern of production. Whether or not the adoption of this model of production will guarantee that the finished programmes show any originality when compared to other British TV work is another question. It depends finally on the kind of politico-aesthetic decisions that are taken within the Channel's own hierarchy.

Hence broadcast TV's very centrality brings it into a close relationship with cinema. Cinema for its part stands or falls on its differences from this central presence of TV. Cinema no longer needs to occupy a central position, with the consequent demands for intelligibility and unexceptionability. Cinema has ceased to be dominated by a simple conception of mass cinema, although certain crucial components of this conception still remain. In particular, the conception of 'a film' developed in the classic period of American cinema still survives in a series of cinema practices. However, it could be said that cinema has become more visibly fragmented than it was within the classic period. In the classic period, the pattern of an American-dominated mass cinema with a series of marginalised practices of film production and exhibition (European art cinema, non-theatrical documentary work, etc.) is the more or less stable pattern for most of the world's cinemas. Nowadays, the term 'cinema' covers a series of diverse practices both of production and exhibition.

To a great extent, a complementarity exists between cinema and broadcast TV: cinema doing (some of) the things that TV cannot, for technical, aesthetic, economic or social reasons. But the relationship between the media is not only one of complementarity; it is equally one of mutual dependence. In performing roles that TV cannot, cinema makes several direct contributions to TV. First, it can develop prototypes for new forms of fiction or new forms of textual construction that TV can then adapt and adopt. The level of automation of TV production makes any dramatic innovation very difficult; just as the Hollywood studio system once made cinematic innovation difficult. So cinema provides a point at which experimentation can be found, which often has a fairly direct influence on TV. Equally, cinema can pioneer and render more acceptable certain areas of representation, certain subject matters, so that they, too, can be taken up by TV. Second, cinema is able to provide a certain amount of material directly for TV: the practice of screening old feature films on TV is established virtually everywhere that TV is used. This provides TV with spectacular material far cheaper than it could possibly manufacture for itself, even on an international level. The practice provides more as well: it sets cinema up as a particular kind of reference point for TV. Cinema is constituted as 'better' than TV (more big stars, more big spectacles, etc.), but also as more adventurous, a belief that some TV channels have used in order to introduce more adventurous material than would be possible if it were made directly for TV only, and within the institutions of TV manufacture. Both ZDF in Germany and the British Channel Four use cinema as this kind of political and aesthetic Trojan Horse.

Cinema needs TV as well: it is a relationship of mutual dependency. Cinema now has a strong financial dependency on TV for many of its diverse financial operations. The financing of large-scale feature film production takes into account the eventual sale to TV, which is often arranged as a 'pre-sale', where the TV channel effectively becomes a co-producer. The financing of radical, independent work also depends on TV financing in various places where TV adopts a 'Trojan Horse' strategy. Often, this dependence becomes excessive, as other possible sources of finance (state funding, private sources) tend to fade away, and the existence of a radical and independent sector becomes dependent upon the internal decisions of a TV channel. Cinema also depends upon TV aesthetically: a certain consciousness of the history of cinema can be gained from TV screening of old films, especially, as on French TV, where this is actively encouraged by screenings of seasons of films along with intelligent critical commentaries of various kinds, both on TV itself, and in critical magazines. Cinema also assumes a certain level of facility of reading images and sounds on the part of its audience; this, too, is a product of habitual use of TV. TV enables cinema to assume rather more from its audiences. These relationships of mutual dependency between TV and cinema are by no means easy ones: there is the perpetual accusation from cinema that TV gets films 'too cheap' and is therefore directly contributing to the financial instability of cinema and the consequent closure of cinema halls. Neither are the relations between the two media the same in each country, and they are, by definition, shifting relations, taking different forms at different times.

In two distinct ways cinema has developed away from the classic model of a mass cinema with marginal forms. One direction maintains many of the features of the mass cinema: its basic conception of 'a film' and its attitudes to the nature of film exhibition. The other, dealt with in the next chapter, tends to move beyond these conceptions to produce a number of 'active audiences', using the public and collective nature of cinema exhibition to develop new relationships between spectators and film or video material. The first direction is that chiefly represented by the so-called commercial cinema, whose products are often re-used by broadcast TV and form a staple of the growing home video market. It produces films which can still be treated as objects for consumption, intelligible on their own to the audiences that they define for themselves. The second direction re-uses material from the commercial cinema, putting it into contexts that can alter its meanings and its nature as experience. It is also the area of independent cinema production and exhibition; and of the use of film or video in a public context that often goes beyond traditional cinema halls. It has a much more hesitant and sporadic relationship with the institutions of broadcast TV.

The commercial cinema has undergone a gradual transformation since the arrival of mass broadcast TV in the early 1950s. A number of strategies were attempted, during the 1950s, to compete with broadcast TV on its own terms, particularly since the technical and aesthetic quality of early broadcast TV in the USA was not great. Cinema emphasised the physical superiority of its projected image in a series of technical 'improvements' (Cinemascope, Widescreen, VistaVision, 3-D, etc.) which resulted overall in a certain loss of projected picture quality. It also boasted the superiority of its capital base in a series of spectacular productions that culminated in the débâcle of *Cleopatra* (1963). Since this initial period, another strategy has emerged, which aims to complement and supplement broadcast TV rather than to challenge it directly. There are two interlinked aspects to this strategy. The first exploits cinema's ability to produce prototypes rather than series: it produces films at a variety of budgetary levels that initiate and develop a particular narrative conception and problematic. Such films can indeed result in TV series being built from them. This conception of cinema is that which is current in the more 'mainstream' or 'entertainment' areas of commercial cinema: it leads to blockbusters with huge promotion budgets like

Star Wars, and *Alien*, as well as more modestly budgeted (but equally thoroughly worked out) films like *Escape from New York* (1981) or *Twilight's Last Gleaming* (1977), to cite random but related examples. Its films are conceived of as entertainment events which require no special skills or knowledges on the part of their potential audiences, apart from the general (and culturally acquired) ability to make sense of the current fashions in narrative film-making, and the more diffuse 'general knowledge' of Western culture. The particular area of this general knowledge that the film exploits will be indicated in the narrative image that surrounds and gives a context to the film. They will also be explained within the context of the film from very basic presuppositions. *Twilight's Last Gleaming* assumes a public knowledge of the fact of silos containing nuclear weapons, the general belief that it is possible for such weapons to be launched by mechanical error or by individual human initiative, and a sense of the massive dislocation to the American military and its personnel caused by the Vietnam War. These knowledges lend plausibility to the film's narrative, and are developed (and hence explained, reinforced and, as it were, verified) during the course of the narration.

But *Twilight's Last Gleaming* is also a rather difficult film for British film exhibition. It was released in a cut-down version in Britain, reduced from 146 minutes to 122 minutes. Its difficulty lies chiefly in its split-screen sequences, which combine multiple images of interlinked spaces and events, shown 'directly' by film, and 'indirectly' by video surveillance cameras. These compress much of the action, and pose severe problems for spectatorship: the problems of knowing which way to look when; the problems of having a de-centred form of attention. Added to this, the film aimed to make an argument about the nature of American political power and geopolitics. Faced with such a film, the British distributors opted to reduce it to its thriller aspects. So the case of *Twilight's Last Gleaming* demonstrates a trend within the commercial entertainment cinema which British interests, notoriously conservative, frequently have difficulty in dealing with. The commercial entertainment film still habitually begins from premises that are cultural commonplaces, and with ideas that have an immediate place in the small change of everyday life. But they can then extend beyond the constrictions of what they can assume everyone will know. Entertainment films can develop their narratives to the extent of launching a critique of the American governmental system that would be impossible on American TV, or indeed on British TV, if it occurred on a programme made directly for TV. They can also complicate their narration by introducing elliptical or enigmatic sequences and encounters; by developing dense thematic parallels between characters and actions; by a limited use of techniques (like split-screen) that disorient the spectator. The demands of immediate and universal intelligibility no longer apply so rigidly and directly to the commercial entertainment film. They apply instead to broadcast TV.

Commercial cinema still maintains a certain level of production that appeals to an immediate intelligibility in its largest scale productions, the so-called blockbusters. Such films become general cultural events through their skilful and massive use of publicity, expenditure on which is planned to exceed expenditure on the film's production. Films like *Jaws* (1975), *Star Wars* (1977), *Raiders of the Lost Ark* (1981) or the James Bond cycle (from 1962) represent cinema's attempt to maximise its audience and to draw in spectators who rarely see films in cinemas. Hence they often conform to a simpler form of intelligibility, substituting spectacular effects for complexity of narration and event. However important such films are to the economics of the industry, and to the maintenance of the general conception of what constitutes 'a film', such productions are relatively rare and isolated events in cinema film production. Signalled in advance, discussed endlessly before they are seen, they can be few in number: overproduction of blockbusters would reduce their cultural impact. Instead, the normal run of films (whose budgets are often large) normally seeks out a certain difficulty and specificity of address.

Blockbusters and more specialised films alike comprise a commercial cinema which has a central marketing function within modern society. Broadcast TV's output is largely resistant to advertising as specific cultural events; however, cinema films depend upon such marketing. So a large component of the current commercial cinema is the ways in which it practises marketing of individual films and of cinema itself. Individual films are established with a particular narrative image which enhances considerably their marketability on TV as well as in cinemas. A notably successful piece of marketing was the film *Jaws* (1975), which in due time attracted a vast TV audience. This audience was much larger than that for Spielberg's earlier made-for-TV film *Duel* (1971) could possibly have been, simply because of the cinema-based marketing to which *Jaws* was treated. But cinema's marketing does not only rebound to the benefit of individual films. Cinema, equally, is the arena in which stars can be created: actors whose contradictory images are constituted as continuing paradoxes for spectators. Cinema still remains the central place for the production of stars because it offers single self-contained films rather than series re-production of the same basic performance. Broadcast TV's patterns of repetition militate against the creation of stars from its performers because they generally become associated with one particular performance and one particular basic problematic. They also appear too intimate and domestic, lacking the dimensions of distance and difference that cinematic performance will tend to give them. Hence TV personalities are made stars through the action of cinema and its marketing devices. They can then return, enhanced, to broadcast TV activities.

The major strategy adopted by commercial cinema both in its marketing and in construction of individual films has been to produce films whose address has been quite clearly directed to a specific fraction of the population. This address does not exclude other people from the audience (i.e. still rests its appeal on generally shared cultural definitions). Rather, it is an approach that guarantees that the films will diverge from the mass conception of thematic material that dominates broadcast TV. Hence a diversity of particular 'interest groups' is catered for directly in commercial cinema production. These are often groups that have a relatively large amount of disposable income, so there is a certain circularity in the process: cinema tends to address its films towards those fractions of the community that recognise themselves in various forms of activity, one of which is cinema attendance. So in addition to the obvious specific audiences that cinema addresses, those of 'youth culture', gay culture, the Women's Movement, one major facet of cinema's address of its films is to the culturally sophisticated. Hence commercial films which cautiously ease themselves into areas which connote 'culture': the use, for instance, of Baroque music in American films about mature problems of married life (Pachelbel in *Ordinary People* (1980); Vivaldi as the organising structure of *The Four Seasons* (1981)). Another index of cultural sophistication is the element of self-consciousness that has invaded commercial cinema. Extensive broadcast TV screening of old entertainment films has created a new 'public memory' of cinema, as well as recreating the images that compose those films by cutting about 15 per cent off their edges (the phenomenon of 'video cut-off'). Despite this loss of edges, the centre still holds, so contemporary cinema can be self-conscious about its narration (making some devices obvious to the viewer) because it can assume a certain knowledge of Hollywood cinema in its audience. The result is a large number of films that trade upon their knowingness, placing the audience in a position of colluding with the film in mocking a supposed naive audience. Such is the position of *Raiders of the Lost Ark*, camping in relation to the B-features and adventure serials of classic Hollywood. Equally, sophistication about the tradition and history of the cinema can lead to the work of a Robert Altman, whose career has consisted to a large degree of un-making the staple genres of classic Hollywood by frustrating and undercutting their presumptions: the war film in *M*A*S*H*, the Western in *McCabe and Mrs Miller* (1971), the private eye movie in *The Long Goodbye* (1973).

Self-referentiality in the more or less commercial feature film has two different facets. One is that which tends to be taken up within a mainstream production that seeks to maximise its audience; the other is a feature of a more overtly specialised cinema, an 'art' cinema. The first, associated still with maximisation of the audience, is a level of reference to the public iconography of the movies: to those figures and genres that have some kind of circulation outside a specifically filmic set of interests. Hence it refers to certain stars whose images (in the form of posters, books of biography laced with stills, etc.) still have a general popular circulation: Humphrey Bogart, Marilyn Monroe. They refer to genres that have a fairly stable identity in the history of cinema: gangster movies, Westerns. It is reference to that small fragment of classic Hollywood that has remained in the public memory, or has been reintroduced as camp or nostalgia. This type of reference is confirming for its audience, in that spectators can 'spot the reference' and tend to feel sophisticated in that recognition; it is safe for the film itself, since it can reckon on a certain level of public awareness of the myth of the history of cinema, and the few images from it that still have currency. This level of reference to films themselves cannot be taken as the structuring principle of the film, what organises it and gives it meaning. At best it can, like *Play It Again Sam* (1972), starring Woody Allen, provide the central obsession for a character in a film. For Woody Allen, the figure of Bogart (impersonated by an actor in the shadows) provides a kind of alter ego, who would do precisely what Allen could never do. So *Play It Again Sam* is another Woody Allen film: playing over the feelings of insecurity and self-congratulating self-depreciation that Allen has made his authorial mark. The reference to Bogart (not to a more obscure star) is incidental to this process. It is a reference to a character that Bogart played only once (in *The Big Sleep*, 1946): Philip Marlowe in a trench coat, an image that has wide currency in the myth of the cinema.

The films of Robert Altman have a rather more complicated relationship to this kind of self-referentiality of modern cinema. To some extent, they remain within the simpler type of reference, which plasters a pastiche of a particular piece of film iconography on to a traditional kind of film, rather like the picture palaces of the 1920s splashed pastiches of architectural style on to brick box buildings. Sometimes, however, Altman produces a more complicated form of reference, which tends to criticise the form that is being pastiched, pointing out the personal inadequacies and idiocies of a man like Philip Marlowe, in a way that is not altogether affectionate. The films have a more uncertain career as a result: they tend to specify their audience, and the demand they make on their spectators in a way that can conflict with the drive to maximise the audience.

Some of Altman's films are characterised by concerns that have more traditionally been associated with the 'art cinema'. This area of production and exhibition has defined its audience as 'different from' the audience for mass entertainment films. To some extent, exhibition defines 'art cinema' rather more than interests within film production. Films from European countries often become 'art films' when exported, where they are recognised as national cinema (and rather superior as a result) in their country of origin. Such was the case with the films produced by Ealing Studios in Britain in the period 1944-56. Seen as notable entertainment films in Britain, they became 'art films' abroad. They had different exhibition patterns: in Britain, they went out on the normal Rank circuit release, as first features in Odeon or Gaumont cinemas, showing for one week only, right across a particular geographic locality (North London, South London, the North-East, etc.). In the USA and France, the career of those films that were released tended to be different: they were shown typically for extended runs (more than a week) in specialised cinemas in major population centres, and were subsequently absorbed by film-clubs, college circuits, etc. Such is the pattern of art cinema exhibition, the kind of exhibition that is given to 'Continental' films that are shown in Britain. However, for various reasons, Britain has scarcely developed a network of art cinema venues outside London.

This pattern of exhibition makes available films that are not considered suitable for the mass cinema circuits, and hence defines a different audience. It tends to produce an area of film production when the cinema network begins to approach financial viability. This 'art cinema' in exhibition and in production has two major tendencies within it, which could be subsumed under the names of two French directors: Godard and Truffaut. The category of 'director' (the creator of the art) is central to the way in which criticism deals with art cinema, so perhaps the use of these authorial titles is appropriate. Truffaut represents a rather more reactionary end of art cinema: his films are (increasingly) conservative in their form, becoming indistinguishable from the more crafted product of entertainment cinema (many of whose young personnel in USA would recognise Truffaut as 'a major influence on their lives'; probably along with their mothers). Truffaut brings a characteristic 'vision' to his films: they are essentially humanist, concerned with individuals trying to make sense of their world, and cautiously testing the ground in personal relations. The terms applied to his films by critics and audiences alike are those of 'warmth and humanity', 'understanding', 'wry humour'. Their concern is with individuals, whose portrayal is considerably aided by the skills in dramatic understatement developed by French cinema acting.

This humanism and conservatism of form contrasts strongly with the work of Godard, whose films throughout the 1960s created something of a scandal each time a new one appeared. Godard's films have a central concern with the problems of representation: character becomes a problem for them rather than a refuge because they seek to portray the character of individuals as constructed by circumstance (and changed by circumstance) rather than as a stable entity to be explored. Equally, the films became increasingly aware through the 1960s first of the limitations of filmic portrayal, then increasingly of the social role of filmic portrayal, and of the ideological role of images and sounds in society. Godard's films can never be said to be conservative in their form: often they are seen as puzzling or obscure, making demands on their audiences that are out of line with their expectations.

These two approaches (from directors with similar beginnings in cinema) can be taken as synoptic of two tendencies within modern art cinema, a splitting of audience into two different perspectives. One seeks a humanistic portrayal of personal problems of a kind that is not considered usual in commercial cinema. The other looks to specialised cinema to provide films that challenge them on a formal aesthetic level as well as providing a radical set of concerns on other levels as well. Both of these 'tastes' still rest at the level of a traditional definition of 'a film' as a self-sufficient entity, though in some areas the work inspired by Godard's films has had to move away from this conception, and much of his work in the 1970s was concerned with the possibilities of broadcast TV and video.

The work of Altman represents a new development that began in the early 1970s in which entertainment cinema, in its search for identifiable audiences, began to produce films aimed more specifically towards the audience which had traditionally identified itself with art cinema. This meant a subtle series of changes in the expectations that films made of their audiences. It became possible to produce highly elliptical narratives which substituted the longueurs and the 'gaps in between' for the classic cinema's concentration on the narratively significant actions and their chains of consequences. This tendency has usually been mollified by the continued demand to maximise audiences within a more adventurous aesthetic strategy. The interests backing such commercial-art features have wanted to hedge their bets as far as possible. Nevertheless, an erosion of the action-centred nature of the classic narrative form has tended to take place during the 1970s in American production. In Europe, the tendency has been far more marked, with major American-owned distributors like United Artists financing the work of established art cinema directors like Fellini or Bertolucci. This is more the acquisition of already established commodities (star directors) than a move into new terrain as has tended to happen in the USA itself.

Commercial cinema's move towards the terrain traditionally occupied by art cinema is one aspect of a general trend within commercial film-making from the latter half of the 1960s. Commercial cinema's response to the prevalence of broadcast TV has been to move out of competition with it. The amorphous mass market has been abandoned to broadcast TV; the commercial cinema has begun to explore and exploit other definitions of audience. This is strikingly similar to the kind of strategy that gave birth to art cinema in several European countries in the 1920s. Commercial film production and exhibition has moved towards different definitions of its audience, in terms of specialised interests ('minority' groups; pornography; specialised interests like rock music; art cinema interests). In doing so, cinema production has cautiously begun to define itself as different from broadcast TV. It tends to be different in the kind of subjects it treats; its willingness to enter into certain controversies, even political ones; its distance from the direct control of state or para-state institutions; its attitude to the kinds of forms of narration and *mise-en-scène* that it can use. Commercial cinema can assume more of its audience than broadcast TV, or can be more exploitative, offering dubious or objectionable material. It can attempt to provide entertainment for those who are dissatisfied with broadcast TV, providing, of course, that they can afford the price of a cinema seat. However, this tendency within commercial cinema remains within the regime of a traditional conception of the film as a self-sufficient entity. It still assumes that a film should be in and of itself intelligible and not require any specific knowledges on the part of its audience other than a diffuse cultural awareness gathered from everyday life. In this sense, all that has happened is that commercial film-making has realised something of the diversity of modern culture, and has begun to realise that 'mass culture' is composed of many specific facets, attitudes and knowledges rather than being a single monolith (as the pessimistic theorists of the Frankfurt School feared).

Equally, the commercial cinema in its diversified form has entered into a close relationship with the institutions of broadcast TV. In this area, there is not a distinct separation of terrains: broadcast TV dealing with a mass audience, and cinema catering to a more specified and distinct set of audiences. Instead, broadcast TV uses cinema as a central aspect of its own output; and commercial cinema looks towards broadcast TV as a vital source of finance. Broadcast TV looks to cinema to provide a particular conception of 'film': not only the self-sufficient, generally intelligible entertainment, but a work at a particular budgetary level and creation of narrative image that broadcast TV institutions can only rarely afford to provide directly. Commercial cinema has tended to integrate the expectation of sale to TV in the overall financing of film production; sometimes this has gone further, with joint cinema/TV production arrangements being formalised. These tendencies keep cinema production within a particular traditional conception of a film, and compromise its moves towards catering for more diversified conceptions of possible audiences.

16 Beyond the Hollywood film: British independent cinema

To some extent, the conception of a film produced within the American-dominated commercial cinema does not realise the full potential of cinema. The Hollywood film is a self-sufficient fiction of about two hours' length, which resolves the enigma presented in its narrative image. It aims to be universally intelligible; it trades upon its newness; it is produced by professionals. Equally, this conception of a film brings with it expectations of a particular level of expenditure on the image, or rather the visual and aural indications of such an expenditure. The Hollywood film uses the cinematic image to provide a level of visual pleasure that cannot be found on the smaller screen and more cursory image of broadcast TV. However, it does not use the public nature of the cinematic event to any great degree; it gathers together an audience who remain anonymous to each other, sharing moments of pleasure, or annoying each other with cigarette smoke and weak jokes at the film's expense.

The work of the last decade or so in British independent cinema has begun to explore some alternatives to this Hollywood cinema: alternatives which use the potential of cinema in new ways, to create new relationships between audiences and the material they watch. These relationships have the potential to produce an active, radical and organised audience for both film and TV material. Independent cinema has begun this work by organising film exhibition in new ways, by reconceiving the basis of films themselves, and by seeking new ways of producing films. There is often no particular unity between different initiatives in this area, with contradictory ideas being pursued side by side with each other. Other ideas have scarcely been followed through. However, this area of cinema work goes further than any other in realising the potential of cinema as a public screening event, and the potential of cinema as a critical and adventurous medium in relation to the centrality of broadcast TV.

Some areas of film exhibition have long been involved with films which do not conform exactly with the conception of a Hollywood film. The traditional art cinema venues have had policies of exhibiting 'old' films, either as calculated revivals or within a repertory policy of exhibiting classics of cinema. A strategy of re-releasing has traditionally been the commercial distributor's response to a temporary shortage of new films: there was a flurry of re-releases in the early days of the Second World War in Britain, and again as a result of the temporary American boycott in 1948. In addition, a very few old commercial films have had regular re-releases based on their very special status in popular memory: *Gone With the Wind* and Walt Disney's feature-length cartoons are the most obvious examples. However, the ordinary strategy of re-releasing tends to deny the age of the film, pretending that it is a new film; only art cinema and the very few films like *Gone With the Wind* will offer the age of the film as proof of its enduring market value.

Alongside these forms of cinematic exhibition that use 'old films', the film society movement in Britain after the Second World War began to offer a more consistent market for films after their initial 'newness' and value to commercial exhibition had begun to fade. Exploiting the 16mm technology made available in the 1930s, film societies tended to remain outposts of art cinema, showing to a small but cohesive group of enthusiasts those films which had had a run in metropolitan art cinema. Developments in film criticism, particularly the magazine *Movie* at the beginning of the 1960s, began to broaden the range of films available in film societies. In particular, old Hollywood began to become acceptable, provided that some of the categories usually applied to art cinema had been applied to the particular films being shown. If a Hollywood film was made by a particular author with a particular style (e.g. John Ford) then it would be exhibited, despite belonging to a despised genre like the Western. In the more advanced film societies, printed material accompanied films, and lectures or discussions were organised.

The importance of film societies lies in the way that they produce an attitude of connoisseurship (it is no accident that one of Britain's main art cinema distributors in the period was called 'Connoisseur Films'). Commercial films are seen against the grain of their Hollywood origins; they are reviewed in the terms provided within the discourses surrounding art cinema distribution. At its most radical, this attitude of reading can see films in ways very different from those in which they were perceived at the time of their commercial release. This constitutes a re-use of Hollywood films which refuses certain aspects of their nature as Hollywood films: it refuses to value newness as a criterion of the worth of a film; it refuses to participate fully in the regime of universal intelligibility in which the films participate. Instead, the films are perfectly legitimately submitted to a form of reading developed within art cinema. The stylistic aspects that go unnoticed in a good commercial film (the ease of narration, the fluidity of cutting and camerawork) are valued over and above the ostensible subject. Sometimes, as with Lindsay Anderson's consideration of John Ford, the style and the subject can be related as coherent parts of a total and individual vision. However, this form of viewing remains, as most of the art cinema institutions, within the model of a film provided by Hollywood. Certain strategic divergences are recorded from it: the divergences which constitute the national art cinema audiences against the dominance of Hollywood. In particular, the Hollywood regime of universal intelligibility is replaced by a particular view of film as art which rests on notions gained from more established critical evaluation of the fine arts and literature.

Further divergences from the commercial model of a film began to be developed by cinemathèques and film archives with extended series of screenings of films organised around either themes or (more usually) the work of a particular director. Such enterprises are usually found only in capital cities, like the National Film Theatre in London or the Paris

Cinemathèque. Their aim has tended to be to screen as much material as possible in whatever form. As a rule, the whole output of a director (reputed disasters along with mythical classics) is put on show, or at least as much of it as still exists. In some ways the apotheosis of the critical models developed in art cinema and film societies, these forms of exhibition did have the advantage, in their indiscriminate screening policies, of providing material that stretched these critical concepts sometimes to breaking point.

Subsidised screening venues, open to the public, began to be developed as a result of the policies of the British Film Institute in the late 1960s and early 1970s. Based on traditional film societies, these Regional Film Theatres began an often difficult transition from the film society policy of exhibition on a film-by-film basis (similar to commercial cinema's 'This week something, next week something different'). The conception of structured programming began to be adopted, in which a series of films were exhibited, linked around a common theme or the work of a particular director. This notion of programming would take the excuse of the 'latest' Buñuel film to show a small number of previous Buñuel films; or the opportunity of a film about adolescent sexuality (*La Souffle au Coeur* (1971), for instance) to programme a diversity of films which could be said to deal with the same topic (*Meet Me in St Louis* (1944), *Lolita* (1961), *Mädchen in Uniform* (1931), *Rebel Without a Cause* (1955)). Such a season, in some locations, would be provided with 'contextualising matter', like programme notes, a booklet, or a speaker and discussion.

Such programming in Regional Film Theatres has always been severely compromised by the overall conception of the screening venue, which in almost all cases hovered uneasily between the exclusive atmosphere of a film society and the anonymity of a commercial cinema. The demands of profitability (subsidies by no means covered basic operating costs) tended to mean that traditional film-by-film programming was the rule rather than the exception. Such problems still remain.

The spread of available art cinema exhibition venues, at least in the larger urban centres in Britain, means that forms of film exhibition are available that break to some extent with some of the forms of commercial cinema. It is possible to see films organised into seasons of related material; it is possible to see films whose life in the commercial cinema has long since been exhausted; it is possible to develop, through reading and discussion, forms of critical attention to films that begin to develop away from the model of universal intelligibility offered by commercial films. Some independent cinema venues have gone rather further, experimenting with forms that refuse the notion of a film as a self-contained entity, and developing rather different forms of audience organisation. Such initiatives are tentative, and, through lack of funding, none has achieved the status of a full-time operation. They are initiatives that are usually linked with film production, and in some cases, film projects have emerged from work in film exhibition.

Independent exhibition has begun to organise two main forms of film season and related activities. One is that of programming films in close conjunction with other organisations: women's groups, political groups, trade union branches, organisations of ethnic minorities, campaigning groups like Campaign for Nuclear Disarmament. The audience for film screenings is thus drawn from the membership of these groups, as well as from the wider public who are interested in the particular issues raised by the film season. As important as the screening of films are the activities that relate to them: activities of discussion either immediately after screenings or at another time; activities of producing written and photographic material that argues for (or with) both the films and the issues around which they are programmed. This form of programming organisation moves away from some of the problems associated with the programming of Regional Film Theatres. In particular, it avoids the sense of producing programmes for an anonymous public who may or may not respond to the particular theme. Instead, programming gains a purpose as it is associated with particular local activities. At its best, such programming and the activities it generates have a series of effects. It enables the group concerned to see their particular interests represented on the cinema screen in a diversity of ways, some of which will be unfamiliar, others perhaps objectionable. It provides a focus for examination of the general forms of representation that are available in our society, and those which predominate. Hence a feminist group can view side by side the representations of prostitution that are produced in commercial films like *The World of Susie Wong* (1960) or *Klute* (1971) with the attempt to examine personal accounts of prostitution in a critical way seen in Jan Worth's *Taking a Part* (1979). From the discussions which are provoked by these screenings of different kinds of films, a more acute awareness of the role of forms of representation in modern society can be developed.

The organisation of such screenings need not necessarily be tied to a permanent cinema venue. In fact, it is often an advantage to be able to use an area that does not have the fixed rows of raked seating normally associated with cinema halls: such organisation of seating often impedes the progress of discussion, orienting it towards whoever happens to be 'leading' from a position under the screen, facing the audience. In other ways, too, the use of non-cinematic venues has distinct advantages. It can take place in the many areas in which cinemas no longer exist. The use of non-cinematic venues also helps to avoid some of the attitudes traditionally associated with cinema-going; the sense of cinema as a private experience that takes place in public. Partly for these reasons, independent cinema predominantly uses 16mm technology, and films are usually made on this gauge as well. With improvements in 16mm projection technology and the general decline in the standards of 35mm projection in the commercial cinemas, the difference between the two gauges is becoming almost unnoticeable.

Discussions after the screening of films have a quite distinct relationship to those films: they work over the memory images of the films. In the case of a conventional cinematic narrative, the memory image of the film is a complete and finished entity: the problematic has been resolved into a coherent order, a sense of completion that usually (but by no means always) contributes to their sense of reality. Other films, often independent films constructed with this kind of use in mind, refuse to present such a resolution of their material. Discussion is sometimes directed against the coherence of the conventional narrative film, exploring the ways in which its conclusion was reached, re-memorising the film as a disparate collection of scenes, characters, themes and pleasures rather than as the unity that it appeared to be. Discussion of more openly organised films tends towards the construction of different possible ways of understanding the material presented in the film, hence towards the activity of constructing a memory of the film collectively. Both kinds of discussion balance between films and their problematics, between the questions of how an issue can be represented and what can be done about it.

The relationship between the narrative image, the narration of the film and the memory image of that narration is maintained in such discussion in a similar relation to that of commercial cinema, although it is radically revised. The conventional narrative image of film-by-film publicity is replaced by various kinds of advertisement for the film, its relation to the overall problematic of the season, and its difference from other films in that season. The memory image is the subject of discussion and dispute rather than a fixed and rather private conclusion. Some experiments with exhibition have begun to work on the self-sufficiency of the individual film, by interrupting the showing of a narrative film. This is perhaps the most radical act to undertake with a narrative film as the aim of commercial cinema has long been that of the unimpeded narration of the film. Hence practices like the suspension of the projection of a film to interpolate other material (slides of alternative views; other sections of other films; a spoken address to the film; an acted scene) break the fundamental ties that bind the spectator into the fiction: it cuts across the relations of identification and voyeurism as well as the coherence of the balancing and rebalancing of narration.

Such exhibition activities have taken place in a large number of part-time exhibition venues, and other kinds of halls as well. At the time of writing, most remain at the level of experiments or individual initiatives. However, their importance lies in the way in which they are rethinking the relations of cinema spectating. This work will be able to produce an active and critical audience, an audience who are not mystified by the methods of cinema or broadcast TV, able to argue and press for changes in the ways in which these two media present the world. Further, they will be able to contribute to the production of new representations, more appropriate to their social situation and to their conception of the world, as it is and as it should be.

British independent cinema's work in the area of exhibition is closely connected with its various forms of film and video production. Film production, like film exhibition in independent cinema, has had a long history of antecedents and examples. In particular, the sector that is known from the outside as 'the avant-garde' has consistently shown other film-makers both new possibilities in the usage of film, and in the ways in which films can be produced. Particularly in Britain, lacking an indigenous 'art cinema', much work has been undertaken within institutions set up by those with a background in the fine arts rather than in entertainment cinema. Hence the London Film-makers' Co-operative was set up in 1966 by an alliance of artists interested in film and film-makers interested in ideas coming from modernist practices in design, painting and music. Many of the concerns with film as a performance activity with which this book has dealt were first developed in the practices of the London Film-makers' Co-operative, in the kinds of film that have been produced and the ways that they have been shown. Equally, the Co-op has pioneered new forms of film production, enabling other film-makers to be able to conceive of producing work with more co-operative methods, involving more than the traditional distinctions between 'the creators' and the 'ancillary technical staff'. The work of independent film-makers in Britain has been directed both towards new forms of films and towards new forms of production. Here again, some of the ideas that have been adumbrated in particular films or in the production of particular films have not yet attained the status of regular practices.

Exhibition in independent cinema has moved away from the indiscriminate conception of audience that still predominates in the commercial and art cinema sectors. Production has therefore been able to assume different things of the potential audiences for films. In particular, the conventions of universal intelligibility need not be adhered to. At its simplest, this means that a film and its surrounding material will not offer the conventional pattern of narrative image completed by coherent film. Hence Cinema Action's *Film From the Clyde* (1977) was offered, by its poster, as a 'Working Class Film', which is not exactly a blandishment that is found in commercial cinema. Further, the film itself offers a sequence of documented events (the workers' occupation of the Upper Clyde Shipbuilders' yards in 1971-2), but does not produce a definitive analysis of them (as a TV documentary would). Instead, the film contains a number of potential analyses, and is designed to provoke discussion of the whole strategy of factory occupation and work-ins. As a result, the narration of events is balanced by a conception of sequences that are separate from each other, emphasising different aspects of the situation of the yards. One sequence presents without dialogue of any kind the conditions of work: noise and physical discomfort. *Film from the Clyde* is a film which identifies its audience and thus has to make none of the usual concessions to a nebulous 'general audience': it takes no pains to explain the technical vocabulary of industrial relations; neither does it identify and privilege the various politicians who appear. As it attempts to be a 'working class film', it feels confident that its audience will have a different frame of reference.

In addition to assuming distinct frames of reference within their audience, some independent films also assume a different attitude of attention to films. Rather than the regime of narrative progression, which tends to unify all the effects contained within the film into a final harmony, some independent films deliberately work in a different way. They promote an attitude of reading the image as a space containing different and conflicting meanings; and the soundtrack as composed of sounds which do not necessarily cohere into an aural 'point of view'. Hence a film like *At the Fountainhead* (1980) presents the viewer with a fictional biography of a Jewish musician who fled Nazi Germany and settled in England; the real character on whom this is based; a present-

22 Photography for the oppressed by the oppressed: *At The Fountain-head*

day family reunion of the fictional character's relatives, some of whom are concerned with the publication of a documentary-fiction book about Nazi Germany; and various kinds of documentary material about Nazi Germany and its post-war division into East and West. Connections between these strands are presented for the viewer to trace a way through, rather than to cohere into one perception. Hence different levels of the experience of nationality and history are allowed to relate to each other. At one point a piece of newsreel footage is presented twice, with radically different voice-overs, both claiming the images as proof of their argument. Such a strategy, multiplied and played through more subtle variations, reduces the authority of image and sound to the point where an attitude of perceiving it as a collection of fragments, each with meaning, none with totalising meaning, becomes the only possible attitude for the viewer to adopt. Such an attitude is not so different from that which is invited by Cubist painting or the photo-montages of Rodchenko. In both cases, representations of objects are offered in fragments of the space of the image, but no overall spatial coherence is offered. The picture does not imitate a real space. Neither does it create a coherent perspective or point of view: Rodchenko's montages offer objects photographed from a large number of perspectives.

Some films have taken these strategies even further. Some, like those of film-maker Peter Gidal, deliberately work on the levels of attention that spectators give to the projected image, presenting radically less information than is conventionally the case. Others integrate this courting of boredom or even infuriation on the spectator's part with sections which provide more conventional amounts of information. Such is the case with Penny Webb's *The Young Girl in Blue* (1978), with a scene with still camera looking at an empty room, a scene of interminable waiting for something to happen, frustrated still further when a character passes into frame but performs no action. Lis Rhode's *Light Reading* (1979) provides too much information at points: a richly punning and alliterative voice-over and one image in particular that refuses ever to resolve into a coherent representation. This film begins to provide shifts in spectator attention, providing different amounts of information at different moments.

Some independent work has been accused of obscurity, or difficulty, precisely because it tries to move away from the assumptions of the Hollywood film. The accusations are usually made from the point of view of those assumptions: that cinema is a place of entertainment (which is a category which is wielded as though entertainment were not concerned with anything); that its entertainments should be universally comprehensible, assuming only ideological common sense in its audience; that its entertainments should conform to a particular model of narration and spectating. Moving images are perhaps the only medium upon which such normative demands are made: other media, whether books, newspapers, photography, even radio, have diversified their audiences to the point where the universalising conception of intelligibility is no longer appropriate. Entertainment cinema has diversified its conceptions of possible audiences only within the model of the Hollywood film and its regime of intelligibility; further change has been hampered by interdependence with broadcast TV and its demands. Independent cinema is moving beyond this constricting model, pointing the way towards new uses of cinema and new pleasures from film and video. A particular kind of cinema is being constructed, one which is appropriate to the increasing sophistication of sections of the cinema and broadcast TV audience.

This sophistication is perhaps the result of an increased availability of film and broadcast TV; equally, it is probably the result of developments within those media themselves. Whilst cinema has diversified its audience, broadcast TV has presented a different model of narration, dependent far more upon the process of segmentation than on the coherent narrative unities of cinema's typical procedures. Segmentation in broadcast TV remains a means of securing attention within the context in which TV is used. The overall coherence of a particular segment is finally provided by the impression that it creates that it is the representation of a particular reality. However, independent cinema seems to have realised that the segmental procedures of TV have opened the way towards a new form of spectator attention which is not so much geared to the overall coherence of a narration, but is willing to treat a film as a series of diverse segments. The form of attention that cinema can generate, extended over a considerable period of time, enables the generation of comparisons between different segments. Such a sense is much more difficult to achieve with broadcast TV. Hence the large number of independent films which offer different generic attitudes to the same basic question: *Rapunzel* (1976), with its four versions of the same fairy tale; *Riddles of the Sphinx* (1977), with its incomplete narrative fragments and series of attentions to related problems (ranging from near-documentary to near-abstract film); *News and Comment* (1978) with its deliberate play with a series of different expository devices favoured by broadcast TV. This segmental procedure, with its possibilities for comparison and contrast between each segment, generates an attitude of reading the sound and image as a constructed representation rather than the impression of a pre-existing reality. This attitude is then naturally extended to seeing each image and sound as a separate signifying entity, to tracing meanings rather than receiving an illusion.

This is to argue for the formal properties of independent films, for the attitude of reading that they tend to promote. These formal properties are the result of the political impulsions behind the making of the films: to produce means of representation that can develop new and radical points of view on and in society. The powerful drift towards common-sense views of reality that is inscribed within the forms favoured by commercial cinema and broadcast TV has to be countered by those whom common sense deems 'abnormal' or outside the ideological consensus. The powerful pull of these representations of 'normality' upon individuals has to be countered by implied or direct criticism of those representations. In these circumstances, the possibilities of juxtaposing different and contradictory representations of the same phenomena offered within the ideological consensus can produce a sudden burst of subversive humour that is often worth hours of serious argument.

Independent cinema has a commitment to finding new means of producing films as well as new forms of film. In particular, the intention to explore ways of representing those groups which are deprived of regular representation in cinema or broadcast TV has led to the beginnings of work with such groups. Some films have been produced around the Women's Movement in Britain that have involved radically different means of production. For the Film and History Project's *Song of the Shirt* (1979), the film-makers operated as co-ordinators, drawing in contributions from a wide range of women, both historians working on women's work in the early nineteenth-century garment industry, and women working in a number of different jobs today. This project involved a large amount of discussion of the ways in which the clothes trade and women's work within it has been represented, and the ways in which the film could present materials for a historical analysis of it. Hence the process of construction of a melodramatic serial novel in a Chartist paper is shown: the agonising of its writer, concerned with questions of morality; the comedy of seamstresses enacting and lampooning the story. United by common feminist concerns, co-ordinated by the central group of ten film-makers, the Project drew in a wider range of contributions than is usual for historical series produced for broadcast TV. These contributions were not limited to advisory roles, providing information when requested, but played an active part in conceiving the whole three-part, 135 minute film.

In another way, a screening project at Four Corners cinema in Bethnal Green has led to the production of a film around the theme of 'Mothers and Daughters'. This film, still in production at the time of writing, springs from an imaginative series of screenings and related events that took place in 1979. Thematically organised screenings of diverse material formed the central core for discussions and for the production of written and photographic material which was found and/or produced by members of the 'audience' as well as by the organisers themselves. A programme around the education of women to become mothers at the turn of the century included early films like *A Victorian Lady in her Boudoir* (1896-7), some Chaplin films and a film about young girls' ambitions *Serve and Obey*. This was supplemented by displays of photographs from local archives, and, crucially, interviews with local women who grew up during the early years of the century. A central group of regular participants developed, along with a more casual audience.

In this case, what is normally accounted to be the 'research' stage of a film was dramatically changed. The film-makers did not search for pieces of reality that could be soldered into a representation. Research was a collective discussion about reality as representation, involving both representations from various periods of cinema history, and the representations that are often mistaken for reality: people's memories, their accounts of their own experiences. This activity of comparing representations both formal and informal, appropriate and inappropriate for various individuals' lives, then produced the project for the production of a film.

These examples point to a possible general production strategy which would enable the production of representations that various minorities would see as appropriate to their situations. Programming of film and video material in public exhibition can produce a fairly regular audience group who follow through the season and its discussions. In such circumstances, it is possible that a group consisting predominantly of, for instance, single parents, pensioners, or blacks would be able to explore the kinds of representations of themselves that are available to them in cinema and on broadcast TV. Hence both the radical absence of black faces on British TV can be identified, together with the American 'tokenist' strategy in imported soap operas; then a series of different representations: the classic Hollywood nigger; liberal Hollywood of *Guess Who's Coming to Dinner* (1967); 'blaxploitation' films like the Shaft series; examples of the work of African film-makers; isolated British commercial films like *Babylon* (1980); and videotaped examples from TV news and current affairs together with the banned documentary from US TV, *Blacks Brittanica* (1978). From the problems with current representations, where they do exist, discussions can produce a sense of possible representations more appropriate to the condition of the particular individuals concerned. From this, the project for some kind of film or video work can be developed: not necessarily a 'feature film' in the conventional sense, perhaps a series of videos for use in a particular place, in teaching or for various kinds of public meeting. This conception of production would intend to produce representations by and for those who are ignored or treated solely as jokes and problems by broadcast TV's institutions.

Another form of production has also been developed by some independent groups who have worked with people who are already politically organised: with trade union branches, with particular factory occupations, with organised tenants' groups or youth groups. The films that have been produced can be direct campaign films, designed to provide a vivid synopsis of a particular campaign while it is still under way (films for a series of pro-abortion rights campaigns like the Newsreel Collective's *A Chicken is not an Egg* (1975) or

23 An image yet to infiltrate British TV: *Pressure*

Jeff Perks's *The James Whiter than White Show* (1975)).
Alternatively, film-making can take a more reflective form,
looking at general issues rather than a particular campaign.
Such a film is the Newsreel Collective's *Divide and Rule —
Never!* (1978), with its acute dissection of the problems of
teenagers faced with unemployment and National Front
recruitment. Such films usually receive very little finance
from the major financers of independent cinema, arts funding bodies like the British Film Institute. Instead, they are
financed from donations, subsidies from the political group
sponsoring them, or, in the case of the Sheffield Film
Co-op's *Jobs for the Girls* (1979), from the Equal Oppor-
tunities Commission (who disclaimed the film, despite
its popularity).
 A variant on both strategies is represented by Cinema
Action's *So That You Can Live* (1981), where the group's
initial involvement in a film about campaigns around the
Equal Pay Act enforced in 1975 produced a continued

contact with one woman shop steward in South Wales after her eventual redundancy. The resulting film follows her and her family through its history over the following five years. Though Shirley and her family provide the central strand of the film, the particular events within the family (work, unemployment, leisure, growing up, moving house) are intertwined with sequences that demonstrate the historical circumstances for this family in South Wales: its traditions of working-class solidarity and self-improvement, and the current de-industrialisation of the area.

In all of these examples, the work of the film-makers results from forms of close association with people who are involved with the subject matter of the film in various ways. This rhythm of production is very different from that of a conventional film, whether fiction or non-fiction. In fiction, there is usually no sense that the producers of the representation should have any contact with the people they are representing through various fictional devices: it is very rare for a fictional film that centrally involves gay characters to be made in consultation with gay men and women. For non-fiction films and broadcast TV programmes, the relationship between the crew who film and the people who are the subject of the film is (except in very rare cases) one in which the crew descend upon a place, film in ways that they decide, and disappear again. In such a situation, the activity of being filmed tends to become an imposition for those who are being filmed, alleviated only by the supposed glamour of being seen on the screen. The opportunity presented by the fact of being filmed is wasted. It could be an opportunity for reflection on and analysis of the situation that is being filmed. If the filming involves the exploration of work processes or labour relations in a factory, for example, then the preparation for filming will involve producing an account of these processes. Currently, it tends to be the researcher's job to find out what happens, to piece together the accounts of individuals, or to find a dependable and authoritative source (usually, then, a member of management). Filming could be an opportunity for the workforce themselves to assemble fragmentary experiences into a coherent account, to think through the production process, and possible ways of improving it. The result would be that filming becomes an integrated and important part of a process of change, rather than an isolated event of photographing something that is supposed to be unchanging.

Independent cinema in Britain is currently involved in work at the levels of exhibition and production (as well as the implied work of distribution) which in various ways moves away from the model of cinema exemplified by the Hollywood film. As the inheritor of different forms of exhibition work, it has produced means of using exhibition to analyse forms of representation rather than as a single isolated event. It has pushed cinema's tendency to diversify to the point where the notion of different audiences implies different kinds of films: ones which no longer conform to a model of universal intelligibility, but address themselves to audiences whose frames of reference can be assumed to work differently, and to audiences who are becoming attuned to methods of reading sounds and images as productive of meaning rather than representations of a reality. Finally, production methods have begun to move away from the isolation of film-maker face-to-face with subject; instead, means are being developed to produce films in ways that involve the subjects of representations within the production of those representations. Such work is dependent on grants as its aim is not straightforwardly to produce profit. The grants that tend to be available are either directed towards the development of film as an artistic activity (towards the production of 'new kinds of film work') like the funds of the British Film Institute or Regional Arts Associations, or are directed towards conceptions of community arts or social work. Much independent film, particularly work over a long period with groups in exhibition or production, falls uneasily between these two definitions. The funds that are available cover the full cost of the work involved only in a few exceptional cases, so much of the continuity that is so important in developing new methods is lost between projects. However, independent cinema has managed to demonstrate that cinema need not be equated with the model of the Hollywood film and its means of production and dissemination. In doing so, new social roles for cinema have been sketched. These will become increasingly important as various forms of new video technology begin to be used.

17 Postface (1992)

This book was originally published ten years ago: in the month that my first television production was broadcast. Since then, I have worked as an independent television producer, running my own small production company. The way that my partners and I have made programmes does not particularly conform to the system I describe in Chapter 14. More precarious and marginal, a product of the very particular circumstances of Britain's Channel 4, it is more like the way the film industry tends to work.

Both our successes and our difficulties have come from this hybrid way of working. We, along with several hundred other independent production companies, have helped enlarge the scope of British television as television itself expanded the hours it broadcast in the 1980s. Through that period, almost all of the finance for productions has come from the British TV channel commissioning the programmes. Co-financing was the exception rather than the rule. But as the future unfolds, it seems that the investment-based financing models of the film industry are set to become a more normal basis for television production as well, especially for larger projects. The television commodity is about to come of age.

Our conscious choice ten years ago was to establish a small, highly specialised company with a filmic approach to its work: a kind of bespoke tailoring of the image. This remains possible only so long as the economic and aesthetic conditions exist for it, as, in purely financial terms, it remains a relatively expensive way of making programmes. Those independent companies that have grown large, however, have done so to the extent that they have adopted the more industrial model I described, in which economies of scale begin to be made. I remain convinced that both forms of production will continue to be needed, and that a more complex form of investment financing need not exclusively favour those larger companies.

Since even the largest of independent production companies tends to specialise in a few areas of production, the sector as a whole has become an example of the 'post-Fordist' industrial strategy outlined by several analysts, most notably Robin Murray. Small and flexible production units are able to survive because they exist within a complex network of transferable skills and information. These range from a strong trade association (PACT: Producers' Alliance for Cinema and Television) which pools information and conducts political lobbying on behalf of its members; to specialised companies offering services ranging from budgeting and accountancy to programme distribution and finance; to a wide range of skilled freelance production personnel who move from company to company as the availability of work dictates. A degree of geographical concentration (mainly in London) has hitherto been vital to this sector, but now several cities around Britain are basing their development strategies for media around such a conception. Such a 'post-Fordist' approach tends to suit an industry which produces prototypes rather than runs of identical items.

More generally, the creation of independent television production in Britain has proved again what the American industry had already discovered: that it is relatively easy to separate the functions of production and broadcasting.

Production and broadcasting have historically been conflated because of the circumstances in which television was born, as a transmission rather than as a recording medium. The divorce settlement between production and broadcasting is subject to frequent revision of maintenance agreements and disputes over the custody of the children (the programmes), but it was a relatively easy operation compared to changing television itself.

Very few viewers care whether a programme was made by its broadcaster or not; what they care about is the

satisfactions it yields them. Crucial to those satisfactions is
the degree of intelligibility of the programme. This depends
on the particular internal organisation of each segment to
make it immediately accessible to as much of the population
as possible. If there is one thing that should be revised in this
book, it is this point. As some critics have pointed out, the
section on broadcast TV reaches the point where it should
discuss the multiplicity of ways in which broadcast TV and its
viewers negotiate their complex relationship; and stops.

From my own work as a producer and from the general
reception of this book's ideas, I know that the notion of the
segment and the particular sense of the primacy of sound over
image remain valid. But they are not the only defining factors
of broadcast TV. There is in addition the 'instant recognisability factor' of most of broadcast TV. This obviously links
into the level of repetition involved in the construction of
a TV programme and series, but there is more to it than that.

Young children and channel-hoppers alike can recognise
types of programmes within seconds of selecting them,
whether or not they are acquainted with the particular format
they have glimpsed. By contrast, there is often a high level of
confusion among both audiences and critics in relation to the
meaning and nature of a large number of cinema films. This
implies no judgement of value. I am not imputing a relative
richness of ambiguity to cinema. To a purely textual analysis,
the television soap is a positive riot of ambiguity (this is one
of the luxuries of having no need for narrative closure). The
TV soap, though, is instantly recognisable as a genre, together
with its day-time, early evening and peak-time variants. It is
much more clearly recognisable than the cinema melodrama,
the genre that dares not speak its name. Such coyness is
necessary in cinema, but it would spell disaster for an
individual television programme, let alone an entire genre.

This instant recognisability in TV has something to do with
the level of repetition, the primacy of the segment over the
sustained narrative structure, the assumed distracted nature
of audience attention and the other factors I describe as
characterising broadcast TV. But what I failed to appreciate
(both as writer and, to begin with at least, as producer) is the
formidable and subtle organisations of meaning to which they

have given rise. In the chapter on TV I use TV news as a prime example of the ordering of voices, but the example of news tends to run away with the argument a little.

Broadcast TV's formidable output of material contains many different forms of organisation of voice and image; of gesture and writing; of editing and visual effects; of image superimposition and compositing; of on-screen time and space; of music and sound effect; of emotional affect and physical presence; of frame edge and image detail; of the accidental and the calculated; even of broadcast time and duration. So subtle and pervasive are these different combinations of characteristics that television is adept at parody and plagiarism. Just compare the precision with which a TV drama can imitate a particular TV documentary style (not just 'documentary' in general, but, say, the particular form of the caring, socially committed, observational style that British TV has developed) with the lumbering and even embarrassing way in which most major feature films will fail to catch the subtleties of a genre as obviously mannered as the TV news report.

Many of cinema's attempts at parody of TV fail, even when they are legitimately required by the narrative rather than inserted as satirical side-swipes at an 'inferior' medium. The reason lies midway between film-makers and audiences. Viewers used to broadcast TV are highly attuned to the least shift in the combination of elements in a particular TV form, precisely because those forms, and particular examples of them, are so ingrained in the everyday. They are instantly recognisable to the extent that they conform to particular routines of meaning. These routines provide the basis from which a particular programme departs.

Broadcast TV is as much a matter of routines in its reception as in its typical, semi-industrial, methods of production. Such familiarity is necessary to sustain the sense of co-presence of the act of TV enunciation and the activity of TV viewing: the high degree of self-referentiality and direct address which I describe in Chapter 8. The routine of the broadcast schedule is not unlike the routine of the working day: periodised into groups of hours, segmented by hour and fraction of the hour, and different at the weekend and public holiday from the ordinary weekday. Such scheduling routines both imply and depend upon routinised systems of meaning.

In much writing about TV, such a statement has been linked to some variant of a denunciation of the capitalist work ethic which bases management strategies around the routinisation of tasks. However, two questions have to be asked: what do these broadcast routines achieve, and what are their limits?

Factory routines are arrived at as a means of breaking down complex tasks into manageable and repeatable activities. They involve sophisticated analysis on a once-and-for-all basis, rather than having to go back to basics each time. Factory routines can produce the Fordist regime of the production line (as seen in *Modern Times*), or more flexible forms of specialisation. The analysis from which they are derived can be undertaken by 'experts' (management consultants), or by the workforce themselves, or by a combination of the two. They are not essentially wrong or undesirable in themselves, however inhumane some of their variants have been and continue to be.

So it is with the routines of meaning in broadcast TV. They enable a complex sorting operation to take place instantaneously (at least, for those who are TV-fluent), so that the particularity of the programme can become intelligible. These meaning-routines occupy a similar position in the institution of broadcast TV to that of the narrative image in cinema, described in Chapter 2. But there is no direct equivalence, as has been discovered by the numerous studies which have tried to transfer the diffuse generic concept of 'melodrama' in cinema to the very different systems of recognition used by broadcast TV. The narrative image of a film serves to summarise its difference-in-familiarity, its distinctive place and appeal within a known institution. Meaning-routines in broadcast TV do not. Rather, they aim entirely and only to establish the ground of familiarity from which the individual programme will depart.

This explains the immense public outcry on the issue of 'repeats', the 'second chance to see', which is the first resort of the broadcaster strapped for cash. Broadcast TV operates a sharp distinction between its routines (its patterns of repetition) and the individual executions of those routines (its programmes). To see, week after week, a successful situation comedy like *Birds of a Feather* running its same situation through another variation is perceived as substantially different from seeing again an individual episode as a 'repeat'. From outside the viewership of broadcast TV, there might seem to be a fine distinction between the two activities. From outside, the similarities of format and underlying meaning-routines seem to overwhelm the distinctiveness of each episode; from inside, it is the reverse.

This is how broadcast TV keeps at bay the nostalgia which is so prevalent in the photo effect of cinema. Old television remains old television; old movies become classics. Very rarely does a television series achieve the status of a *Hancock's Half Hour* or a *Fawlty Towers*, whose formats retain an appeal despite their age; despite having been seen 'before'; despite the shifts in underlying meaning-routines which have taken place since their initial broadcasts. More often an old series becomes an *I Love Lucy*: a mild distraction, a curiosity from another age, subject to the vagaries of camp and cult. These rely exactly on the perceived inappropriateness of their object to the critical attention and adulation which is heaped upon them.

So precise are the meaning-routines of broadcast TV that the slightest departure from them, or deliberate muddling of them, can, if supported by a sufficient advertising and public relations effort, make itself appear a startling innovation. So something as mundane as David Lynch and Mark Frost's series *Twin Peaks* can be hailed by serious critics as 'post-modernist television'.

In reality, there was little that was new in *Twin Peaks*. It simply took the soap's habitual lack of narrative closure and applied it to a murder mystery narrative and so produced a shaggy-dog story. It then mixed in a few running gags and tag lines ('damn fine cup of coffee'), the staple of every successful long-running comedy. These make the series 'archly knowing', giving the impression that someone somewhere was 'being had' by the whole confection and taking it seriously. Of course this made it necessary to indicate that the joke was at the expense only of the 'unsophisticated viewers', and not of the entire audience, which is the basic principle of the shaggy-dog story. So it mixed in a generous dollop of metaphysical mystification, but in an intentionally surreal form, marking it out from the 'mundane' metaphysical carryings-on which are another staple characteristic of the TV soap. This careful combination of very familiar televisual elements is then cemented by the vaguely cinematic feel that comes with a high budget and leisurely cutting style. This last element has long been used to pick out 'TV with cultural value' from 'the rest'.

In other words *Twin Peaks* was scarcely novel: it was snob TV. It used pieces of existing TV genres to try to convey the impression that the TV audience divides along traditional lines of material and educational privilege into the culturally sophisticated and the culturally naive. If anything, the lines of division between the sophisticated readers of TV and the naive ones are more or less the opposite. You only have to hear the average parliamentary debate about TV or a lecturer in literature's views to realise that. Of course, this is not the same as saying that certain kinds of programme, or certain series, are of interest to different segments of society. It is a question of fluency in TV and consequent pleasure in it.

Perhaps the initial reception of *Twin Peaks* was really an indication of the lack of analytic resources behind the term 'post-modernism'. But equally, the notion of the TV viewer as far as it is developed in Chapter 14 of this book would provide an inadequate means of analysis.

The problem of how to experiment successfully within broadcast TV can only be addressed with a more differentiated conception of the ways in which broadcast TV attempts to deal with the vagaries of its viewership. I met the problem in my own early experiences as a producer of TV programmes. Making a series on a 'new' subject for a new channel in a new way without the benefit of a fixed slot proved, in retrospect, to be one or two innovations too many.

The series, *Visions*, ran for a total of 32 editions on Channel 4 between November 1982 and November 1985. Its brief was to cover non-Hollywood cinema (largely unfamiliar to a UK television audience at that time) using a fresh approach. The series had no on-screen presenter, nor had it a standard narrating voice. Some programmes consisted of a standard documentary *tour d'horizon* of a national cinema (e.g. China, Brazil) or a film festival report (Cannes, Ouagadougou); others were magazines containing contrasting items such as long review of a single film, like *The Company of Wolves* or *Tootsie*, plus a meditative essay by a film-maker like Chantal Akerman or Raul Ruiz. It was often very good, if reviews, festival screenings and sales of programmes abroad are anything to go by. But the series made a virtue of instability; it refused to be pinned down; it refused to make many presentational concessions to its potential viewers.

The *Visions* approach might have been able to establish itself as a 'format', given its assumed audience and the familiarity of its ostensible subject, 'cinema'. But we wilfully ignored the problem of finding viewers. The series dodged around the schedules (which were naturally not under our control) so that only five programmes in all ever had the same starting time on the same day of the week. We should have seen this level of unfamiliarity as one of the determinants of what we were able to do. Unfortunately for the long-term viability of the series, the only familiar thing about *Visions* turned out to be its constant, all-round unfamiliarity.

Worse, all of this took place within the blizzard of novelty that characterised the launch of Channel 4 in Britain: the same blizzard that attends the launch of any new channel, whether or not it sets out, as Channel 4 did, to be consciously new and different. For part of the familiarity of broadcast TV lies in its regularity, the predictability of its schedules. A new station, by definition, lacks any public knowledge of the overall pattern of its schedules, even the points within those schedules that it intends to become familiar. *Channel 4 News* or the peak-hour soap *Brookside* are now accepted parts of the broadcasting landscape in Britain. But they were, to begin with, just as unfamiliar as *Visions*.

Scheduling position, and the marketing effort which comes in its wake, therefore, also contributes to the definition of the meaning of a programme, to the establishment of its generic and specific meaning-routines, and so to the mutual expectations that viewer, programme and programme-maker all have of each other. But what happens when the television consumer is faced by a dazzling multiplicity of channels? The run of *Visions* had ended by the time that Britain experienced the promise of an 'explosion of TV channels'. This took place substantially later than the USA, Scandinavia, France, the Netherlands (the list is long). Neither has it taken place to the same extent. There are many probable causes, ranging from the very high domestic penetration of video cassette recorders (over half British households); the infamous decision of the British government not to invest in developing a cable infrastructure, unlike most other European nations; the problems of launching satellite-to-dish broadcasting in the depths of the recession of 1989–92; the tradition, dating from the mass introduction of televisions in the latter part of the 1950s, to rent TV equipment rather than to make capital purchase; even the physical nature of British cities and home ownership.

Multiple channel television has usually gone in two directions, both of which are complementary to the major national freely available network channels. One is to produce, often with meagre budgets, programming which addresses segments of the market rather than the whole market. This is particularly valuable in situations of cultural diversity; and it would be more so if the potential audience were not so often 'at the bottom of the heap', with little money over to pay subscriptions for TV services or to make them attractive to corporate advertising. Nevertheless minority channels of various kinds, from ranting preachers to culture-vultures, from Hispanics to sex-therapists, now provide American TV viewers with a number of standing examples of questions and voices, different fluencies in TV, other tastes and lives that are often conveniently ignored. This in no way prevents them from being written off or considered marginal by more powerful forces in television, of course, but it makes such a writing-off a wilful act rather than a casual omission.

In the richer parts of the multiple channel environment, three areas of complementarity have been discovered. One is to broadcast, live and in full, sports and suchlike events whose duration alone makes them problematic for networks which depend upon a continuous spread of diversity to underpin the universality of their appeal. Lucrative and powerful new channels have emerged from this simple philosophy of providing a constant output of one kind of programming: Ted Turner's CNN (Cable News Network) is a good example. Sometimes these services require some kind of payment from the viewer, usually subscription, rather than relying on advertising revenue. Such premium financing is crucial to the other mainstay of complementary programming, the film channels.

Cinema films have long had a pattern of declining price of admission, depending upon the time elapsed from their first release. Television extended this, by adding the TV showing as a final full-stop, because it involved no direct viewer payment. Home video introduced a further refinement (small-screen and domestic versus large screen and public), which in turn produced both a distinction between films on video for rental only and 'sell-through' (where the tape is 'yours to keep'), and a new outlet for B-movies, replacing the drive-in with the stay-in. Subscription broadcasting adds another level. It provides a superior form of broadcasting to the networks, not only by showing the film before its first network broadcast, but also by enhancing that showing. So in the USA, subscription movie channels show films with fewer or no commercial interruptions. In France, Canal Plus had to define itself against networks showing films without breaks, so it moved towards abolishing the tyranny of the TV schedule. However much the schedule may underpin the universality and multiplicity of the broadcast networks, it does imply the message that 'you watch it when we want you to watch it'. Canal Plus' alternative is simply to show each month's menu of films several times at radically different hours of the day and night, so that accessibility and convenience for the viewer is much increased.

Such a strategy does not work to the same degree with television programmes, whose use of routines of intelligibility would seem to rule out repeats. But television in the USA (especially) has found a way of re-using TV programmes successfully: by intensifying their routines. The syndication of long series which have already been shown on the networks is now crucial to the economy of American TV, as most

high-cost entertainment series from soaps to comedies are
no longer paid for entirely by the price paid by the networks.
If (and that is a big 'if', given the number of cancelled series)
a show is successful on the network, it can then begin to make
up its deficit and earn profits in syndication – repeat showings
on local stations, usually not in prime-time. But the syndicated
show nowadays is habitually 'stripped', shown every weekday at the same time. This makes the show even more routine
than it was on its once-a-week network airing, intensifying
the intimacy and directness of the relationship between
viewer and narration.

Even in markets more sophisticated than Britain, a stable
system of different levels within the television market
(comparable to the stages through which a cinema film
can pass) has barely been established. Yet, given the multiplication of channels, such an arrangement into tiers is vital,
offering distinct kinds of service, some specialist, some universalist, some based on first use, others on subsequent use.

The multiplication of channels in Britain has so far produced
only marginal changes in the nature of broadcast TV,
in the very precise sense that the margins are not as tightly
drawn as they were ten years ago. The wild and the wonderful
sometimes gets broadcast, and even funded, simply to satisfy
the TV systems' hunger of something to show. Old programmes are repeated; films from non-Hollywood sources are
shown; subtitling has at last become acceptable to a viable
British TV audience. Such things are not only the result of the
conscious policy of diversity espoused – and sometimes put
into practice – by Channel 4. They are also the side effect of
the expansion of broadcast hours into the all-night ITV
service; of experiments aimed at finding ways of diversifying
and segmenting the TV audience to find commercially viable
markets; and of the tentative search for novelty that even TV
must engage in as it has to constantly refresh its routines.

All of this has, unfortunately, hastened the decline of the
attempts to create alternative forms which I sketched out in
Chapter 16. Excellent films have continued to be produced,
most notably from black film-makers, like The Black Audio
Film Collective's *Handsworth Songs* and Sankofa's *Dreaming
Rivers* and *Young Soul Rebels*. But gone is the attempt to

widen from a more collective approach to film-making into the construction of alternative ways of distributing and viewing. Many factors contributed, of course, besides the decline in public funding for, and the emphasis on market viability of, the arts, which was so much a feature of the Thatcher era. There has also been the dramatic spread of home video, which, in Britain, can now be found in about half of the nation's households. However, many of the films and several of the film-makers I mentioned in this chapter have made an accommodation with the television system, and the rise of home video has also enabled the development of experimental video work. But I have no intention of removing my account in Chapter 16. It is in the nature of 'alternative' developments that they are quickly forgotten, and their history and experience is lost. Some British experimental video has set about reinventing wheels forged long ago by the independent film movement (most, on the other hand, has found new directions). Remembering is not entirely a matter of regret and loss: it is, like the photo effect, a matter of presence and absence indissolubly linked.

As for the fundamental changes in broadcast TV, in Britain and elsewhere, they are still to come. A TV broadcast is still an important event, especially on a national network. All nation-states with more than two or three channels have moved beyond the stage where any programme could assume that the 'whole nation is watching'. Brazil is perhaps the last bastion of such a feeling, where TV Globo's novellas can, on rare but symptomatic occasions, command a 100 per cent rating. Each act of broadcasting has become just slightly less important than it was. Marketing of TV programmes to their audience has become a standard feature during the last decade, from paid-for advertising to the more effective, but less controllable, symbiotic relationship between TV press departments and the TV pages of the popular press.

Broadcast TV retains a special place within the social discourse of the nation. Its role is precisely that of broadcasting: it takes ideas which have already become current, or even a little outmoded, in specific areas, and shouts them out to all and sundry. This activity, essentially that of a megaphone, may sometimes offend those whose attention is attracted who then discover something that they would rather not know about. Broadcast TV is a gatekeeper. It has an intellectual and emotional importance in society because it admits ideas and individuals, whether in dramatic scenarios or in factual programming, into the general social discourse of the nation. Such a role tends to give an over-inflated sense of importance to many people who 'work in TV', as anyone who has been contacted by a TV researcher soon realises.

It also defines broadcast TV as we know it as a stubbornly social medium, bound by the rules of good behaviour, just as much as by demographics of audience size and composition. The corporate and cultural existence of broadcast TV is defined by social norms and values. Its calculations are those of what will be acceptable, just as much as of what will be intelligible. But there is a subtle difference between the two. Intelligibility is left to take care of itself within the TV system; acceptability is policed by the state and/or its delegates. For there is a significant difference between the routines of intelligibility and that which is socially acceptable. TV's meaning-routines can be applied to any issue, even those that do not have an easy acceptance. Questions of sexuality are the most obvious area. Even well into the era of AIDS, the British regulatory authorities at the Independent Television Commission do not deem British TV a suitable medium for the advertising of condoms. Such advertising appears freely on the more regulated TV screens of Scandinavia.

Whatever may be the social constraints still laid upon broadcasting, cinema positively rejoices in its role as the playground for the mad and the marginal, whoever they might be. It has triumphantly discovered a distinct role as the vehicle of wish-fulfillment, whether cheerfully (as with Steven Spielberg), or more darkly, as in the intricate forms of dismemberment favoured by the horror genre.

The Spielberg school of phantasy films is a pure expression of the American way in film-making. Since *Jaws* in 1975, he has put his name to a string of films which embody a particularly naked form of wish-fulfillment. *E.T.*: the child of divorced parents finds a playmate who is both naive and endowed with supernatural powers, and engineers his resurrection; *Back to the Future*: an adolescent can at last realise his incestuous desires towards his mother by literally remaking his father; *Gremlins*: the untrammelled expression of the instant gratification of desire. Many such films carry Spielberg's name as executive producer as he has preferred to direct more complex and displaced visions of childhood and its problems, most notably in *The Empire of the Sun*.

Though television joyfully shows these films, they are not projects that television would realise itself. They deal with wish-fulfillment in all its asocial, if not anti-social, complexity. And in each case the films work because at their heart is a disturbed family unit. The conflict of desire within the family, in which the child is more or less powerless, literally produces the wish-fulfillment phantasy solution which then takes over the film. These disturbed families, often with an absent or ineffective father, are of a kind that television finds peculiarly difficult to realise outside of those instantly recognisable 'places for the problems': the social documentary, the serious drama, the soap opera.

The sharp distinction which I drew in this book between cinema and television still holds. The real revolution for television has not yet happened, despite the large-scale changes that have taken place during the 1980s. We have the signs of a revolution to come, rather than the revolution itself. The widespread use of VHS home video has encouraged a greater sophistication in viewing habits, both in choice of material and in the ability to review segments, to skip segments, giving a far greater sense of control over the screened image than was imaginable twenty years ago. The availability of more broadcast channels has also increased choice, but not in the way that investors and broadcasters intended. The overwhelming evidence is that, faced with greater choice, the potential audience exercises greater selectivity and ends up viewing less than they did before. Gradually, broadcast television is losing its peculiar position in the national culture.

Television is busy making itself less important. This is the likely outcome of the revolution in broadcasting which is now unfolding. Once the act of broadcasting becomes more mundane, it will be freer to encompass more, and will be less limited both by the demands of instant intelligibility and by those of the socially acceptable. But there is a trade-off here: television will be less noticed. Not only will the ability to address and perhaps influence the social intercourse of the nation be lost, but with it the claim, by whatever mechanism, on the social funds of the nation. Some few universalist channels will probably continue to exist, of course, especially if a tiered market can be created. But the scale and scope of broadcasting in different markets is almost impossible to predict.

Two things are certain, however: both cinema and television will continue to fail to learn from their own and each other's histories; and, as with all revolutions, the outcome may change rather less than was expected either by participants or by observers.

Films and programmes cited

Even this list is an activity of definition: it involves designating material as either filmic or televisual, a problem for programmes made for broadcast that eventually saw the light of projection in cinema. Such examples are listed, arbitrarily, as cinema films. This list also raises the problem of the best method of designation of broadcast TV series, for which a variety of solutions has been adopted.

Cinema films

Adieu Philippine (1962), d. Jacques Rozier, p. Unitec/Alpha Productions/ Parisfilm, France/Italy.

Alien (1979), d. Ridley Scott, p. Twentieth Century-Fox, GB.

All Quiet on the Western Front (1930), d. Lewis Milestone, p. Universal, USA.

All That Heaven Allows (1955), d. Douglas Sirk, p. Universal-International, USA.

All the President's Men (1976), d. Alan J. Pakula, p. Wildwood Enterprises, USA.

Apocalypse Now (1979), d. Francis Ford Coppola, p. Omni-Zoetrope, USA.

At the Fountainhead (of German Strength) (1980), d. Anthea Kennedy, Nicholas Burton, p. British Film Institute, GB.

Babylon (1980), d. Franco Rosso, p. Diversity Music Productions, GB.

Bad Timing (1980), d. Nicholas Roeg, p. Rank Organisation, GB'

Big Red One, The (1980), d. Samuel Fuller, p. Lorimar Productions, USA.

Big Sleep, The (1946), d. Howard Hawks, p. Warner Bros, USA.

Blacks Britannica (1978), d. David Koff, p. WGBH Educational Foundation, Boston, USA.

Blind Spot (Reise Nach Lyon) (1980), d. Claudia Alemann, p. Alemann

Film Production, W. Germany.

Blue Angel, The (Die Blaue Engel) (1930), d. Josef von Sternberg, p. UFA/Paramount, Germany.

Bonnie and Clyde (1967), d. Arthur Penn, p. Tatira-Hiller Productions, USA.

Bride Wore Red, The (1937), d. Dorothy Arzner, p. MGM, USA.

Carabiniers, Les (1963), d. Jean-Luc Godard, p. Rome-Paris Film/ Laetitia, France/Italy.

Casablanca (1942), d. Michael Curtiz, p. Warner Bros, USA.

Caught (1948), d. Max Ophuls, p. MGM, USA.

Chagrin et la Pitié, Le (1970), d. Marcel Ophuls, p. Norddeutsche Rundfunk/Société Suisse de Radiodiffusion, W. Germany/ Switzerland.

Charley Varrick (1973), d. Don Siegel, p. Universal, USA.

Chicken Is Not An Egg, A (1975), d./p. Newsreel Collective, GB.

China Syndrome, The (1978), d. James Bridges, p. IPC Films, USA.

Cleopatra (1963), d. Joseph Mankiewicz, p. Twentieth Century-Fox, USA/Italy.

Clockwork Orange, A (1971), d. Stanley Kubrick, p. Warner Bros/ Polaris, GB.

Close Encounters of the Third Kind (1977), d. Steven Spielberg, p. Columbia, USA.

Cobweb, The (1955), d. Vincente Minnelli, p. MGM, USA.

Coming Home (1978), d. Hal Ashby, p. Jerome Hellman Productions, USA.

Divide and Rule — Never! (1978), d./p. Newsreel Collective, GB.

Don't Look Now (1973), d. Nicholas Roeg, p. Casey Productions/ Eldorado Films, GB/Italy.

Duel (1971), d. Steven Spielberg, p. Paramount, USA.

Emmanuelle (1974), d. Just Jaecken, p. Trinaca Films/Orphée Productions, France.

Errand Boy, The (1961), d./p. Jerry Lewis, USA.

Escape From New York (1981), d. John Carpenter, p. Avco Embassy, USA.

Expresso Bongo (1959), d. Val Guest, p. Conquest Productions, GB.

Film From the Clyde (1977), d./p. Cinema Action, GB.

Flamingo Road (1941), d. Michael Curtiz, p. Warner Bros, USA.

Four Seasons, The (1981), d. Alan Alda, p. Bregman/Universal, USA.

From the Life of Marionettes (Aus dem Leben der Marionetten) (1980), d. Ingmar Bergman, p. Personafilm/Bayerische Staatsschauspeil, W. Germany.

Front Page, The (1931), d. Lewis Milestone, p. United Artists, USA.

Ghost and Mrs Muir, The (1947), d. Joseph Mankiewicz, p. Twentieth Century-Fox, USA.

Gone with the Wind (1939), d. Victor Fleming, p. David O. Selznick, USA.

Go Tell the Spartans (1978), d. Ted Post, p. Spartan Productions/ Mar Vista Productions, USA.

Guess Who's Coming to Dinner? (1967), d./p. Stanley Kramer, USA.

Harder They Come, The (1972), d. Perry Henzell, p. International Films, Jamaica.

His Girl Friday (1939), d. Howard Hawks, p. Columbia, USA.

Hollywood Canteen (1944), d. Delner Daves, p. Warner Bros, USA.

I Am a Fugitive from a Chain Gang (From the Chain Gang) (I'm a Fugitive) (1932), d. Mervyn LeRoy, p. Warner Bros, USA.

Industrial Britain (1979), d. Roger Buck, p. Northern Arts Association, GB.

James Whiter Than White Show, The (1975), d. Jeff Perks, p. National Film School, GB.

Jaws (1975), d. Steven Spielberg, p. Zanuck/Brown, USA.

Jeanne Dielmann, 23 Quai du Commerce, 1080 Bruxelles (1975), d. Chantal Akermann, p. Paradis Films /Unité Trois/Ministère de la Culture Française de Belgique, Belgium/France.

Jobs for the Girls (1979), d./p. Sheffield Film Co-operative, GB.

Killing of a Chinese Bookie (1976), d. John Cassavetes, p. Faces Distribution Corp., USA.

Klute (1971), d. Alan J. Pakula, p. Pakula/Warners, USA.

Kramer vs. Kramer (1979), d. Robert Benton, p. Columbia, USA.

Kuhle Wampe (1931), d. Slatan Th. Dudow, p. Praesens-Film, Germany.

Leo the Last (1969), d. John Boorman, p. Chartoff/Winkler, GB.

Letter from an Unknown Woman (1948), d. Max Ophuls, p. Ramparts Productions, USA.

Light Reading (1979), d./p. Lis Rhodes, GB.

Lolita (1961), d. Stanley Kubrick, p. Seven Arts/Transworld, GB.

Long Goodbye, The (1973), d. Robert Altman, p. Lion's Gate, USA.

McCabe and Mrs Miller (1971), d. Robert Altman, p. Warner Bros, USA.

Mädchen in Uniform (1931), d. Leontine Sagan, p. Deutsche-Film Gmbg, Germany.

M*A*S*H (1969), d. Robert Altman, p. Twentieth Century-Fox, USA.

Matter of Life and Death, A (1946), d. Michael Powell/Emeric Pressburger, p. General Film Distributors, GB.

Mean Streets (1973), d. Martin Scorsese, p. Jonathan T. Taplin Productions, USA.

Meet Me in St Louis (1944), d. Vincente Minnelli, p. MGM, USA.

Meet Mr Lucifer (1953), d. Anthony Pelissier, p. Ealing Studios, GB.

Mildred Pierce (1944), d. Michael Curtiz, p. Warner Bros, USA.

Millions Like Us (1943), d. Frank Launder/Sidney Gilliat, p. Gainsborough, GB.

Morocco (1930), d. Josef von Sternberg, p. Paramount, USA.

Mystery of the Wax Museum (1933), d. Michael Curtiz, p. Warner Bros, USA.

Ned Kelly (1970), d. Tony Richardson, p. Woodfall, GB.

News and Comment (1978), d. Frank Abbott, p. East Midlands Arts Association, GB.

Nighthawks (1978), d. Ron Peck/Paul Hallam, p. Four Corners/ Nashburg, GB.

Only Angels Have Wings (1939), d. Howard Hawks, p. Columbia, USA.

Ordinary People (1980), d. Robert Redford, p. Paramount/Wildwood Enterprises, USA.

Passionate Friends (1922), d. Maurice Elvey, p. Stoll Film Co., GB.

Passionate Friends (1948), d. David Lean, p. General Film Distributors, GB.

Petrified Forest, The (1936), d. Archie Mayo, p. Warner Bros, USA.

Play It Again, Sam (1972), d. Herbert Ross, p. Paramount, USA.

Postman Always Rings Twice, The (1946), d. Tay Garnett, p. MGM, USA.

Postman Always Rings Twice, The (1981), d. Bob Rafelson, p. Lorimar, USA.

Pressure (1975), d. Horace Ové, p. British Film Institute, GB.

Private Life of Henry VIII (1933), d. Alexander Korda, p. London Films, GB.

Psycho (1960), d. Alfred Hitchcock, p. Paramount, USA.

Raiders of the Lost Ark (1981), d. Steven Spielberg, p. Lucasfilm, USA.

Rapunzel, Let Down Your Hair (1976), d. Susan Shapiro/Esther Ronay/Francine Winham, p. British Film Institute, GB.

Règle du Jeu, La (1939), d. Jean Renoir, p. Nouvelles Editions Françaises, France.

Riddles of the Sphinx (1977), d. Laura Mulvey/Peter Wollen, p. British Film Institute, GB.

Rififi (Du Rififi chez les Hommes) (1954), d. Jules Dassin, p. Pathé, France.

Saturday Night Fever (1977), d. John Badham, p. Paramount, USA.

Serve and Obey (1973), d./p. Linda Dove, GB.

Sing As We Go (1934), d. Basil Dean, p. Associated Talking Pictures, GB.

Song of the Shirt (1979), d./p. Film and History Project, GB.

So That You Can Live (1981), d. Cinema Action, p. Cinema Action/ British Film Institute, GB.

Souffle au Coeur, La (1971), d. Louis Malle, p. NEF/Fides/Franz Seitz, France/Italy/W. Germany.

Spione, Die (1928), d. Fritz Lang, p. LangFilm Gmbg, Germany.

Stagecoach (1939), d. John Ford, p. Walter Wanger, USA.
Stagecoach (1966), d. Gordon Douglas, p. Twentieth Century-Fox, USA.
Star Wars (1977), d. George Lucas, p. Twentieth Century-Fox, USA/ GB.
Suspicion (1941), d. Alfred Hitchcock, p. RKO, USA.
Taking a Part (1979), d./p. Jan Worth, GB.
Time to Love And a Time to Die, A (1958), d. Douglas Sirk, p. Universal, USA.
Toni (1934), d. Jean Renoir, p. Les Films d'Aujourd'hui, France.
Twilight's Last Gleaming (1977), d. Robert Aldrich, p. Lorimar/ Bavaria, W. Germany.
Tyneside Story, The (1944), d. Gilbert Gunn, p. Spectator Short Films, GB.
Victorian Lady in her Boudoir, A (1896/7), d.? Esme Collings, GB.
War Game, The (1965), d. Peter Watkins, p. BBC, GB.
Went the Day Well? (1942), d. Alberto Cavalcanti, p. Ealing Studios, GB.
Whatever Happened to Baby Jane? (1962), d. Robert Aldrich, p. Associates and Aldrich Productions, USA.
World of Suzie Wong, The (1960), d. Richard Quine, p. World Enterprises/World Film Ltd, GB.
Written on the Wind (1956), d. Douglas Sirk, p. Universal International, USA.
Young Girl in Blue, The (1978), d./p. Penny Webb, GB.

Broadcast TV productions

Agony (1979-81), several series, 26 minues ea, d./p. John Reardon, London Weekend TV, GB.
All in the Family (1971-9), many series, 25 minutes ea, p. Norman Lear, Bud Yorkin, Tandem, USA.
Blaise Pascal (1971), 1 x 131 mins, d. Roberto Rossellini, RAI-TV, Italy.
Borgias, The (1981), 6 x 55 mins, p. Mark Shivas, BBC/Time-Life/ Channel 7, Australia.
Bouquet of Barbed Wire, A (1976), 7 x 54 mins, d. Tony Wharmby, London Weekend TV, GB.
Brothers, The (1975-7), many x 50 mins, BBC, GB.
Charlie's Angels (1976-), many series, 54 mins ea, Spelling-Goldberg Productions, USA.
Chinese Detective (1981), 6 x 50 mins, p. Terence Williams, BBC, GB.
Coronation Street (1960-), 26 mins twice weekly, Granada TV, GB.

Crossroads (1965-   ), 25 mins twice to four times weekly, ATV then Central TV, GB.

Dallas (1980-   ), 50 mins ea, p. Lee Rich/Philip Caprice/Leonard Katzman, Lorimar, USA.

Days of Hope (1975), 4 x 90 mins, d. Ken Loach, p. Tony Garnett, BBC, GB.

Edward and Mrs Simpson (1978), 7 x 54 mins, d. Waris Hussein, Thames TV, GB.

Elizabeth R (1970), 6 x 90 mins, p. Roderick Graham, BBC, GB.

Empire Road (1976), 10 x 30 mins, p. Peter Ansorge, BBC, GB.

Father Dear Father (1971-7), several series, 26 mins ea, Thames TV, GB.

Flamingo Road (1980-1), 50 mins ea, p. Edward H. Feldman/Rita Latkin, MF/Lorimar, USA.

Forsyte Saga, The (1966-7), 26 x 50 mins, p. Donald Wilson, BBC, GB.

Gentle Touch, The (1980-   ), several series, p. Tony Wharmby, London Weekend TV, GB.

George and Mildred (1976-9), several series, 26 mins ea, d./p. Peter Fraser-Jones, Thames TV, GB.

Ghost and Mrs Muir, The (n.d.), p. Gene Reynolds, TCF, USA.

Hawaii Five-O (1978-   ), several series, 54 mins ea, Leonard Freeman Productions, USA.

Hill Street Blues (1980-   ), 54 mins ea, p. Steven Bocho/Michael Kozall/Greg Hoblit, MTM Productions, USA.

Kleine Fernsehspiel, Das, weekly, Wednesday 10pm, Zweites Deutsches Fernsehen, W. Germany.

Life on Earth (1978), 8 x 55 mins, p. Christopher Parsons, BBC.

London Programme, The (1978-   ), 40-60 mins, Fridays about 11.00 p.m., London Weekend TV, GB.

Man About the House (1975-6), several series, 26 mins ea, d./p. Peter Fraser-Jones, Thames TV, GB.

M*A*S*H (1972-   ), many series, 50 mins ea then 25 mins, created by Larry Gelbart/Gene Reynolds, Twentieth Century-Fox TV, USA.

Nationwide (1969-   ), 30-45 mins, weekdays about 5.55 p.m., BBC, GB.

Newsnight BBC2, weekdays, starting 10.30-11.00 p.m., 30 mins.

Omnibus (1972-81), weekly, 50 mins, BBC2.

Panorama (1959-   ), 56 mins ea, Mondays 8 p.m., BBC, GB.

Poldark (1975-6), 15 x 50 mins, p. Morris Barry, BBC/London Films, GB.

Prisoner, The (1967), 6 x 47 mins, p. David Tomblin, Everyman Films, GB.

Rising Damp (1975-8), several series, 26 mins ea, p. Ronnie Baxter, Yorkshire TV, GB.

Rockford Files, The (1974-81), several series, 50 mins ea, p. Meta Rosenberg, Universal TV, USA.

Roots (1973), 12 x 55 mins, Wolper Organisation, USA.

Second Chance (1980), 6 x 60 mins, d. Gerry Mill/Richard Handford, Yorkshire TV, GB.

Six Wives of Henry VIII, The (1971), 6 x 90 mins, created by Maurice Cowan, BBC, GB.

Soap (1979-82), 30 mins ea, p. P.J. Witt/Tony Thomas/Susan Harris, USA.

Starsky and Hutch (1975-9), several series, 50 mins ea, Spelling-Goldberg Productions, USA.

Steptoe and Son (1962-73), many series, 30 mins ea, BBC, GB.

Sweeney, The (1976-9), many series, 56 mins ea, Euston Films, GB.

Telford's Change (1978), 10 x 75 mins, d. Barry Davis, BBC/ Astramead, GB.

That's Life (1974-81), 45 mins, Sundays 9.45 p.m., BBC, GB.

Till Death Us Do Part (1966-74), many series, 30 mins ea, BBC, GB. (revived as *Till Death . . .* (1981), one series, 26 mins, ATV/ Clarityscene Productions, GB.

TV Eye (1978-   ), 26 mins ea, Thames TV, GB.

What the Papers Say, weekly, 10 mins, around midnight, Granada TV.

World in Action (1963-   ), 26 mins ea, Mondays 8.30 pm, Granada TV, GB.

Your Life in Their Hands (1960-   ), many series, BBC, GB.

Z-Cars (1962-7), many series, variously 50 mins and 2 x 24 mins, (1967-71), BBC, GB.

Select bibliography

1 Preliminaries

Clive James's selected TV criticism can be found in *Visions Before Midnight* (Picador, London). Cinema semiotics in English has been developed principally in *Screen* and *Screen Education* magazines: a useful compilation of the initial work is *Screen Reader 2* (Society for Education in Film and Television, London).

Realism
A basic set of textual extracts is *Realism and the Cinema*, ed. Christopher Williams (Routledge & Kegan Paul, London). The argument presented here is based particularly on Roman Jakobson's essay 'On Realism in Art' (1921) in *Readings in Russian Poetics* (MIT Press, Cambridge, Mass.), written into cinematic terms by Paul Willemen 'On Realism in Cinema' in *Screen Reader 1* (Society for Education in Film and Television, London). The notion of 'motivation' is developed by Gerard Genette's 'Vraisemblance et motivation' in *Figures II* (Seuil, Paris). Most of Bazin's writing is collected in *What is Cinema?* (2 vols, University of California Press). The BFI Dossier no. 8 (ed. Don Ranvaud) is a valuable source of additional material on Rossellini.

Technology
The classic series of texts on this question is Jean-Louis Comolli's series of essays 'Technique et ideologie' in *Cahiers du Cinema* nos. 229-33 (1971-2). Useful writing on colour can be found in the American journal *Film Reader* nos. 2 and 4. Raymond Fielding's collection of original texts from the *Journal of the Society of Motion Picture and TV Engineers* (*A Technological History of Motion Pictures and TV*) (University of California Press), contains Herbert Kalmus's history of Technicolor on which most other accounts are based. A basic rather undependable book on *Four Aspects of the Film* (including colour and

widescreen processes) is by James L. Limbacher, (Brussel & Brussel).

Effects

The debate about the notion of ideology is too widespread nowadays to be easily referenced. The notion of 'reproduction' is put forward by Louis Althusser in 'Ideology and Ideological State Apparatuses' in *Lenin and Philosophy* (New Left Books, London), criticised from wildly different positions by Paul Q. Hirst's 'Althusser and the Theory of Ideology' (*Economy and Society* vol. 5, no. 4, 1976) and Terry Lovell's *Pictures of Reality* (British Film Institute, London). *Days of Hope* is criticised and defended respectively by Colin MacCabe and Colin MacArthur in *Screen*, Winter 1975-6 and Spring 1976 (vols 16, no. 4 and 17, no. 1). The passage about film, TV and history comes from my review of the film *At the Fountainhead* (*Screen* vol. 21, no. 4).

2 Cinema as cultural event

Writing about film exhibition is scattered in reminiscences and various articles in academic journals. Notable are Douglas Gomery's 'The Picture Palace' in *Quarterly Review of Film Studies*, Winter 1978 (USA), and some of the essays in Tino Balio's collection *The American Film Industry* (University of Wisconsin Press). The notion of 'narrative image' has been developed by Stephen Heath, particularly in his 'Film Performance' (*Cinetracts 2*, Summer 1977, Canada). There are numerous accounts of Disney's grasp of cinematic marketing; notable, perhaps, is Richard Schickel's *The Disney Version* (Simon & Schuster/ Avon Books, New York). Charles Eckert offers a succinct account of marketing in classic Hollywood in 'The Carole Lombard in Macy's Window' (*Quarterly Review of Film Studies*, Winter 1978). Mae D. Huettig's *The Economic Control of the Motion Picture Industry* (Philadelphia, 1944) still remains basic to an understanding of classic Hollywood, despite its age.

3 Cinema as image and sound

A basic introduction to some of the questions raised in this and the next chapter is *Film Art* by David Brodwell and Kristin Thompson (Addison Wesley, Reading, Mass.). Christian Metz's psychoanalytic work on cinema and identification is translated in *Psychoanalysis and Cinema* (Macmillan, London). Freud's concept of 'narcissism' is developed in 'On Narcissism: an Introduction' (*Standard Edition*, vol. 14); that of fetishism in 'Fetishism' (*Standard Edition*, vol. 21); also directly relevant are 'Creative Writers and Daydreaming'.(*Standard Edition*, vol. 9) and 'The Family Romance' (*Standard Edition*, vol. 9). Lacan's writings on the look are found in 'The Mirror Phase' (*Écrits*, Tavistock, London) and chs 6-9 of *Four Fundamental Concepts of Psychoanalysis* (Penguin, Harmondsworth). The debate is extended into cinema by Laura Mulvey's 'Visual Pleasure and Narrative Cinema' (*Screen*, Autumn 1975, vol. 16, no. 3), which has led to a series of developments including E. Ann Kaplan's collection *Women in Film Noir* (British Film Institute, London), and my 'On Pornography' (*Screen*, Spring 1980, vol. 21, no. 1). The notion of the 'photograph effect' is developed by Roland Barthes in his last book, translated as *Camera Lucida — Reflections on Photography* (Cape, London).

4 Cinema narration

The narrative analysis presented here draws upon the Russian Formalist and semiotic traditions. Victor Erlich's guide to the Formalists is still the best: *Russian Formalism: History, Doctrine* (Mouton, The Hague). *Screen Reader 1* (Society for Education in Film and Television, London) reprints a series of Formalist writing on film; Lee T. Lemon and Marion J. Reis have collected *Russian Formalist Criticism: Four Essays* (University of Nebraska Press). Steve Neale's *Genre* (British Film Institute, London) presents a useful, if dense, summary of a series of semiotic arguments about narration. Stephen Heath's analysis of Welles's *Touch of Evil* remains a central practical example: 'Film and System, Terms of Analysis' (*Screen*, Spring and Summer 1975, vol. 16 nos. 1 and 2). This in turn owes much to Barthes's analysis of a short story in *S/Z* (Cape, London), glossed in Rosalind Coward and John Ellis, *Language and Materialism* (Routledge & Kegan Paul, London). The notions of historic and discursive narration are explained and referenced in Seymour Chatman's *Story and Discourse* (Cornell, USA). The conception of repetition and innovation was first suggested by Klaus Wyborny in his 'Random Notes on the Conventional Narrative Film' translated in *Afterimage* (GB) no. 8/9, Spring 1981. Raymond Bellour analyses a specific sequence of *The Big Sleep* in relation to the classic Hollywood narrational style in 'The Obvious and the Code' (*Screen*, Winter 1974/5, vol. 15, no. 4). Colin MacCabe proposes the model of 'the classic realist text' in 'Realism and the Cinema-Notes on some Brechtian Theses' (*Screen*, Summer 1974, vol. 15 no. 2) and 'Principles of Realism and Pleasure' (*Screen*, Autumn 1976 vol. 17, no. 3).

5 The cinema spectator

The outline presented here is considerably sophisticated by Stephen Heath's 'Narrative Space' (*Screen*, Autumn 1976, vol. 17, no. 2) and Jeane-Pierre Oudart's article translated as 'Cinema and Suture' (*Screen*, Winter 1977-8 vol. 18, no. 4) and ensuing debate. Again, Steve Neale's *Genre* provides a useful summary.

6 Stars as a cinematic phenomenon

This chapter was originally a conference paper for a British Film Institute Education Department weekend school in January 1982. Writing on stars is so widespread (mostly repeating the contradictory images of stars rather than analysing) that naming any particular examples is invidious. However, Richard Dyer's *Stars* (British Film Institute, London) offers a summary account of many different approaches. His own suggested approach is itself criticised by Pam Cook in 'Star Signs' (*Screen*, vol. 20, nos. 3/4).

7 Broadcast TV as cultural form

Raymond Williams's *Television: Technology and Cultural Form* is published by Fontana (London). More basic consideration of the workings of broadcast TV, from a critical ex-insider, is *Stuart Hood on Television* (Pluto Press, London). An American 'conspiracy theory' view of TV as a means to sell advertisements is Gaye Tuchman (ed.) *The TV Establishment* (Prentice-Hall, Englewood Cliffs, N.J.). Timothy Green's *The Universal Eye* (Bodley Head, London) describes several national broadcast institutions in the early 1970s as they would like to see themselves. The sociological 'effects' debate is exemplified by Jay G. Blumler and Denis McQuail *Television and Politics* (Faber, London) and J.D. Halloran (ed.) *The Effects of Television* (Panther, London, 1970). The basic facts about family life in Britain are culled from government statistical sources; the argument here is based on Fran Bennett, Rosa Heys and Rosalind Coward, 'The Limits to "Financial and Legal Independence" ' (*Politics and Power* no. 1).

8 Broadcast TV as sound and image

One of the few articles to take a similar attitude to that adopted in this chapter is Stephen Heath and Gillian Skirrow, 'Television, A

World in Action' (*Screen*, Summer 1977, vol. 18, no. 2), analysing a specific current affairs programme. Directly relevant to the argument about TV and casual racism are: Hazel Carby 'Multiculture' in *Screen Education* 34, Spring 1980; Steve Neale's article on stereotypes 'The Same Old Story' (*Screen Education* 32/3, Winter 1979-80); and a series of articles by Carl Gardner, Alan Horrox, Denis MacShane and others in *Screen Education* 31, Summer 1979.

9 Broadcast TV narration

Roger Silverstone offers a structural analysis of TV narratives in *The Message of Television: Myth and Narrative in Contemporary Culture* (Heinemann, London). *Coronation Street* is one of the few soap operas to have a serious book devoted to it (ed. Richard Dyer *et al.*, British Film Institute, London). Mick Eaton opens the serious consideration of situation comedy with 'Television Situation Comedy' (*Screen*, Winter 1978-9, vol. 19, no. 4). *Everyday TV: Nationwide* (Charlotte Brunsdon, David Morley, British Film Institute, London) is also very suggestive.

10 The broadcast TV viewer

The centrality of the concept of 'citizenship' to the position of the TV viewer is suggested by Ian Connell in 'Television, News and Social Contract' (*Screen*, Spring 1979, vol. 20, no. 1).

11 The current situation

The argument about the separate and mutually defining spaces of cinema and broadcast TV was first put forward in my 'The Institution of Cinema' (*Edinburgh '77 Magazine*). The situation of British film exhibition receives periodic journalistic attention whenever more cinema closures are announced. One such piece is my 'What's One Odeon Less Anyway?' (*Marxism Today*, October 1981).

12 The organisation of film production

The effects of cinema's accounting procedures on the various areas of its operation are chronicled by, amongst others, Terence Kelly in *Towards a Competitive Cinema* (London, 1963). The current structure of the film industry is adequately covered in *Anatomy of the Movies* by

David Pirie (Windward, London). Statistics about American distributors are drawn from David Gordon's 'The Movie Majors' (*Sight and Sound*, Summer 1979). The concept of authorship in relation to films is explored in John Caughie's collection *Theories of Authorship* (RKP, London).

13 The dominance of the Hollywood film

Thomas Guback's economic account of Hollywood's dominance remains the best: *The International Film Industry* (Indiana University Press). A basic history of Hollywood's economic development can be found in Robert Stanley, *The Celluloid Empire* (Hastings House, New York), summarising existing knowledges and suppositions. Steve Neale's article 'Art Cinema as Institution' (*Screen*, vol. 22, no. 1) is the best contribution on this subject. Rank's production enterprises in the 1940s are dealt with in my 'Art, Culture and Quality' (*Screen*, Autumn 1978, vol. 19 no. 3).

14 The organisation of broadcast TV production

Basic studio techniques are explained in Gerald Millerson, *The Technique of Television Production* (Focal Press, London). Nicholas Garnham explains *The Structure of Television* (British Film Institute, London) in Britain; Stuart Hood (*op. cit*) the structure of internal decision-making. There are two useful studies of the manufacture of TV series: Philip Elliott, *The Making of a TV Series* (Constable, London) — on the documentaries on *The Nature of Prejudice* — and Manuel Alvarado and Edward Buscombe on *Hazell: the Making of a TV Series* (British Film Institute/Latimer, London). The Glasgow Media Group's controversial *Bad News* and *More Bad News* (Routledge & Kegan Paul, London) describe the industrial production of TV news. A useful collection of annotated source material about American broadcast TV is Lawrence W. Lichty and Malachi C. Topping (eds), *American Broadcasting: a Source Book* (Hastings House, New York).

15 Cinema and broadcast TV together

An interview with Eckart Stein of ZDF's *Das Kleine Fernsehspiel* about the possibilities and limitations of TV is in *Screen*, May 1982. The wide debate about TV news and current affairs includes the Glasgow Media Group's work; Anthony Smith's *Television and Political*

Life (Macmillan, London) about the experience of six European countries, and his collection of essays *The Politics of Information* (also Macmillan); Richard Collins's *TV News* (British Film Institute, London); Philip Schlesinger's *Putting 'Reality' Together* (Constable, London). *British TV Drama* is the title of a book by George Brandt (Cambridge University Press); John Caughie deals with the question of 'Progressive Television and Documentary Drama' in *Screen*, vol. 21, no. 3. *Godard: Images, Sounds, Politics* is the subject of a book by Colin MacCabe (Macmillan/British Film Institute, London).

16 Beyond the Hollywood film

The best single source of writing about British Independent Cinema is ed. Rod Stoneman and Hilary Thompson *The New Social Function of Cinema* (Catalogue: British Film Institute Productions 1979-80). The Independent Film-makers' Association's (rejected) proposals for a new relationship between cinema and British TV can be found in *Screen*, vol. 21, no. 4. *Screen*, vol. 21, no. 3 contains material on independent exhibition and the fate of 'marginal' distributors in the commercial arena. Peter Wollen's writing gives a succinct statement of the more formal aspects of independent film: 'The Two Avant-gardes' in *Studio International* November/December 1975 and ' "Ontology" and "Materialism" in Film' (*Screen* Spring 1976 vol. 17, no. 1). Annette Kuhn's *Women's Pictures* (Routledge & Kegan Paul, London) provides a fine account of independent cinema, both textual and institutional aspects. Some of the films written about can be hired from Cinema Action (*Film From the Clyde*), Cinema of Women (*Taking a Part, Light Reading*), The Other Cinema (*News and Comment, Blacks Britannica*, Newsreel Collective films, *James Whiter than White Show*), Sheffield Film Co-operative (*Jobs for the Girls*).

Further reading

Allen, Robert C., *Speaking of Soap Operas*, Chapel Hill and London: University of North Carolina Press, 1985
—— (ed.), *Channels of Discourse*, Chapel Hill and London: University of North Carolina Press, 1985
Ang, Ien, *Desperately Seeking the Audience*, London: Routledge, 1991
—— 'The Battle Between Television and its Audiences: The Politics of Watching Television', in Phillip Drummond and Richard Paterson (eds), *Television in Transition*, London: British Film Institute, 1985.
—— *Watching Dallas: Soap Opera and the Melodramatic Imagination*, London: Routledge, 1985
Austin, Bruce A., *Immediate Seatings: A Look at Movie Audiences*, Belmont, Ca.: Wadsworth, 1989
Baehr, Helen and Dyer, Gillian (eds), *Boxed In: Women and Television*, New York and London: Pandora Press, 1987
Bordwell, David, *Making Meaning: Inference and Rhetoric in the Interpretation of Cinema*, Cambridge, Mass.: Harvard University Press, 1989.
—— *Narration in the Fiction Film*, Madison: University of Wisconsin Press, 1985
Bordwell, David, Thompson, Kristin, and Staiger, Janet, *Classical Hollywood Cinema: Film Style and Mode of Production to 1960*, New York: Columbia University Press, 1985
Branigan, Edward, *Point of View in the Cinema: A Theory of Narration and Subjectivity in the Classical Film*, New York: Mouton, 1984
Collins, Jim, *Uncommon Cultures: Popular Culture and Postmodernism*, London and New York: Routledge, 1989
Cook, Pam (ed.), *The Cinema Book*, London: British Film Institute, 1985
Corner, John (ed.), *Popular Television in Britain: Studies in Cultural History*, London: British Film Institute, 1991
Cubitt, Sean, *Timeshift: On Video Culture*, London: Routledge, 1990
Donald, James (ed.), *Fantasy and the Cinema*, London: British Film Institute, 1989

Drummond, Phillip and Paterson, Richard (eds), *Television in Transition*, London: British Film Institute, 1985
—— *Television and its Audiences: International Research Perspectives*, London: British Film Institute, 1988
Dyer, Richard, *Heavenly Bodies: Film Stars and Society*, London: British Film Institute, 1987
Elsaesser, Thomas (ed), *Early Cinema: Space, Frame, Narrative*, London: British Film Institute, 1991
Feuer, Jane, 'Narrative Form in Television' in Colin MacCabe (ed.), *High Theory, Low Culture*, Manchester: Manchester University Press, 1986
Fiske, John, *Television Culture*, London and New York: Methuen, 1987
Geraghty, Christine, *Women and Soap Opera*, Cambridge: Polity Press, 1991
Gledhill, Christine (ed.), *Stardom: Industry of Desire*, London: Routledge, 1991
Goodwin, Andrew and Whannel, Garry (eds), *Understanding Television*, London: Routledge, 1990
Gorbman, Claudia, *Narrative Film Music*, London: British Film Institute, 1989
Hartley, John, *Tele-Ology: Studies in Television*, London: Routledge, 1992
Heath, Stephen, *Questions of Cinema*, London: Macmillan, 1987
Hodge, Robert and Tripp, David, *Children and Television*, Cambridge: Polity Press, 1986
Kaplan, E. Ann (ed.), *Regarding Television: Critical Approaches – An Anthology*, Frederick, Md.: University Publications of America, 1983
—— *Rocking Around the Clock: Music Television, Postmodernism and Consumer Culture*, London: Methuen, 1987
de Lauretis, Teresa, *Technologies of Gender: Essays on Theory, Film and Fiction*, Bloomington: Indiana University Press, 1987
MacCabe, Colin (ed.), *High Theory, Low Culture*, Manchester: Manchester University Press, 1986
McDonnell, James (ed.), *Public Service Broadcasting: A Reader*, London: Routledge, 1991
Modleski, Tania (ed.), *Studies in Entertainment: Critical Approaches to Mass Culture*, Bloomington, Ind.: Indiana University Press, 1986
Morley, David, *The 'Nationwide' Audience: Structure and Decoding*, London: British Film Institute, 1980
—— *Family Television: Cultural Power and Domestic Leisure*, London: Comedia, 1986
Mulgan, Geoff (ed.), *The Question of Quality*, London: British Film Institute, 1985
Mulvey, Laura, *Visual and Other Pleasures*, Bloomington: Indiana University Press, 1989
Murray, Robin, 'Fordism and Post-Fordism' and 'Benetton Britain' in

Stuart Hall and Martin Jacques (eds), *New Times: The Changing Face of Politics in the 1990s*, London: Lawrence & Wishart, 1989

Neale, Stephen, *Cinema and Technology: Image, Sound, Colour*, London: British Film Institute, 1990

Polan, Dana, *Power and Paranoia: History, Narrative and the American Cinema*, New York, Columbia University Press, 1986

Root, Jane, *Open the Box*, London: Comedia, 1986

Rose, Jacqueline, *Sexuality in the Field of Vision*, London: Verso, 1986

Rosen, Philip, *Narrative, Apparatus, Ideology: A Film Theory Reader*, New York: Columbia University Press, 1986

Seiter, Ellen, Borchers, H., Kreutzner, G. and Warth, E.-M., *Remote Control: Television, Audiences and Cultural Power*, London: Routledge, 1989

Tulloch, John, *Television Drama: Agency, Audience and Myth*, London: Routledge, 1990

Turner, Graeme, *Film as Social Practice*, London: Routledge, 1988

Willis, Janet and Wollen, Tana (eds), *The Neglected Audience*, London: British Film Institute, 1990